GU00984782

A
SHOOTING
MAN'S
CREED

A
SHOOTING
MAN'S
CREED

SIR JOSEPH NICKERSON

SWAN·HILL
PRESS

Copyright © 1998 Rosie Whitaker and Chapman Pincher

First published in the UK in 1989 by Sidgwick & Jackson Ltd
Second edition published 1998 by David A H Grayling
This edition published 2004
by Swan Hill Press, an imprint of Quiller Publishing Ltd

Reprinted 2006

British Library Cataloguing-in-Publication Data
A catalogue record for this book
is available from the British Library

ISBN 0 904057 55 1
ISBN 978 1 904057 55 0

Printed in England by Cromwell Press, Trowbridge, Wiltshire

Swan Hill Press
An imprint of Quiller Publishing Ltd.
Wykey House, Wykey, Shrewsbury, SY4 1JA
Tel: 01939 261616 Fax: 01939 261606
E-mail: info@quillerbooks.com
www.countrybooksdirect.com

Introduction

As he writes in his introduction, 'Statement of Belief', my father was badgered for years by his friends to write a book on shooting. In his early 70s he eventually gave in and began putting some of his ideas on paper. He knew that if he were to die before writing such a book, much of what he had learned in his long shooting life would be lost for ever. He went about writing the book with gusto, hiring a full time literary assistant, and talking for hours onto tapes which were then painstakingly organised into chapters. He was delighted to see the book take shape and when it was published, in 1989, he was tickled pink that it shot into the non-fiction bestseller list where it remained for several weeks. The book was hailed a success and was reprinted twice.

From his first bird, a magpie at the age of nine, to his last bird, a pheasant, at the age of 75, my father's passion for shooting was unsurpassable. He broke the record for wild English partridge in 1952 at his estate in Lincolnshire and was renowned for being a deadly shot. He regularly amazed his fellow guns by using 20-bores, and in his later years, 28-bores and even .410s to accomplish some incredible sporting shots. To watch him knock down high pheasant at his shoot in Rothwell, even in his last season, was like being a spectator at an extraordinary balletic performance. Although by this time rather on the corpulent side, and suffering from arthritis in his hip, he would dance about on his toes, barrels darting this way and that, pheasants spinning down overhead. All the time his loader would be mirroring his footwork behind him, changing guns in an effortless rhythm, honed to perfection through years of practice. Only rarely did a fellow gun hear a loud cheer echo down the line, as he saluted a bird that had outwitted him.

Born in 1914, the eldest of seven brothers and sisters, my father grew up in the Lincolnshire Wolds, on the family farm in Thoresway, a few miles away from Rothwell, where he made his home. His love of shooting stemmed from a childhood of scrambling through hedges and ditches with his beloved younger brother Sam. Together they declared war on rabbits and vermin, even shooting sparrows in their youthful enthusiasm. Events took an unexpected turn when the family's coal business started to go downhill in the general depression of the late 1920s. My grandfather's health was failing and my father left school early to work for the family business. They all moved to Grimsby and life was very different. They visited the farm only at weekends and had to adjust to living in a town, with fewer luxuries and privileges. Ultimately, the farm was lost and my grandfather died prematurely, leaving a young widow and seven children aged between two and 21. The family's future looked bleak. From this change in lifestyle stemmed my father's ambition. To farm was his ultimate goal, which he achieved four years later .

He bought the Home Farm at Rothwell, some 600 acres which had previously been part of the Yarborough estate. Like so many farms all over the country in the 1930s, Rothwell had been badly neglected. It was a veritable rabbit warren, oozing with vermin and not a single game bird on the place. It is testimony to his hard work and dedication that in less than twenty years Rothwell grew to comprise 2,500 acres and was regarded internationally as a model farm. Farmers and agricultural ministers would come from all over the world to visit. At the same time, Rothwell was gaining fame as a wild grey partridge shoot, visited by numerous politicians and members of the Royal Family. The other great passion in my father's life apart from Rothwell, was Wemmergill, a grouse moor in County Durham which was famous in the early 1930s for achieving record daily bags of over 1,000 brace. My father first shot here in 1942, and later leased the moor from the Strathmore family in 1952. He spent the 35 years as tenant improving it tremendously, building miles of access roads and draining vast acres.

Meanwhile, my father's interest in farming had focused on plant breeding, and after extensive travels in Europe after the Second World War, he set up a plant breeding company in the 1950s. The Nickerson Seed Company still operates from Rothwell although it was sold in the 1970s to Shell. His interest in selective breeding and improved varieties then moved towards poultry and livestock, and he founded Cherry Valley Farms Ltd in 1960, a duck company based in Rothwell. In its first year, it produced 1,000 ducks, nowadays it produces over 10 million, and exports breeding stock to more than 40 countries. Fifteen years later, buoyed up by the achievements of selective breeding at Cherry Valley, he bought the Cotswold Pig Development Company, a pig breeding company whose breeding stock is exported worldwide. In 1983, my father was knighted for his services to agriculture.

As is often the case with men of such energy and ambition, my father had a chequered personal life. He was not an easy man to live with and had extremely exacting standards which were hard to maintain. He married four times and had three sons, one of whom was tragically killed aged 21 in a Land Rover accident; and three daughters, of which I am the youngest, as well as a step-daughter from his last marriage. Although we were in complete awe of him as young children, he became more mellow with age and spoiled us terribly. School holidays at Rothwell were always planned to the last second. A timetable of the weeks ahead would be sent to us at school, and at least one activity was organised each day. Ballroom dancing, riding, dog training, driving lessons, French or maths tuition, a farm tour or a visit to one of the factories. Dinner was always black tie and television was banned until the evening. Looking back on it, it was rather an antiquated upbringing for the '70s and '80s.

All his children were brought up to shoot, the girls encouraged just as much as the boys. With a shooting-wife as well as three gun-toting daughters, my father was often the only male shot in the line. Going shooting with him was like going out on a military exercise. He had every detail minutely planned to the last second. At breakfast he would announce: 'Wheels moving at 09.00 hours'. Woe betide you if you were late. I still have nightmares of the cavalcade of Range Rovers moving off without me, or arriving on the field to realise I had forgotten some vital piece of equipment. Whilst most of us can hardly keep our own tally and mark all our birds, my father had the most unusual ability of not only being able to mark all of his birds down the last yard, but also everyone else's. When in the line with him, it was imperative to concentrate furiously, because he had the most off-putting habit of shouting 'Wake up there!' if a bird sneaked past without you spotting it. He never missed a trick. On the upside, he would always notice your best shots and bellow 'Bravo!' waving his cap down the line.

He did not usually draw for numbers when hosting a day. Because he always knew what was going on in the line, he would place his guests according to their success on each drive so that each one got a similar amount of shooting. Some said it was so he could bag all the best spots, but while that would not have been entirely out of character, this was not the case. Shooting was indeed a serious business to my father, who did not see it as a social sport at all. He loathed coffee-housing between drives, and was always far too busy picking up, speaking to the keeper and planning the rest of the day, for any chit-chat. Alcohol was never served between drives as on some shoots, and at lunch he never offered anything stronger than a light beer. He did not truly relax until the day was over. Even as a septuagenarian, on shoot days he would cram in an hour's work with his secretary before breakfast and another couple of hours after tea. He was in touch with his office throughout the day. His perfectionism was exhausting just to watch, and his energy incredible.

Just four months after the publication of *A Shooting Man's Creed*, my father died unexpectedly of a heart attack while on holiday abroad. I think all children consider their parents to be immortal and it was a huge blow to all of us. Since his death, much has changed in the world of shooting. The tide is turning in favour of small wild bird days, and vast bags are seen as morally reprehensible. My father's view was that reared game birds were like a crop to be harvested – they had enjoyed a good life while it lasted. He felt strongly that shooting was vital for conservation and rural economy and he founded the Josesph Nickerson Heather Improvement Foundation, to promote the role of heather improvement in upland areas. If he were alive today I know he would have campaigned fiercely against the encroaching political legislation which threatens all fieldsports.

His sense of perfection; his instinctive understanding of game birds; his strict approach to shooting etiquette; his genuine love of the sport, as well as his occasional pomposity, all spring out of the chapters that follow.

Over recent years, demand has remained high for copies of *A Shooting Man's Creed*. Our family was delighted to be contacted by Swan Hill Press, for permission to print a new edition. My father would have been so happy to hear his book being described as 'a modern classic'. It is our hope that the book will now be available more widely, and remain in print for many years to come.

Rosie Whitaker 2004

Author's Acknowledgements

To all those who have persuaded me to write this book, those who tried to persuade me for thirty years without success, having now dropped off the perch; to all those who have inspired and taught me so much; and to all those keepers with whom I have shared so much.

I should particularly like to thank Jane Crouch, my Literary Secretary, and Patricia Kerr, our archivist, who has kept all the records so well.

The author's family have requested that royalties from the sale of this new edition be donated to the Gamekeeper's Welfare Trust. (Registered charity no. 1008924)

Foreword

by the Duke of Westminster

On leafing through the pages of this book it will be hard for the reader not to be assaulted by many emotions. It is a fascinating manuscript and one man's experience up against a background of his deep love of the countryside and all that it has to offer.

Joe's enthusiasm and dedication towards the cause of country sports leaps out from every chapter and his lifetime experience in the management of game, whether it be on the high or low ground, makes this book a must for those who wish to enhance their knowledge.

It is only through written contributions such as this that it will be possible to instil in our successors the standards of behaviour, excellence and perfectionism that are required to ensure that our countryside sports have a peaceful, happy and prosperous future. It is also a fine record of the contribution of one man over fifty years, and there is no doubt that we owe him a great debt of gratitude for his work in the Heather Improvement Foundation and elsewhere. He realizes how much enjoyment he has had from country pursuits, a debt which he has repaid in full to the countryside by all that he has done.

This is a fascinating book and I highly commend it to you.

Contents

Statement of Belief

Several of my friends have been urging me to set down some details of my long and varied shooting life, believing that what I have learned and practised would be of interest and value to others. What they had in mind was not only the techniques of shooting challenging targets but how to produce, conserve and present them, along with all the associated issues, such as general shoot management, control of 'vermin' and handling of gundogs.

I have been diffident about doing this because of the difficulty of describing experiences and offering advice without appearing to be immodest or even boastful. Once I passed seventy, however, the increasing pressure from friends to get on with the task became irresistible. The fact that I have a complete set of records – game-books and detailed diaries – going back more than fifty years, covering virtually every bird I have ever shot, the cartridges expended and the lessons learned, has made the task easier and ensured the accuracy of my narrative. Nevertheless, I feel I must apologize in advance if these records, to which I will frequently have to refer, make me sound vain or pretentious. There is one feature of my nature, however, for which I will make no apology – I am a perfectionist, some might say almost to the point of eccentricity. If that becomes apparent in this text, as I expect it will, all I can say is that it is the way I am made and it has paid off for me in sport – in ice-skating and skiing as well as shooting – as it has in business. Organization, efficiency, enthusiasm and dedication are the names of both games.

To me, as the title of this book suggests, shooting has long been something of a religion. As all religions do, it requires discipline, reverence, ritual and, above all, love. Many people like and enjoy shooting. A smaller number, of whom I am one, love it in the sense that life would be much less rewarding without it.

My reverence is for the wild surroundings which make challenging shooting possible and for the splendid quarry, which is something non-shooters find hard to understand. I have abounding admiration and respect for game-birds, but a farmer's attitude to killing them because they are a crop which has to be harvested like any other. A pheasant, partridge or grouse has a far more pleasant life than a chicken that is reared for the pot and a much greater chance of survival when its time comes to pay for its keep. The satisfaction of shooting does not come from killing birds *per se* but in the practice of hard-learned skills – as in any other sport. The satisfaction of knocking down, dead in the head, a distant, high, curling pheasant with a 28-bore gun has to be experienced to be understood. A double, or even four, at partridges or grouse is extraordinarily gratifying.

When I say that shooting is a religion I do not mean that it supplants what is usually meant by that word. On the contrary, for me it is an adjunct to my fervent belief in the Almighty and I am eternally grateful for his bountiful provision which has given me so much enjoyment and excitement and continues to do so. After more than sixty years of holding a game licence and shooting more than my share, when I go into a grouse butt or duck hide or stand waiting for the partridges or pheasants, I am as excited as the first day I ever did it. I still experience that tingle of delight when I wake up and know that I am going shooting.

I stress the enjoyment and excitement because shooting should always be fun – as indeed business can be – and the secret is to be able to harness organization to maximize the pleasure and not become such a slave to it that the fun suffers. In the field, as opposed to the clay shooting ground, the spirit of competition, which can generate irritation and frustration, should be taboo.

While shooting has become increasingly expensive it can, quite sensibly, be regarded as an investment in health – both mental and physical – as well as an investment in pleasure. One of its strengths in that respect is that, having accepted an invitation, or being the host, you have to get up and go. I am deeply grateful for having been able to spend so much time in the open air.

Shooting is also about giving pleasure to others and I owe it an immense debt as a fount of enduring friendships which have enriched my life. I would never have met many of my friends but for shooting.

People like the Marquis of Ripon and Lord Leicester, who established shooting records many years ago, inherited their estates and the wealth to run them and to do little else, but most shooting men these days have to work, as I have always done myself and, unless they can do so effectively, cannot afford to shoot. Most of those I know frequently have to decline or cancel invitations because of pressure of work and do so with good grace because they know that it is the work that makes the shooting possible.

I am especially grateful for the opportunities shooting has given me to share open-air enjoyment with my family. My two brothers and I have shot together all our lives. It is a particular joy to me that my wife, who is much younger than I am, shoots and shoots well and that my sons, sons-in-law, three of my four daughters and my grandson are keen shots. Recently it has been wonderful to see three of my young daughters shooting well, safely and without greed, and then picking up with their own dogs.

The prime purpose of this book is to transmit my enthusiasm to others in the hope that they will derive a similar degree of pleasure and satisfaction. As far as possible, I have restricted its contents to what I have learned from personal experience. No doubt there will be many who disagree with some of the things I have to say. They are perfectly entitled to do so: all I would claim is that this is what has worked for me and some of it may work for others.

I appreciate that, as a life-long farmer and country-dweller, my attitude is necessarily different from that of a town-dweller who goes into the countryside to shoot. I am part of the country, bonded by nature and experience to its fields and woods. It is my workshop and my laboratory as well as my playground. I enjoy visiting towns on occasion but only briefly. I have admiration for fine architecture but it cannot compare with the grandeur of the architecture of the open country, which I can humbly mould, though only to a limited degree.

Countrymen have the opportunity to shoot the whole year round if they wish and that is one reason why so many of them are such good shots. When the game-shooting ends on 1 February it is permissible to shoot duck, chiefly wigeon, on the foreshore for another nineteen days. Hare shoots are normally held in February: there are always a few rabbits and plenty of pigeons, which are fair game any time because of the damage they do and because they are so challenging. They can be shot from hides or driven like pheasants from woods right through until August when the grouse come in.

Shooting takes you to marvellous and hidden places. I have seen so many parts of England – especially in my beloved Lincolnshire – parts of Scotland, Spain, France, Italy, Holland, Germany, Austria, Morocco and the United States – all through shooting. And I have witnessed wonderful sights, like the successful stoop of a peregrine falcon on an old hen grouse, on a snipe, on a golden plover, on a pigeon and even on to a pink-foot goose. My memory store of such episodes will stand me in vicarious stead if and when I can no longer get my gun up. Meanwhile I will go on learning about shooting as I have every day since I shot my first rabbit at the age of eight and my first bird, a magpie, when I was nine, because every target is different and there is always room for experiment to improve technique.

There is also unlimited scope for experiment in the management of shoots and this can provide enormous pleasure and satisfaction, especially to someone as fascinated by the practical application of agricultural and scientific research as I have been and still am.

Further, through shoot organization and management, it is possible to make major contributions to the economic life of the countryside and to the pleasure it affords to so many.

I was fortunate in realizing early in life that work is not everything and vowed, at the age of seventeen, to set aside 100 days a year for sport which I achieved through shooting, fox-hunting and skiing. Nevertheless, I have not had the time or opportunity to shoot as many head of game as the old Marquis of Ripon, who killed just over half a million in his long life. But I have shot about half that number and the experience has bred some knowledge and, I hope, some wisdom, which I now set down in the hope that it will help others.

4

Chapter 1

The Object and its Achievement

The intrinsic joy of shooting lies in outwitting the quarry and the wilder it is the more difficult it is to outwit. While large numbers of challenging birds can be memorable, almost as much enjoyment can be derived from outwitting a few birds in difficult situations. Quite often I go out with one or both of my sons or a couple of friends to pit our wits against a few birds, and we return thoroughly satisfied.

In my experience it is an axiom that 'The plan is half the bag'. It is also half the pleasure. The owner can leave both the strategy and the tactics all to the keeper – when he is more than likely to be disappointed – or he can take a close personal interest, as I do, planning the drives for each day with the keeper and pooling our joint expertise.

A day's shooting is rather like a marriage in that when it goes well it is wonderful but when it goes badly . . . I therefore plan each day like a military operation, whether it be for pheasants at Rothwell, partridges in Spain, or for grouse. I do not rely on the keeper to provide what he thinks fit but tell him what I want and how to achieve it. I listen to his views and may accept some of them, but once I have made some decisions he tends to regret it if he goes against my requirements.

The plan must be flexible for changing wind and sun conditions and I often alter the direction of a drive at short notice, before or during the shoot. One goes to some shoots where the same drives are invariably taken in the same way, year after year. Pheasants do not fly high if driven into the sun yet they still tend to be driven the same way irrespective of whether the sun is shining into their eyes or not. Pheasants usually fly low into a strong wind, in an effort

5

to get under it, yet on many shoots even this will not induce the keeper or owner to change the direction of the drive.

If I think that pheasants will fly badly out of a wood, because of the local conditions, I may blank them into a piece of kale on a hill and drive them back to the wood over the guns. I am inclined to change direction almost as a matter of course towards the end of a season when the birds, especially the cock pheasants, are in the habit of flying back over the beaters. I take it the other way and give them a shock.

Field mastership, which can be learned only by experience, is an art in itself. It includes the question of discipline in a sport where danger always lurks and I will deal with that in subsequent chapters. The field master – usually the owner or head of a syndicate – is responsible for good discipline, which not only ensures safety but makes for a more enjoyable day without unfortunate incidents.

The main object of the planning should be to put the required number of birds over all the guns and to make them difficult. The more birds I miss in a day the better the day's shooting because it means that they have been challenging. A good wind, of course, can be very helpful and I drive birds down wind whenever possible to give them the advantage of the extra speed. Birds fly best on a dull day so a sunless day with a good wind is usually ideal. I will cancel a drive, if I cannot change it, rather than drive birds into a strong wind if it is going to make them too easy. I hate to see a lot of birds killed when they are struggling against the wind – 'flying hares' my brother and I used to call them. When one hears of big bags, especially of grouse, the question that needs asking is: 'How many were killed up wind?' The answer, if given truthfully, is often revealing.

There is delight and satisfaction in going to a well-run shoot, and the reverse when a shoot is a shambles. At a new shoot I can usually tell from the start, before a shot is fired, how the day is likely to turn out. It is the meticulous attention to detail which makes all the difference. Chance is bound to intrude itself enough into one's plans, however well laid – so it pays to reduce its ravages to a minimum.

If a shoot is properly organized one does not need to rush between drives to kill a lot of birds, and rushing can reduce the pleasure, especially for the older guns. It is a matter of controlling the beaters through close contact with the keeper throughout the day. There is little that is more frustrating than to arrive at a stand and see good birds – perhaps the best of the drive – going over before you can make ready to shoot. There should also be reasonable time for the pick-up, though one should always avoid holding up the other guns by searching for some difficult bird or runner, especially when there are pickers-up to do the job for you. Excessive haste is one of the main reasons why birds are left behind, especially those near the pegs, which the pickers-up may reasonably ignore. When birds have cost so much in time and effort to rear and present they should not be left to rot or attract vermin. I shall have more to say about the important matter of picking-up in further chapters.

Most shoots in Britain – and even more so on the Continent – are spoiled by having too many guns. In my view, seven is the maximum number of guns that should be accommodated at any shoot in Britain, including walking guns, and six is much better. A larger number is unfair on the birds, which must have a reasonable chance of escape, and on the guns, some of whom are bound to be 'in Siberia' on several drives. Too many guns for the terrain also means that they are too close together, which makes for displeasure and a feeling that guns are 'poaching' each other's birds.

The optimum distance between guns for shooting normal grouse, partridges or pheasants effectively is forty-five yards but, when birds are really high, guns should be sixty yards apart. Pegs should never be closer than about forty-five yards. When this is unavoidable, as it may be on some drives, it is better to double bank with the front guns perhaps shooting cocks only. So often, when there are too many guns and they draw for places, one or more may be out of the shooting for several drives in succession and for the majority of the drives in the day. The luck of the draw is supposed to even out over the day but, very often, it does not. There are people who seem to be particularly fortunate at drawing good numbers, and those whose experience is the reverse may become rather disenchanted, especially in a syndicate. I appreciate that in some syndicates a large number of guns, say eight or nine, reduces the individual cost but it might be wiser to pay a little more for better sport and

7

less frustration. There are some rag-time shoots where extra guns turn up, usually half-guns, claiming to have mistaken the day, and are accommodated as back-guns instead of being sent home.

For several years now I have restricted the guns at Rothwell to a smaller number – five or, more often, three – and this has greatly increased the enjoyment of those taking part. I am also inclined to reduce the numbers on the grouse moor. This might appear to increase the difficulty of ensuring that the birds fly over the guns but it is surprising how consistently a well-trained team of beaters, flankers and keepers can drive the birds over three guns. A smaller party of tried and trusted friends gives greater pleasure as I grow older and I think that others may follow my example.

On pheasant shoots I place the guns, individually, usually with myself behind, where I can watch what is happening and try to finish off any wounded birds. Placing, provided he watches what is happening, enables the field master to ensure that everyone gets a share of the good shooting. It also enables him to split the better shots down the line so that the weaker ones are not all together. (It may not necessarily be a compliment if a host who is a good shot puts you next to him!)

When I ask guests to draw cards bearing the numbers of their stands, as I often do on my partridge shoot in Spain, I have carefully weighted the drives so that, in the course of the day, each gun should have the opportunity to fire roughly the same number of cartridges.

One needs to choose guests carefully, not only to ensure safety and avoid greedy shots, but because some guests do not take to each other or have had some mutual problem in the past. I take care not to have them on the same day because nothing is worse at a shoot than atmosphere. Shooting is about enjoyment.

Birds can be shot by walking them up or driving them towards the stationary guns. Walking up grouse over dogs is good sport and very exacting physically, when properly done, and the behaviour of well-trained dogs is a joy to watch. Walking up pheasants or partridges and shooting them going away is usually an obscenity, though going-away quail put up by pointers are a different matter, providing extremely challenging targets.

To me the driving of birds has been – and remains – a most fascinating study and I will deal with it at some length in ensuing chapters.

As regards the weather, I take the farmer's philosophic view; the weather has to be accepted as part of the natural scene. The keeper and I therefore make two basic plans for each day to suit different conditions. Unless the weather is totally atrocious, which happens very rarely, we press on. As a rule, only dense fog, which is dangerous, or very deep or drifted snow, which is impossible for the beaters, would make me delay or cancel. With wildfowling, of course, one opts out in freezing weather after a prolonged frost in deference to the quarry and other birds which must not be frightened away from the feeding grounds at such a tough time.

I am a great believer in the blanking-in of hedgerows, stubbles and coppices before the shoot proper begins in the morning and later before drives. It can add a great number to the bag yet on some shoots blanking-in is neglected, usually because of laziness or lack of supervision on someone's part or, as is often the case, because the owner demands too many drives in the day.

Stops are usually thought of as people placed somewhere in a wood to tap away and prevent birds from running through, but there is much more to them than that. The main function of stops is to prevent birds from leaving a wood which is to be driven that day. They therefore need to be put out very early in the morning before the birds have strayed out of the wood. All too commonly, stops are told to stand near the edge of the wood but they should be well away from it where the birds can see them when they fly down from roost. Stopping is a lonely and boring business, but if properly done it can make all the difference to a drive.

Nothing alarms birds more than the sound of the human voice or the slam of vehicle doors once the season has started and the birds have begun to realize what it is about. During most drives the only noise that should be heard – apart from the discharge of the guns – is the sound of the sticks in the hands of the beaters and stops. The only time beaters should make a lot of noise is when a field of roots or thick cover has to be driven up wind. Partridges in particular

9

will want to fly with the wind if they can, and will otherwise go back over the beaters, especially if they cannot see them.

As I have said, it is a common belief, heard on many shoots, that some people attract pheasants and other birds in some mysterious way so that an unfair proportion of the birds flies over them. There may be something in it and the explanation may lie in the fact that such people are usually good shots and, therefore, experienced shots. They will tend to be quiet and about their business, not moving about unnecessarily at the stand, while some other guns seem incapable of remaining silent, chatting and guffawing with their neighbours, and usually paying for it.

Having dogs running free with the beaters is a very mixed blessing: they are just as likely to put birds back as forwards. What keeps the birds coming forwards is the continuous tap-tap of the beaters' sticks or, in the case of partridges and grouse, the sight of the beaters and their flags. Beaters with dogs are often very competitive in trying to pick wounded birds from a previous drive and in the process many birds which have never been shot at all are grabbed. I will not permit dogs with beaters on my shoots unless there are extenuating circumstances such as a drive where brambles, or fallen boughs after a storm, are so thick that the beaters cannot get through: then spaniels do valuable service. But, really, on a well-managed shoot the undergrowth should normally be 'swiped' to avoid such situations.

No sportsman worthy of the name shoots low pheasants, unless there is a need to do so right at the end of the season because too many birds would otherwise be left and cause crop damage. On my shoots, when we are about to shoot in an area where some pheasants may be low, I sometimes avail myself of a gambit devised by my brother Sam and say to my guests in a loud voice: 'Shoot whatever gives you pleasure.' It usually works!

Guns should always shoot as a team, pitting itself against the quarry. There should be no competition in the game-shooting field. Indeed, for most businessmen a day's shooting is a release from competition. Those who need competition should concentrate on clay-pigeon shooting which lends itself to it. A host has gone to great trouble to stage the day, whether it be big or modest, and he usually wants as good a bag as reasonably possible. It should be the team's purpose to oblige him, as well as for individual members to enjoy themselves in the process.

A good shot should concentrate on the difficult birds. There should be no exception to the rule that one should never shoot at a bird which is going to make a more difficult target for another gun. Leave any bird that will fly better over your neighbour or further still down the line.

What should one do, if you are the host or syndicate head, and a drive goes really badly? Most assuredly, one should not bawl out the keeper in front of the guests, whatever you may care to say to him later in private. It may not have been his fault. My advice is to move on to the next drive, explaining the cause for the failure to the other guns if you happen to know it. Don't waste time doing the same drive again on the theory that the beaters must have walked over the birds. This can make you look foolish, as happened to a host once at his shoot in Hampshire. On one usually productive drive only one pheasant and a jay came out. The pheasant was shot, the jay escaped. The host immediately decided to beat the drive backwards and the guns were duly deployed on the far side of the wood. Only the jay came out.

At some shoots a sweepstake on the total bag is standard practice. For my part I think sweepstakes are inappropriate in the shooting field because they introduce an air of competition and the size of the stake can get out of hand. Normally the stake is modest but there are shoots where the winner can go home with £100, which is not what shooting is about. Certainly only the host should ever suggest a sweepstake. For a guest to do so might offend some people who are opposed to any form of gambling.

Because of the upsurge of terrorism, security is a new factor when certain VIPs are present at a shoot. It is an appalling development, so alien to the British countryside, but if you invite a cabinet minister or anyone currently or formerly connected with Northern Ireland he will arrive with a couple of detectives who will insist on standing with him. The same applies to a member of the Royal Family. They usually make their own arrangements for the accommodation of their bodyguards but the shoot owner may need to take account of their transport and lunch-time needs. A particular aspect of the security requirements is the need to avoid the leakage of any advance information about their attendance.

It hardly needs saying that there should be complete confidentiality on the part of guests and staff about what may be said by VIPs in the field or at lunch.

Chapter 2

Behaviour in the Field

If manners make the man, they certainly make – or break – the shooting man. Shooting is the sport above all where good manners matter most and where bad manners can have such devastating impact on everyone's enjoyment, confidence and safety. We all know the feeling on spotting a well-known greedy shot: I hope I'm not drawn next to him! Generally speaking, manners at shoots are of a high standard but 'rogue' guns are known to all of us. I call them 'anglers' on two counts – they fire outside the 90-degree angles allotted to them, in front and behind, and they are always angling for other people's birds. The worst angler I have ever encountered was also the best shot I have ever seen, which made his offence so much worse.

On receiving an invitation to shoot you should answer it as quickly as possible, whether you can go or not. It is particularly important to reply with haste if you cannot go so that the host can ask another gun without making his invitation look like a second choice. While it may be invidious to introduce any commercial consideration it is only realistic to appreciate that, because of today's costs, an invitation to shoot is something particularly precious and a great favour. So, once having accepted a day, it is essential to honour it, whatever better invitations may accrue. It may sometimes be really necessary to cancel because of unforeseeable business or domestic problems, but they must be serious and genuine. Illness, of course, is always a viable reason and affects us all at times. Nobody will thank you for turning up at a shoot with a highly infectious cold and this is especially true when some of the guests are elderly, because what may be only seven days of snuffles for a young man may be six weeks of bronchitis for an older person. A last-minute cancellation gives a host the irritating problem of finding a quick replacement, so while you may cancel for a sound reason you should never do so for an excuse.

If the weather is appalling you should still turn up, properly equipped for it, unless you receive instructions that the shoot has been cancelled or delayed. In bad conditions, especially of snow, it is permissible to telephone the host to confirm that the shoot is still on – he may have tried unsuccessfully to telephone you – and to ask whether access is still possible, especially if you do not have a four-wheel-drive vehicle.

In some syndicates it is permissible to send someone in your place but this should always be arranged with the syndicate head. It is embarrassing both for the gun and the rest of the syndicate for a stranger to turn up unannounced.

If you are not asked to shoot when you expected an invitation do not assume that you must have offended, unless, of course, you have good reason to think that you did. Take comfort in the fact that you were ever asked at all. With people whom you do not see regularly it is really necessary to keep in some sort of touch, socially, if you expect to be asked to shoot and are not in a position to return their invitation. But don't make it too obvious by ignoring them all the year and then writing to them or asking them to dinner just before the shooting season! Try to offer reciprocity of some sort because people like to be asked, whether they can accept or not.

It is unforgivable to turn up late to a shoot because, if the shoot is well run, the beaters will have been out some time before the first drive is due to begin and the drive should not be held up. If you are late there will be a gap in the line and it often happens that the birds will stream through it. So, when going to a shoot for the first time you must find out exactly how to get there, the precise meeting place and how long it will take. Make sure that you have accurate instructions. If you have a keeper of your own he may be able to find out the way discreetly when your host has provided a doubtful map. If meeting at a house, make sure that you have the telephone number with you when you set off so that in the event of a breakdown or something else outside your control you can warn of your late arrival.

In this connection, it is wise to pack your vehicle, except for guns and dogs, the night before unless you have a man whom you can trust to do this for you. It is the most certain way of ensuring that you don't leave without some essential item of equipment and have to turn back.

You will usually be told if you will be expected to shoot one or two guns. In the latter instance you need to let your host know if you are not bringing your own loader and would like him to arrange one for you.

On a two-gun day you will need to take full cleaning equipment if you wish and can trust the loader to clean your guns immediately after the shoot, which is the usual arrangement. In any case it is wise to take two guns, if you have them, in case one becomes defective. I have arrived at one-gun shoots where the owner – realizing, perhaps, that the conditions are likely to produce more birds than he had anticipated – has offered his guests the option of using two guns if they wish.

I invariably take a third gun, wrapped in cloth and stowed away out of sight in a strong wooden box made to fit the width of my Range-Rover, simply because, when shooting two guns, one may go wrong. Not only would I feel frustrated at being reduced to one gun on a big day but I would be letting my host down.

Always take plenty of cartridges – you will be a nuisance if you run out – but do not make them obvious and thereby give the impression that you are expecting more birds than you may get. The occasional host has been known to regard it as an insult when a gun turns up with far too few cartridges. One has been heard to say: 'You have had what you expected. Now you had better walk as a beater.'

It also pays to have a special bag of heavier-shot cartridges, say number fives, in case the host suddenly announces that there will be one or two drives at high ducks.

Some shoots provide hot soup and drinks, like sloe gin, at mid-morning, but as you cannot count on this, take a flask of hot coffee or Bovril. I do not approve of alcohol in the shooting field and never provide it for 'elevenses', as so many shoots do. At some shoots too much alcohol is taken at lunch for safety.

Do not forget to take enough money in a trouser pocket for tips in notes of such value that you will not be seeking change at the end of the day.

If attending a new shoot ask permission to bring your dog and then make sure that it has plenty of time to empty itself before you arrive at your host's lawn. There is little more embarrassing than having to watch some hapless servant – or even the host himself – removing a canine offering on a shovel. This rule also applies if you walk your dog at night when staying at a house as a shooting guest. Take him on a lead some distance from the front of the house. It is surprising how thoughtless some people are in this regard and then the guns are picking their way through unpleasant hazards in the morning. If you are staying the night a kennel will usually be available for your dog: if not he may be required to sleep in your vehicle. If you have a dog which is inclined to howl or bark at night, leave him at home where, incidentally, it also pays to black out any kennel at full moon, when most dogs are likely to howl.

Do not arrive at a shoot too early. Judge it so that you just have enough time in which to ready your kit without bothering anyone until the host appears. Do not go into the house unless you have been specially asked to do so. If you do go into the house make sure that your dog cannot follow you.

If other guns are already there introduce yourself and if the keeper is there have a word with him, too, for the quality of the day will very much depend on him. Usually, a good keeper will not be around at such a time because he will be with the beaters or placing stops. I can generally tell what sort of a day is in prospect when I eventually shake hands with the keeper. A calloused hand, good day: soft hand, poor day. This, I find, is a sure indication.

Many people now have their own four-wheel-drive vehicles. Do not assume that you will be able to take your vehicle round the shoot. It is usually a great convenience to do so and the best insurance that you do not leave any item of equipment behind. However, you must be prepared to transfer to some other vehicle if the host does not want too many in convoy or has a large wagon in which he likes to transport all the guns together, which does make for good fellowship.

It is an eloquent commentary on changing values that I have frequently seen so many expensive vehicles at shoots that their value would once have bought the whole estate. Most of the land in England over which I have shot could have been bought for about £20 an acre just after the Second World War. The cost of one Range Rover today would have taken care of the first thousand acres! Sometimes there may be seven such vehicles plus cars.

One way of increasing the chance that you will be allowed to take your vehicle is to offer to ferry one or more other guns. You should do this anyway to be sociable. Shooting is a wonderful way of making new friends and one never knows where the chance event of offering a lift to a strange gun may lead. Some of the people who have been important to me in my life have been first encountered through shooting.

Before asking an individual to share your transport make sure if he has a dog or not and whether you can accommodate it. Always decline to have dogs in the front of the vehicle because when they get muddy they make a mess and an obstreperous dog could cause an accident.

Never allow a dog in the back of your vehicle where there are guns in slings lying on the floor. A heavy labrador can easily break the stock of a gun at its thinnest part, occasioning very expensive repairs. A gun rack will avoid this kind of accident so long as proper use is made of it.

If the host fails to make it clear, always ask whether ground game are to be shot or not and whether partridges are excluded, as they well may be on some shoots trying to conserve their numbers. It is common practice to ask if both hens and cocks are to be shot when attending a shoot after 1 January but some owners shoot cocks only at the beginning of the season. So it is wise to establish that too. Some owners bar the shooting of woodcock, which are such lovely birds, so it may be wise to ask about that as well.

Before moving off you will need to know the lunch arrangements, not only for yourself but for your loader or carrier. If you are returning to a house or pub you will need shoes to change into and a bootjack will be helpful. A couple of plastic bags to prevent

17

shoes from becoming muddy can save a lot of work, especially if they are going into the back of a vehicle where dogs are. An old blanket to cover your equipment in the back can save you or your man a lot of extra work after a wet day.

At most shoots there will be a draw for numbers to establish your position for the first drive and it is worth making a note if your memory is not all that reliable to avoid argument, should you forget it at some point of the day. Make sure your loader or carrier, if you have a man with you, knows the number so that, if travelling in a different vehicle, he does not go to the wrong peg. It is astonishing how often one goes to the correct peg to find someone else standing there.

Once at your peg do not leave it unless you are at one end of the line and your host has asked you to move to cover birds which are breaking out, or you are so familiar with the shoot that you know this is what your host would like you to do. It is quite customary to ask your host whether you are permitted to move – and how far – in such circumstances. Some guns – happily rare – are inclined to move several yards right or left of their pegs as a means of 'cashing in' on birds which really belong to neighbouring guns. Such people should never be invited.

If you do move from your peg, either sideways or backwards, always let your neighbours know – in your own safety interests as well as in theirs.

It is the usual practice to move up two numbers after each drive but there are variations on this custom – some of them ludicrously complex and calculated to cause confusion – and you need to establish what the owner wants. Some provide a card showing the drives for the whole day for each gun, even computers being used in these high-tech times in an effort to ensure that everyone has a reasonable share of the good shooting. Others prefer to achieve this by placing the guns personally at each drive, as I tend to do myself. An observant host will note who is getting the most good birds and who has been 'out of it'.

One fault with the moving-up-two system is that, on some shoots, a gun who picks an unfortunate number can be out of the sport almost all day while others are consistently deep in it.

There are shoots, better not named, where those running them seem determined to put themselves in the best positions particularly on a big killing drive. If they have drawn a number which puts them in an unpromising place they are known, suddenly, to fit in an extra short drive, maybe no more than a bit of kale containing half a dozen birds, to get themselves two numbers nearer to the action. When you see this happening you will know not to go to that shoot again.

Never fire your gun into an area, such as a hedge, bush, wood or ditch where you cannot see for the whole distance of its danger-range – *a couple of hundred yards*. You never know where there may be a stop, a picker-up or somebody working sewelling or some other device to make the birds fly. It is not their fault if they are struck by your pellets. Always remember that, at short range, the shotgun is the most dangerous weapon yet invented. On stony or frosty ground it is also important always to be aware of the possibility of a ricochet. In law a gun remains responsible for any injury he inflicts even if it is by the most unlikely ricochet.

For that reason always carry a shotgun with the breech broken and empty of cartridges, which also gives peace of mind to the other guns. If someone, other than your loader, passes you a gun which is not broken always break it, irrespective of the importance or experience of the person handing it to you. Some people are prone to walk, or even to negotiate an obstacle, with a broken gun which still contains two cartridges. Such a gun is not completely safe.

When you close the gun bring the stock up to the barrels, not vice versa which can point them in a dangerous direction, and see that loaders do likewise.

Do not load your gun until you have zipped or buttoned up your coat, put on your ear defenders and safety spectacles if you wear them, and pegged down your dog, if it needs it. There is a great temptation to slip two cartridges into the gun as soon as you arrive at your peg in case an early bird should come over. Resist it because when pegging down the dog or doing something else after you have loaded, your gun barrels can touch the ground and become lethally clogged with mud. It has happened many times! Further, you should not fire at an early bird before the rest of the guns are properly in place because you may start the drive off prematurely if a shot is the signal for that to happen. Incidentally it is your responsibility, not your loader's, to look down the barrels of the gun you are holding before you start each drive and to make sure that they are clear of obstruction. A good loader will check his gun and I train mine to take that precaution. The pair of you cannot be too careful.

I like to put my ancillary equipment – gun covers, thumb-stick etc. – in front of the peg so that I am not in any danger of falling over if I move back a yard or two. The same applies to dogs, which should be set far enough in front so that they are not showered with cartridge cases.

The safety catch should be on safe at all times until you are about to fire, which is the only time when it should be pushed forwards. *Always pull it back on safe before you hand it to your loader whether one or two barrels have been fired.* This is a most important aspect of discipline which must be learned and practised. It is perhaps more in your own interest than in that of others because the person most likely to kill you with an accidental discharge is your loader, as he is so close. As I shall be at pains to point out again, a gun is not completely safe when the catch reads Safe. The catch only locks the triggers while the rest of the mechanism remains cocked. So if a part of the mechanism called the sear happens to be badly worn, the tumbler or hammer can slip forwards if the gun is jarred, firing a cartridge.

Needless to say you should never rest your gun on your boot with the safety catch on or off. It sounds ridiculous but people have been lamed for life this way on many occasions. If you have to put your gun down always unload it first and leave it broken and out of the way of dogs.

The most important aspect of sportsmanship and safety is knowing when *not* to shoot – at the low bird or at the dropping bird near the end of its trajectory when a second barrel could be dangerous.

It is wise practice never to shoot ground game when standing in a line, whatever the rules of the shoot. There is always a risk of a ricochet from stones. Incidentally, dangerous ricochets from the beaks of birds are not uncommon.

Some guns seem unable to resist shooting at a hare when it is in a dangerous position. They should never be asked to a shoot and I would never go to a shoot where I knew they would be present.

Of course, the most dangerous act is to swing through the line when following a low bird. This happens most frequently on grouse moors and at partridge shoots when the birds are coming low, as many of them do.

Some people who occasionally shoot dangerously try to excuse themselves by saying that when they fired the second barrel, which is usually the dangerous one, they were 'already committed', meaning they could not stop themselves. What such a person is really admitting, at best, is that he was not in control of his gun.

It is a common belief that a shot at a pigeon before a drive begins will stop game-birds from coming forward. This is nonsense. What is the difference between shooting at the first pheasant or partridge which comes over early in the drive and at a pigeon? On the day that we shot more than a thousand brace of wild English partridges, on my land at Rothwell, we fired at every pigeon that came near the line before the drive started. The only time you need to hold your fire at a good pigeon is when the host asks you to do so. He may have an arrangement where he fires one or two shots to signal to the keeper that the guns are in position. In my experience a complaint about shooting at pigeons usually stems from keepers who are seeking an excuse for a drive which has gone wrong for other reasons.

It is also important to shoot at jays, crows or magpies at any time in a drive, except in the circumstance just described.

Always leave a bird which is likely to make a more challenging target for your neighbours in the line and, hopefully, they will do the same for you. There is nothing more sickening than to see a shot gunning down a rising bird when it is a few yards off the ground and about to lift and fly down the line, yet some are unable to resist it. They are never asked twice by me.

There has usually been a misjudgement when two guns fire at the same bird. It is better to let the bird go than to subject it to a barrage. A pheasant, partridge or a grouse is better spared than shared. If you have fired simultaneously with your neighbour at a bird which was plumb between you or at one which has changed

21

course always declare, loudly and quickly, 'Your bird!' even if you know you killed it.

Some men are adept at apologizing for taking another gun's birds but continue to do it. Many people who have shot with me wonder why they are not asked again. The usual reason is that they are inveterate poachers of their neighbour's birds. To me it is a form of theft, like stealing from somebody's wallet.

We have all been subjected to such greedy guns and very often they are accurate shots – I would not use the word 'good'. It is very tempting to complain, but that can cause problems for the host as the offender always comes up with a denial or some excuse. My response, if any, is to wait until there is no bird in the sky and fire off a couple of shots in quick succession. At the end of the drive the greedy neighbour invariably asks what I was shooting at and I reply: 'I was just letting you know that I have a gun as well.'

In my view, it is fair to take a bird which another gun has missed or wounded, provided he has had two barrels at it, but it is better not to make a regular habit of it. There are some trigger-happy people who will only allow the next gun to miss with one barrel before firing themselves, and this is most unfair and off-putting. There are some hosts, however, who disapprove of a bird being fired at by another gun after it has escaped two barrels, unless the guns are double-banked, and his requirements should be respected. Usually 'wiping the eye' of a friend on an odd occasion does no harm.

If you find you are so near to the next guns that some confusion about the oncoming birds is inevitable it is sensible to come to an arrangement so that one shoots hens only and the other cocks only. Or you can arrange to shoot the birds over each other's heads. But it must be agreed first!

It is also quite inexcusable to shoot at birds which the next gun has allowed to fly by because they are too low, yet this is commonly done, even by dukes, several of whom are notorious for it.

There is nothing like shooting for revealing a person's true character so quickly and so patently. Many people lie about what they have knocked down. The pickers-up and the keepers soon recognize them and will go so far as to make sure they have a bird in their pocket before setting out for yet another 'mythical'.

On several counts, shooting is a remarkably reliable environment for finding out whom you can trust.

On some drives where there may be many difficult birds it is common practice to double bank the guns so that some are standing behind the others. If there is a great weight of birds and you are one of the front guns then the host will want you to shoot as many as you like but if the birds are in moderate numbers it is good form to shoot cocks only and leave the hens for the gun behind you, unless, of course, you get a really high hen, what I call an Archangel Gabriel. (There was one well-known accurate shot who invariably killed everything he could so greedily that anyone placed as a back-gun behind him was advised to take a good book.)

It is humane to finish off a bird which you have wounded by firing a second barrel at it, provided it is safe to do so. But do not get into the habit of doing this as a matter of course, as so many Continental shots do. They will consistently fire a second barrel into a dead bird and spoil so many pheasants that my staff can tell who has been in the line by examining the birds. It is of course an essential aspect of etiquette and sportsmanship that you ensure that any wounded bird is collected and painlessly dispatched. It is fortunate for us that wounded game-birds are silent, unlike a wounded hare which proclaims its pain and the lack of skill of the person who shot it.

Do not fire at really low pheasants, whatever anybody else may be doing. A low pheasant close to is a cowardly shot and unworthy of a sportsman. Leave it to fly better another day. If you are drawn at the end of the line a distant bird that happens to be fairly low can be a testing target if it is safe to shoot but, in general, low birds should be shot only at the end of the season if there are too many birds left and the host wants them culled.

For your own satisfaction and in the interests of picking up all the game, equip yourself with a counter which can be in the form of a wrist device like a watch or like a small odometer with a press-button. This can be carried on a belt or in the pocket and is pressed after each bird is shot – it is easy to get into the habit. Try to memorize where your birds have fallen, either to speed the pick-up by your own dog or to help the professional pickers-up. Do not expect your loader to know where the birds have fallen. He may remember some but he should not really be watching, for his job is to ensure that you always have a full gun ready for action and to push it firmly into your hand when you need it. On the other hand, if there is a lull, it is a good idea to ask him to keep watch on the left while you watch the right for oncoming birds.

Never leave your peg or your butt during a drive to pick up a bird or for any other purpose. It is extremely dangerous to do so.

When the end of the drive is signalled – not before – ensure that your guns are unloaded and in their slings before you begin to pick up. Never go picking up holding a loaded gun – something I have seen when shooting abroad – because some guns think they may need it to finish off a bird that runs. Nothing could be more dangerous.

It is your responsibility, not your loader's, if you have one, to see that your guns are safe at the end of a drive. Before using them again in the next drive always look through the barrels again to ensure that there are no obstructions. This is particularly necessary in snowy weather because an obstruction of snow almost always causes a burst barrel with consequences which can be fatal. (My loader carries a pull-through for such occasions.)

Do not let your dog begin to pick up until you have collected the birds close to the peg by hand. Otherwise he will be confused and drop one bird to pick up another, which is a nasty habit because if he does that when you send him into a wood another dog may then refuse to pick up the bird. Send the dog for the birds that are not visible or are lying some distance away on the plough or over a fence. He is there to save your legs as well as to enjoy himself. Using a good dog sensibly greatly adds to the satisfaction of a day's sport.

Avoid picking up a neighbour's birds unless you ask permission or are asked to do so. Some guns are more fussy about having their birds picked up by someone else than they are about being 'poached'. It is certainly annoying to have a few nice birds to collect and find that neighbours have picked the area clean, usually adding the birds to their own line. This is particularly common on grouse moors. I ask my guests to pick up what they know they have shot and put them on their butts and then to carry any others to the nearest neighbour's butt.

Good pickers-up stay well behind the line and do their job after the guns have left for the next drive but some are in the habit of sending their dogs forward during the drive to increase their string of birds. If challenged they will usually claim that the dog ran in but they have nearly always sent it. If you are a guest it is wise not to complain, but if you have a dog you are perfectly justified in asking the picker-up behind you to leave a few for yours to pick. A good dog at a peg has waited very patiently for its moment and it is disheartening for it to be sent and to find nothing.

Never send a man to pick up a bird which you would not be prepared to pick yourself if you had the time. Ask yourself: 'Am I so sure that it is down that I would go and pick it?' Otherwise you will quickly get a well-deserved reputation for claiming mythical birds. On the other hand, if the pickers-up trust your word, they will walk half a mile or more, knowing that there is purpose in it.

I once sent a picker-up into some kale to retrieve a partridge which I knew had been shot in the left wing. He came back with a runner which had been shot in the right wing. I assured him that was not the bird we were looking for and that he should go back in. He did so, willingly, and came back with the right bird. (That did a lot for my reputation among the pickers-up and keepers!)

You need to be careful what you say to keepers and pickers-up. On one occasion I told my keeper where there was a partridge I had shot and that it had just one pellet in it – in the head. Unknown to me, the keepers plucked that bird while they were having lunch and, happily, they found only one pellet – in the head. A similar circumstance occurred in Spain during the 1988 season. I had shot a high partridge and had seen it fall dead in some thick bushes. After a long search the pickers-up, who usually pick by hand, assured me that there was nothing there, but as it was my shoot I declined to move until the bird was found. Further, I told them that the bird had been killed by one or two pellets on the left side of the head. I was sticking my neck out because, by that time, all the other guns had clustered round my butt. Dogs were brought and they quickly found the partridge which was examined by all and found to have one pellet wound near the left eye.

I like to lay my birds out in a line after the end of a drive to make them easy to count, not for ostentation, but to make sure they have all been picked. I also like to see all the pheasants shot in each drive laid out in two lines, cocks and hens, and admired. I hate to see birds thrown on a heap. They have given you good sport and should be treated with respect. But do not tell anyone how many you have shot unless you are asked. If you are asked simply say you had a good stand or a very good stand, depending on how it was.

It is always a grave mistake to make suggestions to the owner about how, in your opinion, a drive might have been carried out more successfully. There are some guns, who have shoots of their own, who cannot resist doing this and they soon get a name for being a know-all – and also get few repeat invitations. If your view of how to improve a drive is requested and you have some constructive suggestions then give them by all means, but not in a didactic manner.

Try to keep a smiling face even if the day has been a disaster for you.

Make sure that you thank the host and hostess, if she is present, for the lunch and tea as well as for the sport (you will, of course, follow up with a letter) and see the keeper personally to thank and tip him. The size of the tip can be decided by yourself depending on the size and quality of the bag or it can be a matter for mutual agreement among the guns. Sometimes the host can be approached for advice but some decline to give it, though I always give a generous guideline if asked. A regular attender at the shoot, if you are new there, will give you some indication of what is expected and then you can add extra if you wish, if you have had a particularly good day.

Do not penalize the keeper for a poor day when it is clearly not his fault. If the wind or excessive warmth are against him he has probably worked even harder to provide the birds you do get, and tips are part of his livelihood. On most shoots the keeper will appear at the original meeting place with a card giving the full count of the game shot, and that is normally the time for the guns to see him. On some, however, and often on grouse moors, he disappears after the end of the last drive when the braces of 'grace' birds are handed

26

out to the guns. You need to find out if that is to be the case so that you can thank and tip the keeper then.

The size of tips varies from shoot to shoot but is usually linked to the size of the bag. This is not always fair because a keeper may have to work as hard or harder to show his birds on a small shoot. Keepers who are tipped so much per hundred birds have an incentive to show easier and fatter pheasants. I tip according to the *quality* of the birds and, on a pheasant shoot, though not on a partridge shoot or grouse moor, I give something extra if I have seen a fox on the ground, for reasons I will explain later. If I see swarms of vermin or evidence of rats, however, I reduce the tip.

On some shoots the tips are collected and handed to the keeper but I still seek him out, shake his hand and thank him with a few words to show my appreciation. I try to recall some specific incident that redounds to his credit and mention it to him. On a grouse moor one can comment on the flanking, if it has been well done. Always remember it is not just his work that day which has given you sport but, on a well-run shoot, unremitting effort the whole year round.

Never offer advice to the keeper of another shoot unless he happens to be someone with whom you are on especially friendly or familiar terms.

If you are running a shoot the keeper should be instructed to select the grace birds during the lunch interval, when there is time to hand pick them and they will have a few hours to hang to cool before the shooting finishes. When guests are shooting for two days the grace birds should be selected from the first day's bag because they will travel much better. If possible they should be dry because wet birds do not hang so well or so long.

I always like to thank the beaters when they come in on their wagon or at some earlier convenient time. Though beaters are paid, few of them beat for that reason alone: they come to enjoy a day out and watch the birds and the shooting, and some of them are keen shots themselves. A shoot cannot operate without them and they deserve to be thanked by the owner and, in my view, by the guns. We should never cease to be grateful to beaters. We would have poor sport without them.

If your host has provided you with a loader there will be a 'going rate' for his services and you need to find out what this is. The host will usually tell you. If you have enjoyed your loader's company and his efforts by all means give him a little more. Some loaders can be very talkative, to an extent which can be boring and can interfere with the sport. They should not be encouraged to talk unless you want them to.

At the end of the day always make sure that you have all your equipment – and all your clothes if you have been staying as a guest. The person who habitually leaves his over-trousers or his cartridge bag in someone else's machine is a nuisance. If you have been travelling in someone else's vehicle or your guns have been in a gun-room make absolutely sure that you leave with your own guns. Mistakes happen most often when guns are in slings which look alike but guns can even be packed in the wrong gun cases though, thankfully, this has never happened to me. To find yourself with someone else's guns – perhaps someone who lives in Norfolk when you live in Cornwall – will certainly mean a great deal of inconvenience and, perhaps, having to cancel out of one or more shoots until the exchange is effected. Never to be separated from your guns is a good golden rule, though on some shoots one has to be separated between drives because the loaders travel together in one vehicle.

It is not bad manners to leave straight from the last drive provided you have told your host that you need to get away quickly, perhaps because you have a long journey or an evening engagement. If you do go in to tea make your stay brief because your host may want a rest or have things to do.

You may find that your grace birds have been put into your vehicle. Make sure that your dog cannot get at them. It is a great temptation for a bored and hungry dog on a long journey to have a brace of birds under his nose and he may develop a taste for them, with ruinous consequences.

You need to check your equipment when you arrive home and I will deal with that in the next chapter.

As regards the grace birds I like to have them labelled, giving the date and place where they were shot, before hanging them in a cool, fly-proof place. They should, of course, be young and not badly shot and it is up to the keeper to ensure that old birds are not given to the guns.

There are times when one is drawn near to a house or cottage and, of course, one should do everything to avoid causing any nuisance or damage to tiles or windows. Should it happen that you do so then, obviously, you must apologize and offer restitution. It can be embarrassing but must be done. I once shot a cock-pheasant which carried on straight through a cottage window. I sent my loader to apologize immediately and, when the drive was over, went myself. The mess in the kitchen was unbelievable. The lady of the house was mixing a cake with all the ingredients around her when the glass and feathers arrived as extras.

Finally, under the heading of behaviour, I should perhaps explain my habit of having all the empty cartridge cases collected and counted after each drive, for some people seem to consider this as bad form. Firstly, I think it is as dirty a habit to litter the countryside with cartridge cases, which so many do, as to leave tins lying about after a picnic. I have introduced the habit of collection and disposal on my partridge shoot in Spain where the spent cartridges used to be left on the ground.

Secondly I like, for my records and my curiosity, to know how many cartridges are expended by the whole team on each drive – not by different individuals – under different weather conditions. I do not do it to embarrass anybody and I do not note the number of shots fired by individuals. As long as my guests enjoy themselves, which is the prime purpose of their visit, I do not mind how many birds they miss, so long as they do not wound too many. My guests are not asked because of their accuracy but because I like them.

Chapter 3

The Means to the End

Since this is in no way a technical handbook, I will restrict my general comments about guns to my relevant experience with them and will deal with how I use them in ensuing chapters.

Good shotguns are expensive these days but, if cared for, they are a most worthwhile investment. It is quite possible to shoot well and safely with a much cheaper foreign gun but there is something about the feel of a good English gun which imparts the confidence so necessary to successful shooting. I cherish my guns and derive much pleasure from handling them. When I am using them they are extensions of my arms and I treat them with care and consideration accordingly.

I have been something of a pioneer in Britain in popularizing the over-and-under gun for game-shooting, as opposed to the traditional side-by-side, in the 12, 20 and 28 bores. As Richard Beaumont's book, *Purdey: the Gun and the Family*, records:

> In 1948 Mr Joseph Nickerson (now Sir Joseph) ordered the first Magnum 12 bore over-and-under. Built with 28 inch barrels this gun was delivered in 1950 and weighed 7 lb 12 ozs. Sir Joseph is one of the few English customers to shoot game and wildfowl with guns of this design and has trios of them in 12 bore, 20 bore and 28 bore sizes. His great bags of wild greylegged partridges and grouse scores have all been achieved with over-and-under guns of our make.

The best 12 bore over-and-unders were made by Woodward, whom I knew and whose guns I used for many years. One should hesitate before saying anything is the best but Woodward was a fine craftsman. Purdey over-and-under guns based on the Woodward patent, which they bought, are very good but not quite as satisfactory as Woodward's originals in my experience. I cannot speak for makes other than Purdey and Woodward. Both are superb.

I ordered three over-and-under 20 bores from Purdeys and, having fixed the price – then £3,750 for the trio – told them they could take as long as they liked to make them so long as they delivered them by the time I reached sixty. Purdeys stood by their bargain; They arrived early and since 1972 I have not used a 12 bore, save on an odd shoot. For the last few seasons I have used nothing but trios of Purdey 28 bores, beautiful $5^{1}/_{2}$-pound over-and-under guns which suit me very well.

Strangely, some people still look down on over-and-unders, perhaps because they are used so much by the clay-pigeon shooters. But, surely, that almost universal use in such a highly competitive sport would suggest some decided advantage. With an over-and-under the barrels can be shorter – down to 26 inches without loss of range or accuracy. Because of the design one is holding wood with the left hand and not metal, so one does not have the disadvantage of hot barrels. I think that I am quicker on to the target with over-and-unders, and a bit more accurate, but the total advantage is probably only small. Anyway, I have used them with general satisfaction for forty-four consecutive seasons.

I wore out the barrels of a pair of new Woodward over-and-under 12 bores and Purdeys rebarrelled them. They were so reliable that from 1946 to 1972 I had very little occasion to use the third gun.

To save weight I have had my over-and-unders made with the barrels joined only at the front and back, eliminating the usual full-length bar joining them together. The Purdey 20 bores weigh six pounds and, though they can discharge an ounce of shot with no problem, thirteen sixteenths of an ounce is quite adequate. The retractable front trigger fires the top barrel. On one gun I have this barrel very heavily choked for grouse so that I can get a chance at the first bird a fair way in front and have a bit more spread of shot for the second barrel when I take the nearer bird. Ideally, perhaps, with the tendency of any barrel to whip and lift, the first trigger should fire the bottom barrel.

When I moved to 20 bore guns, in 1972, that calibre was generally thought of as suitable for ladies, boys and men with a disability. I had damaged my shoulder in a hunting fall, and again in a Land Rover accident, but apart from finding them lighter and easier to move quickly, I took them up to make the sport more difficult and to give the quarry a more even chance, as I was finding game in general a little too easy to kill with a 12 bore. The 16 bore is a nice size of gun but in my view not sufficiently different from a 12.

If you have been using a 12 bore all your life, switching to a lighter gun is quite an exercise but worth the effort in the satisfaction it provides. The advantages of a lighter gun when one is older are quite pronounced, permitting a faster swing. I am now down to 28 bore guns for all types of shooting and am killing birds as difficult and as far away as ever I did with a 12 bore, as many friends can testify. Over the last four seasons, at grouse, wild Spanish partridges and English pheasants, the average number of cartridges expended per bird has worked out at 1.8, using a pair of guns and taking on all shootable birds, not just the easy ones.

I recall taking the Purdey 12, 20 and 28 bore guns, all over-and-unders, and using all three against woodpigeons, from a hide, on the same day. There was not much difference in performance but it was decidedly more pleasant to shoot with the lighter guns and, in theory at least, the quarry had a better chance.

It is my view that in the years ahead more and more people will switch to the lighter guns and that the days of the 12 bore may be numbered. It may well go out of fashion as the 10 bore did.

Choke, which is a constriction reducing the diameter of the gun in the top inch or two by leaving more metal there when the barrel is bored, is very much a matter of personal preference and its value depends on the accuracy of the user. Its purpose is to concentrate the pellets in a denser pattern, enabling them to kill birds at greater distances. The more accurate the shot the more he can use choke to advantage. Most people are better off with very little choke, but a choked spare pair of barrels is very useful for specialized use on shoots with extra-high birds.

32

Whatever the calibre, the fit of the gun to your body is all important and must be done professionally at a shooting school if it is to become an extension of your arm, as it should be. As your body changes over the years, and especially if you put on weight as, sadly, most of us do, the gun may need to be refitted. I make sure that my guns continue to fit me and when I miss a bird I know it is not the fault of the gun.

Single or double triggers are a matter of personal preference. The single trigger would be excellent but is not sufficiently reliable so I always have my guns fitted with two triggers.

The weight of the pull is also a personal matter. About three pounds is average. It should need firm pressure because a feather-light pull can be dangerous. The pull of the rear trigger should always be slightly heavier.

Dwelling on the trigger is one of the commonest reasons for missing a bird, so anything that delays the pull is to be avoided. In this connection my loader, Will Jacob, and I have noticed that guns tend to have some sideways play in the trigger and if, like me, you slide your finger down the trigger to pull it, this side movement can take up a fraction of a second. This extra delay, though brief, can be crucial in dealing with a very fast bird. Some leading gun-makers are now examining this observation for which Will Jacob deserves the credit if it proves to be a flaw, as seems to be the case.

While most of the million or so people who shoot in Britain manage with only one gun, for shooting in what one might call the First Division a matched pair of guns is needed or, better still, a trio. The purpose of this is quickly appreciated when one gun is unserviceable and a different one has to be used in its place. I have my guns made in matched threes simply because I do so much shooting and if one of them needs repair I still have a couple which are serviceable.

When the two guns are not exactly alike, swinging and mounting are almost certain to be affected. Some people seem convinced that they shoot better with one of the matched guns than with the other but this should not be so if they are identically bored and otherwise perfectly matched.

While many women shoot with 12 bores, especially at clays,

a lighter gun, such as a 20 bore, is more suited to the physical strength of most, and subjects them to less recoil. In general terms I would say that a lady begins to know she is shooting well when the men stop telling her that she is!

Young boys and girls also need small-bore guns when they learn to shoot, say at age thirteen or even as early as nine if they are under really good supervision, though I was bitten by the gun-bug when I was only eight. The .410 remains a good starting gun with one firing pin removed so that only the right barrel and the front trigger can be used.

The weakest part of any shotgun is the narrow part of the stock where it joins the barrels. It may seem hard to believe, but stocks have been broken there when a gun has been used by a beginner to try to kill a wounded hare! Good stocks are made of walnut, and the best come from the root of French walnut trees. The wood should be chosen so that a pair or trio of guns all match in grain pattern, so far as possible. This will not affect the way they handle but it will affect their value as well as their appearance.

Walnut, though beautifully grained and delightful to handle, is soft and easily scratched or dented. Such damage can take hundreds of pounds off the value of a gun so steps should be taken to avoid it. I have found that much damage is inflicted by the buckles on cartridge bags when loaders are carrying guns. For that reason I have simple slips of soft leather which cover the buckles on my bags, having first taken the precaution of having the sharp points of the buckles filed down. It costs very little to have them made by a saddler.

It is as much to protect the stocks as the barrels that guns should always be carried in fleece-lined slips or slings, as they are also called, when not in use. A cheaper, unlined slip is a poor investment. Like all your equipment, slips need to be marked boldly with your name or initials. I also have mine and the rest of my kit marked with a colour I can instantly recognize.

The initials on a gun are not a conceit but a way of ensuring that you get the right guns back when several are being cleaned in one gun-room. I do not let my guns go into anybody else's gun-room unless in the care of a loader whom I trust. As I have already remarked, it is wise to check, personally, that you have the right case put back in your vehicle and the right guns inside it because of the appalling inconvenience of a mistake.

Any gun, whatever its value, must be cleaned meticulously after shooting or at least pulled through and cleaned as soon as possible later. One cartridge can foul and corrode the barrels as much as five hundred if its remains are not quickly removed. Any water, leading to rust, can be extremely damaging and must be removed the same day – the sooner the better – and replaced by proper gun oil. A feather is often useful for drying parts which are not easily accessible and for putting oil there. Thorough cleaning is specially important if you have been wildfowling and your gun has been exposed to the action of salt, which is extremely corrosive.

You may come to rely, with sound reason, as I – with Billy – have been able to for many years, on a trusted employee to clean the guns properly and take responsibility for their care. With guns the price they are and repairs so expensive I would not like to entrust them to a stranger and would prefer to clean them myself. In the event of damage, such as an accidentally dented barrel, a stranger may well not report it.

Most people, however, are prepared to entrust their weapons to a strange loader, and the least they should do when they get home, or at the latest, next day, is to examine them carefully to make sure he has made a good job of it.

After a wet day it is a wise precaution to leave your gun case open all night in a warm, locked room with your cleaned guns inside and then to check them again for dampness in the morning. It is also essential that your gun slings are dried out by opening them up and leaving them overnight or even longer in a warm room. Many a gun has been severely damaged through having been left for several days, or longer, in a damp slip. Your guns will be much safer in their case.

If you think about it, a gun takes a tremendous amount of punishment during a heavy season, with the various moving parts and springs inevitably suffering some wear. This will not usually be visible so it is essential to have guns examined and overhauled, with weakened parts replaced as soon as possible when the season ends. Do not leave it until the summer because then you will find the gunsmith overloaded with work from all the others who have done the same thing. And, unless you are an expert, I urge you not to attempt the maintenance yourself. Choose a reliable gunsmith as you would choose a reliable jeweller to repair an important brooch. Your guns are not only valuable but need to be kept that way and there is nothing more irritating than a gun which becomes unserviceable in the middle of a big shoot. The gunsmith will discover any faults, dangerous or otherwise, and warn you when the barrels are becoming thin and at risk of failing the proof requirements. Make personal contact with your gunsmith if you can. You will learn a lot from him and he will be more likely to undertake simple repairs quickly during the season. An occasional brace of birds in his direction may repay you.

When you possess only one gun, as so many enthusiasts do, it is obviously more important to keep it well maintained. There are few worse fates than having to put your one gun in for repair in the middle of the season. You may be able to hire a replacement but it is unlikely that you will be able to shoot as well with it.

For security reasons, a gun should never be left in the body of an unattended car. It must be locked in the boot where at least it cannot be seen. These days a stolen gun can cause enormous problems for and with the police.

With loss and accidental damage always a possibility, guns need to be insured for their full replacement value. To take proper account of inflation, this value should be reassessed each year. If you insure a pair of guns make sure that you are covered for their replacement as a pair, which would be more expensive than two separate guns.

A gun is designed and made to kill and the shotgun is especially lethal at close ranges. So it must be treated with respect at all times. No liberties can ever safely be taken with a gun. I will repeatedly return to the subject of safety but, at this point, would stress the absolute necessity of personal insurance against the risk of accidentally injuring another person. In view of the heavy compensation sums now being awarded by courts for injuries you will need a big policy, but they are extraordinarily cheap.

Under the new laws guns must now be stored in a securely locked place and there are special cabinets firmly fixed to walls made for this purpose. It is important to have one because the police have the power to examine the gun-security precautions of anyone holding a gun certificate. It is a great convenience to have a secure, well-lit gun-room with a good bench surface where guns can be cleaned with minimum risk of damage. One occasionally sees guns being cleaned by loaders after a shoot in some dimly lit barn or in the backs of vehicles with a high risk of barrels being dropped. The gun-room also serves, on occasion, as a warm place where guests can change and leave their clothing.

For fun, over my gun-room door I have two Latin notices. The one on the way out translates as 'About to be humbled'; that on the way back as 'Having been humbled'.

A boiler room where wet clothes can be dried during the lunch interval is a great asset. Outside the gun-room at Rothwell I have the luxury of a tap delivering really hot water where muddy gum-boots can be washed so much more easily and quickly. It is especially comforting on an icy day.

Britain used to lead the world in the production and sale of cartridges but sadly, as in so many fields, the manufacturers do not seem to have kept pace with foreign competition. Most cartridges are satisfactory and the differences between them are minimal when compared like for like. Perhaps the one exception is American, for the long distance, out of range shooting the Americans specialise in.

Incidentally, very few gun-makers make their own cartridges though they sell them with their names boldly stamped on them. These are usually British, made to order by ICI and are reliable. There are also, however, some excellent brands loaded by small firms.

Whatever the make, the weight of the load needs to be balanced to the weight of the gun. Too heavy a load in a light gun is likely to give you a headache. An ounce of load is the heaviest you should use in a six-pound gun.

Number six shot is the best for all round purposes with a 12 bore. For the 20 and 28 bore I use the American equivalent of the English six and for higher birds number five. Using anything bigger will handicap you. Some people prefer seven shot for grouse and partridges but I would still use number six.

Under the security requirements cartridges should be stored separately from guns and this is a sensible precaution anyway in view of the incredible extent – according to newspaper reports of accidents – that guns seem to be handled, and even cleaned, with live cartridges in them.

It is absolutely essential that cartridges be stored in a dry place, which should also be cool. Otherwise the metal bases can corrode, making the cartridges dangerous. A sensible temperature is the one you would use to store claret or leather-bound books.

If you attempt to dry damp cartridges on an Aga stove it will make them kick more severely when fired. This effect has been used for giving a slight shock to another gun but I would not recommend any jokes involving guns or ammunition. I have been told – though, happily, I have no first-hand experience – that it is possible to buy joke cartridges which when fired produce a whistling sound, and a small parachute then descends. Such cartridges must be inherently dangerous and the shooting field is no place for pranks of any kind.

Cartridge bags are in constant use yet one sees designs which are hopelessly unsuitable to quick and easy loading. A bag must have a very wide mouth that will stay open so that a loader – or yourself – can easily get his hand into it. For this reason the mouths of my bags are stiffened with metal so that they remain open.

To increase the speed of loading, which is so helpful on a grouse moor or in a heavy partridge or pheasant drive, I devised the spring fitments shown in the photograph on p.10 many years ago, and all my bags are fitted with them. The loader replenishes the clips during lulls in the shoot. These simple but highly effective devices may have been thought of before but if so I had not seen or heard of them. They are now widely obtainable.

A game-counter is a necessary item of equipment. Nobody can count accurately what they have shot without a counter. You can remember five or six out of a flush but, even then, you must get them on to the counter. Some counters are like a wristwatch but the one I use now (having worn out a wrist counter) dangles from a buttonhole on my left-hand jacket pocket. It is easy to get into the habit of clicking it after each kill or each flush. Knowing how many there are to pick can save a lot of time, increase the size of the bag and avoid the leaving of birds for vermin.

The right kind of clothing is an essential adjunct to successful shooting. In my long experience the really satisfactory shooting jacket has yet to be made. I have tried dozens and most of them have a fault. Those which resist the rain become very wet outside – and inside through condensation – and it is extraordinary how the standard of shooting declines along the line when everyone is in wet coats. Some of the waterproof tweed-covered coats do not let rain through but they absorb it and become excessively heavy.

Cotton jackets, which the Piccadilly firm of Cordings used to make, are the best because you can really swing about in them. They soon let the rain in, however, so I carry two or three and change them when they get wet. Whatever the coat, it is wise to have a change or even two in your vehicle. In a real deluge I don a paper-thin waterproof over my shooting coat and it is tolerable for short periods.

I have proved to my satisfaction that the nearer the butt of the stock is to the skin the better the shot, so I do not like shoulder pads and I even pluck the down out of the lining of a jacket on the gun shoulder. I also cut out the right shoulder of my waistcoats and jerseys.

I do not like a belt on my jacket because, when fastened, it impedes movement. Nor do I like dangerous buttons on my outer clothes because they might actuate triggers.

On many jackets the pockets are too small to get a hand in when you want a few cartridges stored there or the flap on the pocket will not fold in far enough to make extraction of the cartridges easy.

The secret of keeping warm when shooting in winter is to wear several thin layers which trap the air. I have a record of what I wore to shoot ducks on Read's Island, in the Humber Estuary, in rather cold weather recently – Aertex vest and underpants, silk vest and silk long johns, thermal short woollen underpants and knickerbockers, a woollen pullover, a cashmere polo neck jersey with long sleeves, a 'goose' waistcoat, and two thin jackets. It sounds ridiculous but I could move easily because most of the garments were extraordinarily thin and you cannot shoot well if you are shivering with cold. Too many thick clothes will make you look like the Michelin man and you won't be able to swing sufficiently.

It is easy to take things off if you get too hot and not at all pleasant if you have brought too few clothes, especially when you are older.

The ideal footwear for shooting in dry weather is shoes, especially if worn with spats. The latter are old-fashioned but immensely practical for keeping out dew, stubble and heather twigs. If more people realized how practical they are more would wear them. I indulge in the luxury of having my shoes hand-made because they fit better and last longer. If you think about it you spend your life either in bed, in your car or in your shoes. They should all, therefore, be the best you can afford: and, as happens so often, the best, in the long run, usually ends up being the cheapest. 'Buy cheap and you buy dear' is a good axiom in shooting.

For really wet and cold weather, of course rubber boots are essential. The best, in my view, are the French leather-lined boots with zip fasteners up the sides which make them easy to put on and remove, ridiculously expensive as they are. I have one pair of 10s for warm weather, a pair of 11s which take an extra pair of stockings when it is colder, and one pair size 13 to accommodate extra-thick quilted socks for extreme cold.

Clean footwear is an absolute must and to turn up with unwashed gum-boots or dirty shoes is, in my view, an insult to the host and the other guns, and rarely goes unnoticed. There was a well-known cabinet minister, now deceased, who never cleaned his shoes from one season to the next, arguing that it was pointless when they were going to get muddy anyway. This quickly became his trademark – a reputation for laziness which pursued him into his political life.

For changing boots and shoes a bootjack is invaluable and it is worthwhile to have a small one in one's vehicle.

I always shoot in gloves, even in warm weather, a very thin one for the right hand and, sometimes, a thicker one for holding the gun. A glove for the left hand is essential when shooting one side-by-side gun because the barrels soon get unbearably hot. If the right hand becomes only slightly numb with cold one can dwell on the trigger without realizing it. In my experience gloves are a safety measure because if fingers are numb and do not have the natural feel of the trigger a gun can be accidentally discharged. Most shooting gloves, now available from most gunsmiths, have a slit in the right index finger so that the top joint of the finger can be protruded to pull the trigger. With thin gloves this is unnecessary and defeats their purpose. I get round it by buying pairs made for left-handers. I find that one always shoots better when the wrists are warm, especially as one gets older. For that reason the wrists of the gloves should be made of wool. When the wind really bites I wear, in addition, the old-fashioned wrist muffs out of sight under the sleeves of the jacket.

I have several extra pairs of gloves in my vehicle or in a bag with the loader. Dry gloves after each drive in wet weather are a great pleasure and make for greater safety because slippery gloves can pose a danger.

It is possible to buy very thin silk gloves which can be worn, with advantage, under leather gloves in extremely cold weather. It is difficult to shoot in thick gloves, and woollen gloves and mittens do little for the fingers.

I hate shooting in waterproof over-trousers but they are essential in some weather conditions. The most convenient are those which have zip fasteners at the bottom of the legs, making them easier to pull over boots. I always have an extra set of over-trousers so that I can change at the lunch interval and go out dry in the afternoon.

Being the item which is most often left behind in a vehicle or a changing room, over-trousers must be marked with your name – in the interest of the person who finds them as much as in yours.

A hood is a necessity for really wet weather, especially on the grouse moor, but it needs to be made of very thin material in a light frame to fit round the face so that you can turn your head and neck easily. I used to shoot in a trilby hat in the past but for many years have found a flat cap to be the best all-round headgear, with an alpine hat in reserve for particularly cold conditions.

Everybody perspires in waterproof clothing so jackets and over-trousers should be turned inside out and aired, preferably outside in the breeze. Otherwise they will become anti-social.

Excessive perspiration, causing a loss of body salts, can cause extremely painful cramp, especially in the legs. Thankfully, I do not suffer from it but many people do and experience excruciating pain, usually when they get to bed. I am told that one pill, of a kind which can be bought at a chemist without prescription, taken as soon as a shooting day is finished, will prevent cramp. Another, just before going to bed, may be a wise extra precaution.

For most of my life I never used a shooting stick because I thought I might miss chances when getting up. Instead I preferred a thumb-stick which serves as a third leg and is essential as you get older, especially on the grouse moor. A shooting stick is pretty useless to walk with but a long, stout thumb-stick can save you from some nasty falls and is very helpful in negotiating styles, fences and bogs. It should be of such a height that when gossiping or surveying the scene, in between drives, you can lean on it. However, I have now reached the stage in life when taking the weight off the legs and hips is sometimes desirable and for that I have found a shooting stick welcome.

The majority of people who shoot regularly become deaf, especially in the left ear. Strangely, though I have fired a very large number of cartridges, my hearing remains almost normal for my age. I must be a fortunate exception, however, and there can be no doubt that ear defenders are a wise precaution with earplugs rather a poor second. It is never too late to start using them. Defenders should, in theory at least, make one less likely to flinch when the gun is fired. People who have become used to them find it very noisy to shoot without them. I have not yet tried them and shoot with no ear protection. I do, however, recommend my family wear them.

Shot-proof spectacles are an absolute essential in my opinion. One needs a yellow pair for ordinary or dim conditions, such as duck-flighting at dawn and dusk – it is surprising how they can light up a bleak grouse moor – and a black pair for bright sunlight. I have mine made abroad, to prescription, and they are said to be proof against number six shot at twenty metres range but, thank God, I have never had to test them. There are also quite cheap, and apparently effective, plastic shot-proof glasses to be had from gun shops but they are easily scratched and stained and soon become blurred and have to be replaced.

Spectacles are helpful to the older shot in preventing the wind from making eyes water. Nobody has yet solved the problem of rain on spectacles.

Finally, there is one additional object among my shooting accoutrement. In my vehicle I have a wooden box about three inches deep, twelve inches wide and fifteen inches long with many small compartments. If I am away from home it goes into the bedroom where I am staying and contains everything that I hope that I will not need – from candles and matches to magnesia tablets. I have stayed in too many remote houses where we have been plunged in darkness through a power failure – usually when everyone is bathing and putting too heavy a load on the system.

It is an interesting and informative exercise to tot up the total value of your shooting equipment. The sum may surprise you and spur you on to take better care of it.

Chapter 4

Facing the Challenge

It is futile to pretend that shooting is not sometimes cruel: this has to be true when birds are wounded. So it behoves us all to improve our accuracy so that wounding is reduced to a minimum. Every bird not shot cleanly – preferably in the head – should be a spur to that end.

Shooting is a fine art in which the competent performer can take pride and satisfaction. What I have learned – and I am still learning – might help others to comparable enjoyment. There are many styles of shooting and I can only describe the ways which have suited me.

You must *want* to kill the bird, so grip the gun strongly and move it purposefully. A half-hearted shot will usually mean a miss. This is the reason why so many low birds are missed: the gun knows, in his heart, that he should not be shooting them and therefore does not concentrate. You must try hard with every bird. It is easy to become complacent and miss easy birds. It may be an illusion but a gun seems to shoot with more effect if firmly held and strongly moved with determination.

A wounded bird is worse than a miss, so do not shoot at birds which are too high if you are not confident that you have a fair chance of killing them in the air. The ideal shot is to hit a bird in the head only and you should train yourself to think in terms of the head rather than the whole bird. This can, however, result in missing in front so, perhaps the average shot should be satisfied by shooting them in the front end of the body.

Your gun must fit your body properly and it must be mounted so that it fits snugly into your shoulder and comes into your cheek.

To shoot consistently well you need to be standing on firm and level ground. Stamp it down if necessary and, if you have a loader, get him to help you. He also needs a level patch if he is to load quickly and safely. For steep sloping ground, if a flat standing area has not been dug out, it pays to have a small entrenching tool, as is common in Spain. The Spanish also make regular use of mats constructed with spirally wound thick ropes, but these are not practicable if there is much of a walk from vehicles to stands. A considerate host will have straw bales near the pegs on deep wet plough to help provide a better footing.

A narrow stance gives more freedom for movement than a wide one and it pays to stand with the left foot pointing a few more degrees towards the left than would seem to be natural. You will be surprised how much this little trick will help you to swing to the left.

For a bird on the left, the left foot needs to be moved to the left and then the right should be placed in front of it. The reverse should happen for the bird on the right. This was a general tip offered by that legendary shot, Lord Ripon, and I would endorse it.

When birds begin to fly in a drive I like to cradle the gun so that it is pointing upwards. From this position it can be mounted more quickly and smartly than from the usual carriage under the arm. There used to be a farming good-wish – 'God speed the plough': perhaps 'God speed the gun' should be the counterpart for shooters, as fishermen wish each other 'Tight lines!' You don't need to be hurried but you do need to be sharp.

Keep both eyes open to make maximum use of perspective judgement. A few may find that they shoot better with one eye closed or partly closed, but they are penalizing themselves in ways which can affect performance at long-range birds. Binocular vision assists in the judgement of both distance and speed. If I had three eyes I would keep them all open. The estimation of the quarry's flight – whether it is very fast, fast or fairly slow – is most important. Often, when watching on the grouse moor, I see a procession of birds behaving in what might be described as a normal manner and then spot one moving faster or more slowly. I remark to my loader, 'That one will get missed,' and it is surprising how often it turns out to be correct.

While accurate shooting is a matter of the co-ordination of hands and eyes, perfect vision is by no means necessary and, indeed, few of us possess it. As long as your eyesight, with or without spectacles, is good enough to permit you to drive a car safely, then you can see and shoot most game. Much nonsense is talked about 'master' eyes, right or left: they do exist but my advice is to shoot with both eyes open, unless a visit to a gun school has shown, beyond doubt, that you need to close one of them. The problem is that if you start squinting with one eye closed you will tend to drop your head and sight down the gun, which is fine for rifle shooting but hopeless with a shotgun. Dropping the head is a common fault and source of misses, as is dropping a shoulder. Try to bring up the gun to the cheek and shoulder while standing erect. The shoulder nearer the bird should be the higher of the two. In a right-handed shot this is usually achieved with the bird moving to the left but the shoulder is commonly dropped with the swing to the right, resulting in a miss underneath.

Lifting the cheek from the stock as the gun is raised is, perhaps, the commonest and the worst fault – almost bound to lead to a miss. Once that happens your eyes may still be aligned on the bird but your gun will not be. If you are unaware that you are doing it you cannot understand why you keep missing birds.

Mount the gun to the cheek and shoulder in one movement, with both arms sharing the work, and the left arm and hand doing the indicating. Again, have confidence, do not check or look down the barrel but, keeping your eyes solely on the bird, mount the gun and pull the trigger without hesitation. Press the trigger as the gun comes into the shoulder. I cannot overstress this advice. *Press the trigger as the gun comes into the shoulder.*

Though the movement should never look hurried, fast reflexes are essential to really good shooting. A good partridge shot will have two dead by the hedge while a slow starter is wondering which bird to engage. Identify your target and stick to it even if you think that an easier one has suddenly come into view.

If your gun fits you, first aim is always the best aim. Have confidence in it. Do not try to correct it by checking the swing, which nearly always causes a miss.

As regards the general position of your body with respect to the target, I have found that it pays to suppose that you are wearing a tie pin. Then you should always move your body, preferably your whole body, so that the pin faces the bird you are going to shoot at.

Do not be afraid to miss but try to understand why you did: much can be learned from misses. What we must avoid when we miss, perhaps successively, is becoming despondent about it.

The best single piece of advice that I can offer to reduce misses is to press the trigger quickly and earlier than you would, perhaps, think of doing. Dwelling on the trigger is probably the commonest cause of misses or wounded birds. When people see a high pheasant jink because it has been hit behind they immediately assume that they have not given it enough lead, but had they pulled the trigger a fraction earlier with the same lead they would have killed it in the head.

I have already stressed the need for safety in what is, intrinsically, a dangerous sport, and will only repeat here the need for proper use of the safety catch. The safety catch should never be pressed forwards to the On position until you are actually taking a shot. It should be pressed forwards with the side of the first joint of the thumb, not by the ball of the thumb, so that you do not have to change the position of your hand round the stock. (As a result of doing this so many times I have a little permanent lump on the side of my right thumb which I look upon as a visitation from the souls of more than 300,000 birds.)

Some people seem to fiddle with the safety catch as they stand waiting and this is always to be deplored.

Always remember – indeed tell yourself repeatedly – shotgun shooting is about movement – movement of the gun and movement of parts of the body and, often, the whole body. You will not shoot much with a stationary gun in any position. A stationary gun at a stationary target is likely to connect: a stationary gun at a moving target is most unlikely to do so.

I attribute what success I have had to moving the gun more and faster than most people whom I have observed.

The reason why so many people, including myself, kill with the second barrel after missing with the first, is that we have not started swinging *fast* enough. With a bird suddenly brought to one's attention, one moves faster, snaps at it and down it comes because the gun was put up to it in one quick movement. A very high bird missed with the first barrel often falls to the second if the gun is pushed really hard in the same direction and almost without the bird being seen.

The reason so many miss with the second barrel at a second bird, having killed one with the first, is because they fail to remount the gun. You can follow through on the first bird to kill it with the second barrel, having missed it with the first. But for a new bird in a different position you need a new mounting – though not totally; i.e. keep the gun up but remount into the shoulder. It should be a conscious second shot rather than a continuation of the first.

Are there occasions where one should use the choke barrel first at a flying target? I do so, if I want to take an approaching bird well in front.

It is possible to intercept a fast-moving bird by aiming at a spot in front of it with a stationary gun but it will happen so rarely that the practice must be avoided. If you are trying to bring down a very long-range crossing bird, such as a pigeon or high pheasant, you may look at the sky in front of the bird, bring your gun through the bird and see daylight in front of it as you pull the trigger, but you need to swing and still be swinging when you fire. This is the best advice I can offer to anybody for dealing with really long shots. They look very impressive when they come off.

To some extent, shooting is like batting at cricket: there are different strokes for different birds, and a skilful exponent is pleasant to watch. At any bird well up in the sky always shoot high, imagining that the bird has a top hat on. Oddly, it is not easy to remember to do this and it is worth saying aloud 'Shoot high' as you swing. That way you will kill more birds and kill them cleanly.

At the distant crossing pheasant, which is usually missed underneath, remember the top hat. It is almost impossible to shoot high enough, i.e. what would seem to be above the bird. In fact most birds, of all kinds, which are missed, whatever their position, are missed below and behind. When a pheasant is hit in the right place it should put its legs out in front – feet first – and spin down.

Do not hesitate to move the whole body when it helps. For

example when shooting a pheasant behind you can swing from the waist and try to take the bird over the shoulder but you can also turn round completely. Remember the tie-pin tip. Your aim and chance of a clean kill will be so much better if you are facing the going-away bird, as it will be with partridges and grouse. But, of course, when doing this you must point your gun skywards as you turn, to avoid swinging through the line.

With a low-flying grouse or partridge taken behind bring the gun down, and with it still moving, shoot deliberately underneath the bird. Just as the advice for shooting a high, crossing pheasant is to imagine that it has a top hat on, with a pheasant, grouse or partridge behind, imagine it is wearing spats and shoot at them.

One sees some good shots who hardly ever move the whole body when they are shooting pheasants, but if you watch them carefully you will usually see that they are selecting those birds which are easy for them without much movement. This is possible when large numbers of pheasants are coming over but it is much more challenging, much more satisfying and more sporting to take the difficult ones which require movement as well. Many of the Edwardian 'Big Shots' only took the birds which came 'between their eyes'. I like to shoot at every good bird that is legitimately mine and which I can kill safely.

The right-handed person really needs to *move* to kill the bird crossing to the right. Most people are too leisurely and do not make enough effort to get through the bird. Swing the gun with force, as though you were going to knock somebody down with it, and keep swinging with follow-through. That is the real secret of successful shooting.

As I have said, when one is older it is easier to swing fast with a lighter gun – a 20 or even a 28 bore. This is a great advantage when large numbers of birds keep coming at you in a drive, especially with high pheasants. The arm muscles can get really fatigued and the only thing to do is to rest and let the birds sail by for a minute or so. A really good keeper will know, from the weight of birds he is showing, that the guns must be tiring and should slow the drive down accordingly.

A lighter gun is also less likely to cause the common fault of bringing the head down to the stock.

When a high-flying pheasant is approaching do not start mounting the gun too early. Decide where you want to kill it then extend the left leg well forward and swing back, pressing the trigger as the gun comes into the shoulder and keep swinging through the bird. When a high approaching bird can be seen from a long distance it is very tempting to line it up with the gun at the shoulder but this usually means a clean miss. Watching pheasant shots at a high stand I can tell who is going to miss from the timing of their gun-mounting.

Never put the gun to the shoulder until you are ready to pull the trigger. But then treat the pheasant as an express train coming at you so that you really have to move fast to beat it. When a high bird is coming with the extra speed of the wind, start your movement just that little bit earlier and give a really good swing. The gun should be in your hands pointing straight up and when the bird gets almost overhead slide the gun to the shoulder and pull. The commonest fault with such high birds is *dwelling on the trigger*.

The person who puts the gun to the shoulder and then starts to swing looks wrong and wooden and, with that technique, will rarely, if ever, become a good shot.

The high pheasant coming at you over the left shoulder, when you have to take it late with the second barrel, having already taken another one, is more difficult than the bird on the right. My advice is not to swing the gun to the left at all but to pull the gun back strongly behind your left ear. You need to be shooting at the inside of the bird's left wing. Such a bird if taken in what would seem to be the proper manner, by turning and swinging at it, is usually missed a long way to the left. That may sound strange but I have found it to be true.

With the curling bird it is necessary to allow for the curl and shoot to the side, moving with the bird whichever way it is going. It is a good idea to talk to yourself, silently, saying, 'Curling to the right, so I shoot to the right,' and so on.

With extremely high pheasants, like those at Helmsley in North Yorkshire, and Tugdale at Rothwell, I use number five shot and shoot them overhead, shooting into the sky in front of them, while keeping the gun moving strongly, and pressing the trigger the moment the gun is in the shoulder. In the process I lift the weight off the left leg and bend the right leg, sometimes lifting the left leg clear off the ground. Kick the left foot up as you bend backwards and you can bend your back just that much more. This may sound ungainly but it is an extra trick which often gets these spectacular birds. Using that technique at Helmsley, while a guest of Lord Forte for three days in 1979, I see from my game records that I shot 390 very high pheasants with 783 20 bore cartridges. (Up to 1974 I had used 12 bore guns there with about the same ratio of kills to shots fired. In recent years I have used 28 bore guns at Helmsley with a similar, and even a better, ratio.)

The bird that is high and gliding is moving at the top of its speed though it may seem to be slow, but remember that it is also almost certainly losing height. A bird that is losing height is going that much faster under the influence of gravity and allowance must be made for that.

In a flush of pheasants, or of any other birds, shoot a high bird first, the second barrel usually being more difficult. For the same reason, when two birds present themselves, shoot the further one first. Most people take the nearer one.

While a very long-distance shot is spectacular and may bring praise, it more often results in a wounded bird which is always to be avoided. This is due to excessive spread of the pellets and their lower velocity at long ranges, unless heavy choke is being used.

With partridges the secret of success lies in quick firing. Put your gun up at the bird and fire immediately and you will be surprised how often it will fall down. With practice you will move your wrist to compensate for the bird's twists and turns – what I call the 'wrist twist'.

With grouse and partridges coming at you at head height, as so many do, it is essential to get two shots into them very quickly – pop-pop – without moving much at all. Let them come fairly close in and snap shoot with minimum delay between the shots. It requires confidence but if you can bring yourself to do it you will be surprised how many more birds you will knock down.

Partridges are sometimes missed in front and below. They are usually slower than pheasants – the bigger the bird the faster it flies – so one should shoot at them. You can hardly shoot too high above a crossing bird. If you keep your gun moving and high it is surprising how far away you can kill a crossing partridge or a grouse cleanly.

I made a few notes about shooting partridges in Spain recently. They read as follows:

Generally speaking, if your gun fits properly, you should get it up and get the trigger pulled much more quickly than most people would ever dream of doing. For the bird that has got behind you and is angling away you need to be into the daylight to the side of the bird and I have only just learned to do that. (After all these years I am still learning.) When taking a bird behind, after it has gone straight over your head, you need to shoot well under them.

For a distant crossing partridge exaggerate the swing, the bird going to the right needing even more swing than the bird going to the left. Don't shoot at birds when they are too far in front or you will get too many runners.

Grouse behind the butt are almost always missed over the top. I can see this repeatedly when other guns are shooting from the way the pollen goes up from the heather. Shoot at the legs and bring the left hand down so that the gun is moving. Master this trick and you will double the number of grouse you kill in a drive.

The grouse flying upwind is often missed in front, as is any slow flier like a magpie or jay.

Some people develop a sore chin or a bruised cheek, especially in the early part of the season and, provided that their gun fits, this can only be the result of failing to mount the gun properly.

A sore or bruised shoulder is also the result of faulty mounting, causing the gun to strike the body on the recoil which should be taken up painlessly if the shoulder is properly cushioned up against the stock. If a bruised shoulder is being experienced persistently, the odds are that the gun is too short in the stock.

A bruised or blistered trigger finger, which can be very painful, is also usually due to a badly fitting gun. This can be corrected by a visit to a shooting school, alleviated by a small rubber pad fitted behind the trigger guard or by the wearing of thin gloves. The side of the thumb which slides on the safety catch takes a lot of wear but this too can be prevented by letting the wear be taken by a glove.

Gun headaches are usually caused by firing cartridges which are too heavy in load for the weapon. The lighter the weapon the lighter the load should be. Gun headaches can also be caused by cartridges which have been stored at too high a temperature, especially if they have previously been damp, because the powder has been affected.

There can be no doubt that for most people in most sports the factor called form really exists. There are days when they perform well and others when, for no reason which they can discern, they perform badly. Nobody really knows what form is and it has been the subject of very little research, which is surprising considering the extent to which it affects multi-million-pound industries like cricket, football, golf and tennis. I have been told that some British psychologists did some preliminary work on clay-pigeon shooters and, apparently, their only firm conclusion was that the quality of the previous night's sleep made little difference. People who had slept badly were as much on form as those who had slept well. Personally a good night's sleep before a big day suits me very well.

Form must be linked with confidence which, in turn, is linked with experience. If you are confident of killing a bird you will probably do so because you will not be hesitant. However, some people find being confident easier said than done. At the start of a season, when a gun has not been touched during the spring and early summer, confidence may have to be re-acquired, as even professional cricketers who have taken a winter break usually find.

Happily I am not much affected by form and cannot remember having a really off day, a fact which astonishes most of my friends who are plagued by form. Some days I miss more birds but that is, almost invariably, because they are more difficult, either due to the terrain or the conditions. Even just a little wind makes a great difference. I think this is usually why some people can shoot brilliantly at one stand and then miss badly at the next. They may think the birds are the same but they are not. I may miss two or three difficult grouse on the trot but, according to my loader, I seem to be able to sort out the problem and rectify it fairly quickly.

At the end of a drive in Spain recently, the gun next to me, who had shot well at the previous drive, asked, 'What was I doing wrong there, Joe?' I replied, 'You weren't doing anything wrong. It was the birds that were doing it right.' I am sure that was correct. I had missed quite a few myself because they were just far more difficult.

Many people find that they shoot consistently well at some shoots and indifferently or erratically at others. I can only think that this must be connected with the atmosphere at the shoot which, in turn, may depend on the company. A relaxed atmosphere generates confidence and a relaxed approach. An excessive determination to do well – trying too hard – is often counter-productive because it causes tenseness when relaxation is required; so is a competitive atmosphere. It helps to think, consciously, that one is shooting as part of a team and that a bird cleanly killed is down to the team, not just to the individual who shot it.

It may be that the company – the other guns – affect one's form.

I find that I tend to shoot best on Mondays when I have had a good rest on Sunday, which I do now as a matter of discipline, not letting anything, however pressing, interfere with it. However, this extra advantage of a day's rest has never deterred me from shooting several days on the trot. I have always been aware that in this life I have a finite number of days on which Fate will allow me to shoot and I have never wanted to miss one of them. That, of course, is just the view of someone who may be excessively devoted to shooting. Many people simply do not want to shoot more than one or two days a week, even if they can afford the time. They find that they can shoot too much to an extent which interferes with their form and their enjoyment. Happily I have not been one of them and, however many days I have shot, 2 February is always a sad day for me and comes all too soon.

In view of my frequent mention of 20 bore guns, it is incumbent on me to stress the most dangerous situation which arises when a 20 bore cartridge is introduced into a 12 bore gun, because it can slide up the barrel and stick there out of sight. If a 12 bore cartridge is then inserted and fired the result is a tremendous

The author with his two sons, Robert (left) and Charles, who both acquired their father's love of shooting at an early age

A line of five Nickerson guns. Left to right: The author with his wife (right) and (left to right) daughters, Rosie, Eugenie and Louise

The Rothwell keepers who made the record partridge day possible

The 'Big Six' who shot the record bag of 2,119 wild partridges at Rothwell, Lincs., or
3 October 1952. Left to right: Samuel Nickerson, Richard Dennis, Leonard Lamyman
Peter Dennis, the author and Frederick Davy

Three generations of the Jacob family with the author at Rothwell

Above:
The Rothwell hedges all trimmed to an A-shape to maximise their value for wild life

Left:
The commemorative stone to A. W. Jacob in the valley where seven guns accounted for 105 brace of wild partridges in one drive on 1 October 1959. The author with his brother, Sam

A right and left at wild partridges at Rothwell. Note the almost straight left arm with the right leg moved forward for ease of swing on to the second shot. Loader, Ben Jacob, who was remarkably fast, has three cartridges in his right fingers and is moving to hand over the second gun before the author has completed his second shot. (The spats are excellent for keeping out straw)

THE LOADING SEQUENCE

Will Jacob is ready with the second gun (pointing skyward) as the author takes the first bird

Will's left hand is stretching out to take the spent gun and, whilst standing close, he is not interfering with the author's action

The author does not need to take his eye off the next bird as Will exchanges guns. Note the dog, unpegged and unconcerned, at that stage

Will reloads with the barrels pointing down

Taking a high bird overhead. The whole body must lean backwards with the left heel raised to follow through

Shooting really high pheasants. Not raised position of left leg and foot. It is th last flick of the wrist that brings the bir down

A wide-mouth bag stiffened with steel and fitted with a dispenser greatly helps the loader. Also note the leather covers over the buckles to prevent damage to gun stocks

Reeth Moor – the Pulpit Butt. Three labradors and Sweep, a large cocker, wait for the drive with the author and loader George Graham

'Tug', a Rothwell stamp labrador

'Sir Ben', one of the author's best

At Reeth Moor, August 1987

Nilo Plantation, Georgia. Featuring the kind of horse-drawn wagon used for quail shooting in the Southern United States

explosion. Clearly there should never be a situation in which 12 and 20 bore cartridges can become mixed, and they must always be stored separately.

This is also the right place to discuss that other crucial factor in safety and performance – the loader. I know that the majority of sportsmen use only one gun but there are still many two-gun shoots if, perhaps, not so many as in the past. And with the likely increase in shooting, as farmers have to look around for alternative income, there may well be more.

Speed is essential for a loader but safety must take precedence. As I have already said, anyone can pepper you but if there is an accident the person most likely to kill you is your loader, because of his proximity.

Over the years I have paid special attention to the techniques of loading and have been wonderfully served by my loaders, who have worked with me as a team. I offer the following advice:

Never let the loader load your first gun at a stand – always load that yourself with a couple of cartridges. Then you are ready if a bird comes early while the loader is busy loading the second gun: he can't conveniently hold two guns at once. At the end of the drive you should also unload the gun with which you finish and hand it to the loader broken. Put the two cartridges into your right-hand jacket pocket and keep nothing else there. If you are in doubt about whether your gun is safe or not you can simply feel the two cartridges and know that all is well. You will *know* that you have taken them out.

Never let your loader touch the safety catch. Always pass the gun to him with the catch pushed back to Safe whether you have fired one barrel or both. Make it an unbreakable habit.

Make sure that your loader holds the second gun pointing to the sky and that he turns away from you when he loads; and watch a new loader to see that he brings the stock up to the barrel and not vice versa.

The loader should thrust the gun *hard* into your hand, not just pass it to you. Sometimes one sees a loader holding out a gun and gaping into the sky. I am never without a loaded gun in my hand and can, therefore, deal with more birds than most shots, especially in a grouse butt, for that reason alone. The gun is slapped into my left hand so strongly that my arm is on its way to the gun-mounting position.

Very few loaders are quick enough to be able to change guns to allow the shooter to have a second gun in his hand to fire at the same high bird, if he has missed it with both barrels of the first gun. Mine have been able to and I have killed many difficult birds with the third shot. Some may think it unsporting to fire three barrels at one bird, but sometimes eight barrels may be fired at a bird which has gone down the line and been missed.

Provide the loader with a cartridge bag with a wide opening that he can easily get his hand into. As I have said, I have the bag mouth fitted with a metal rim so that it stays open.

It is a great help to the loader if you can kill consistently with the first barrel. No loader can keep up with an inveterate bang-banger. At the end of a drive a good shot will have spent half the cartridges, or less, than the poor shot who doubles the work for his loader. (At one particular pheasant shoot a man had fired fifty-four cartridges and killed only four birds. His loader scratched his head and remarked, 'Fifty-four for four! Sounds more like a cricket score!')

Smaller lighter-weight guns also ease the loader's burden both in carrying and loading and are a further advantage to their credit.

You should help your loader by carrying one gun as long as you remain fit enough to do so. No young man should expect a loader, sometimes twice his age, to carry two guns, a heavy cartridge bag and perhaps other equipment up a hill, yet one sees this all too often. Nor should you expect your loader to be responsible for your shooting stick, thumb-stick or dog-lead.

It is rarely now, in this country, that one needs to shoot with three guns and two loaders, as used to be the case when there were so many birds that two guns became too hot to handle. We did so on The Great Day when we shot more than 2000 wild grey partridges, as I describe in the next chapter, and had to experiment. My chief loader was the redoubtable Ben Jacob, then probably the fastest in Britain. My second loader was Bob Johnson but Ben had most of the work – so much so that his left-hand glove was worn out by the end of the day – but he coped magnificently.

Without outstanding loading we could never have killed so many birds in one day.

I owe a great deal to good loaders not only for helping me to shoot more and difficult birds but for their friendship. When you spend hours alone in a grouse butt or a duck hide with the same loader in all weathers a special bond of companionship develops. I have been wonderfully served by the whole Jacob family, Billy's sons Will and Benjy being both superb loaders now, and regard them all with affection and warm friendship. I like to think my feelings are reciprocated, even if, at times, I may have expected too much of them.

I would also like to pay tribute to George Graham, my forester at Rothwell who, for the past several years, has loaded for me on the grouse moor with great speed and skill. A real countryman, he is a most knowledgeable and helpful companion in the butt.

On the subject of shooting technique, should one attempt to teach one's own children or, even more controversially, one's wife? One is always advised not to teach one's relatives to drive.

I taught my sons to shoot with some help from various members of the Jacob family, who are all highly competent. Provided children are of normal physique, they can start to shoot before they are nine, as I did myself, provided they are closely supervised. The best gun to start with, in my opinion, is a double-barrelled .410 but with the firing pin of the left-hand barrel removed and put away to be replaced at a later date. This will accustom a child to a double-barrelled weapon, and save expense later, but make him concentrate on killing with the first barrel. We all see too many adult shots who are overly dependent on their second barrel. This fault is expensive and doubles the work for both shooter and loader.

For practice it is useful, if you have a fast stream, to put a net across lower down and fire at floating tins. Children can see where the shots are going in the water and this is very illuminating.

It is important that young people should not be given too much shooting or they may come to be bored with it or actively dislike it. There are several sons of landed people to whom this happened. With young VIPs, shooting as guests, the danger is that they tend to be put in the hot seat at almost every drive and experience too much of a good thing.

I also taught my wife to shoot, though whether this a wise practice in general, I am still not sure. I think that the best way to teach a woman is to stand about fifty yards behind her and knock down all the birds she misses. This makes her so mad that she becomes determined to succeed!

Nothing can really replace experience in the field because marksmanship depends on confidence and confidence comes only with experience at live game. I had the good fortune to learn to shoot entirely at live targets and so do not feel competent to say much about training and practising with clays. Nevertheless, I am convinced that shooting schools are a valuable adjunct not only in teaching the tyro but in correcting the faults of the experienced shot, especially just before the season starts. A visit is very worthwhile to ensure that one's guns still fit the body, as it changes with age, and that mounting is being done properly. Clay shooting is also fun in itself for a lot of people and is a great way of entertaining if you have a trap of your own.

The clay bird can never really simulate the live bird because, from the moment it leaves the trap, it is decelerating, while the live bird is usually gaining speed or at least not losing it. One also learns to sense the easiest position to shoot a clay because you can anticipate its trajectory. It cannot change its path or its mind like a grouse, partridge or curling pheasant does, so it can never be so challenging. Some guns can certainly shoot well at clays one day and poorly at birds the next or vice versa. I have also noticed that clay-pigeon shooters, who train to hit their targets bang in the centre, do the same when they are shooting at game, when they should concentrate on the head. The clay which is chipped on the front edge is not so highly regarded as one completely smashed to powder but, in fact, it represents a better game shot.

Recently it gave me great pleasure when my youngest daughter, Rosemarie, helped the Cambridge University 'C' clay-pigeon team to beat Oxford. I have also been delighted to have the opportunity to create a memorial for my late son, John William, by presenting a cup to be contested by clay-pigeon shooters at Middleton-in-Teesdale.

Dry practice at mounting can be done at home with advantage. It is a good idea to have a gun in your bedroom or dressing room (properly secure when not in use) and, on regular occasion, especially during the closed season, swing it up suddenly, from the left or right, up to the picture rail and then along it. When doing this I have noticed, repeatedly, that when swinging to the left one usually ends up about four inches below the rail and when swinging the other way about four inches above it. So in the field there may be a natural tendency to miss the bird on the left below and the bird on the right above – an observation which I have proved to be true in practice and for which I make due allowance.

When I travel abroad on business or pleasure I take a walking stick which has a very heavy metal duck's head as a handle. Its purpose is for personal protection – it would make a formidable defensive weapon – but it can also be used for dry gun practice. When I was cruising on a yacht recently I got the engineer to make the stick temporarily into a mock gun weighing six pounds so that I could exercise my shoulder in anticipation of the 12th!

Physical condition and fitness are as important for shooting as for any other outdoor sport, especially for grouse shooting and wildfowling. For shooting, the muscles are very important and I find an hour's shoulder massage each evening very helpful. Above the desk in my study there is a ceiling hook carrying a pulley with a rope. This enables me to exercise my arms while I am reading: the rope pulls up each arm in turn.

Some people laugh and think that I go to extremes but the same people tell me that I am shooting as well at seventy-five as I did in my prime. Expertise is neither acquired nor maintained without special effort and application.

At what age should you give up shooting? It depends entirely on your state of health and your emotional attitude. With respect to the latter, perhaps, some people should never start, they get so distressed and grim if they are having a bad day.

The book *Purdey: the Gun and the Family* shows a photograph, taken in 1933, of five customers who shot happily and safely together aged 80, 83, 80, 71 and 82 – a total of 396 years. On 16 December of that year they shot 114 pheasants, 9 hares, 1 teal, 1 snipe, 3 partridges and 36 rabbits!

It is sad to see a once fine shot missing repeatedly when in senile decline, but what does it matter so long as he enjoys it, is safe and is not interfering with anyone else's enjoyment? I hope that people will understand that, if and when they see me shooting badly, though if it means that I start wounding birds excessively, then I shall pack my guns away.

Lord Ripon dropped dead on a grouse moor after shooting fifty-one grouse and a snipe at his last drive. I can think of no better way to go unless it was on a partridge drive at my beloved Rothwell.

Chapter 5

Thinking like a Partridge

My passion for the grey partridge (*Perdix perdix*) approaches that of Mr Jorrocks for the fox – a kind of love-hunt relationship – and it dates from my boyhood. When I was eight or nine my father, who had been impressed by the works of Ruskin, said that he wanted me to choose a subject and learn so much about it in the course of my life that I would eventually know more about it than anyone else in the world. He gave me a fortnight to make a choice and I told him I had chosen the partridge. He was surprised, perhaps disappointed, but, as he had given me complete freedom, he did not try to dissuade me. This, of course, was long before bird behaviour was the accepted study which it is now.

From then on I began to think like a partridge and imagined myself as a male hatched on 20 June on the Lincolnshire Wolds along with twelve brothers and sisters. My parents were extra-ordinarily attentive and when any weasels or predatory birds were about they clucked us up, ushered us into cover and protected us. Whenever it started to rain – and usually before – we were all clucked in under our parents – six of us under father and the rest under mother.

We stayed close together and near to where we had been born. Though one or two of us died, the rest of us grew rapidly, feeding on insects in the short grass. We began to dust our feathers in the dry, chalky ground and soon learned how important it was to keep an eye open for danger. My father was very watchful for the hen sparrow-hawk that would suddenly dip a wing and lift over the top of a hedge: his brother had been killed by one. It is in the early months of the year when sparrow-hawks take their main toll of us partridges.

How well I remember my first flying lesson! We were taught to fly low because if the wind caught us it could take us too far away. When any of us were separated beyond the sound of the cluck-cluck of our parents we suffered casualties.

Later on we liked being in turnips or mangoldwurzels because there were plenty of insects and knot-grass seeds but we did not like sugar-beet fields because we could not see through the thick cover of leaves, or even hear if the wind was rustling them. It was also usually too wet for us, though the pheasants seemed to love it.

Best of all, later still in the year, we liked a stubble where we could peck at the undersown clover and still see around us. In the winter we lived on grass fields and leys, depending to a large extent on food put out for us by keepers. Without that many of us would have perished in the hard weather.

Most of us males were paired up with a female by St Valentine's Day, 14 February, and we remained attached to her unless she died or was killed.

That was how my childhood thinking went and I have continued to put myself in the position of any game-bird I am trying to shoot. When planning a drive or standing at my peg I look around, test the wind and ask myself, 'Which way would I fly under these conditions?'

I used my accumulated knowledge and that of my keepers and friends to build up what became a huge stock of wild English partridges by modern standards and eventually, with five other guns, was able to account for more than 2000 of them in one day, a record that is never likely to be approached now that this wonderful bird has virtually disappeared from so many areas where it used to be common. The Ely cartridge company is on record as saying that, years ago, the sale of their cartridges depended more on the partridge than on any other quarry, including the rabbit. I believe that about two million were shot each year without any diminution of the future stock. That gives some idea of the numbers which used to grace Britain's fields.

The only shoots for nearly a half-century which have held really large numbers of wild grey partridges were my brother's, at North Ormsby, and my own at Rothwell, both being in the steep, hilly

Wolds of Lincolnshire. Though I helped to shoot more than 300 brace of wild partridges on a very sporting day in Norfolk, there were not more than 75 brace of young greys among them.

The reason we achieved such large numbers was our deliberate policy of creating an ecological environment suited to the grey partridge's needs.

On 2 October 1950 six of us, who were close friends, first shot 1000 partridges in one day at Rothwell. The guns were all Lincolnshiremen who lived nearby, Peter K. Dennis, the late Richard F. Dennis, the late Frederick R. Davy, the late Leonard Lamyman, Sam Nickerson and myself.

The weather was against us, very wet in the morning with a strong wind – up to twenty-eight knots, which made for tremendous sport – yet we finished the day with 1091 partridges – all wild and less than 5 per cent French – 42 pheasants, 114 hares and 13 various.

Tired as I was, I spent two hours handling and ageing every partridge. There was only one brace of thin birds and only three small ones, which were Frenchmen. (For those who are interested the way to tell the age of a partridge is to examine the wingtips. On each wing the outermost of the flight feathers of the juvenile plumage are not moulted early and replaced as the others are, but are retained. These feathers are sharply pointed while the replaced ones are more rounded. So birds with those two sharply pointed feather are juveniles. Other fairly reliable indicators are beak colour – dark in young and light grey in old – and leg colour, olive brown in young, silvery grey in old. Also, the lower part of the beak will support the bird's weight in an old bird but will bend with a young one.)

Two years later, on what we came to call The Great Day, 3 October 1952, the same team of six guns, each using three guns and two loaders this time, accounted for 2119 wild partridges, 56 pheasants, 151 hares, 11 rabbits, 2 pigeons and 3 various – a total of 2342. Of the partridges only 50 were French the rest being wild greys, of which 1379 were young birds.

The day was fine, though not warm, and with a fresh wind. The team always stood in the same sequence shown in the photograph in the plate section. This was arranged by having only one of us draw a number, which established his position, and the rest stood accordingly, moving up two after each drive. Its purpose was to ensure that the better shots would not be drawn next to each other but dispersed in the line.

The main purpose of shooting with three guns and two loaders was to cope with the heat of the barrels if the day went as expected. There was a huge population of wild birds, for reasons I will describe later.

We took the English wild partridge record which still stands, is listed in the *Guinness Book of Records* and is never now likely to be broken. All the game killed was wild and 95 per cent of the partridges were greys. There were no reared birds. And not a single 'squeaker'.

I should, perhaps, point out that more than 5000 people had visited Rothwell during the summer to inspect the crops and the management system, for farming has always come first with me. In addition, during the green pea season, I was employing more than 600 casual labourers. So the whole area can hardly have been said to have been left undisturbed in the interests of shooting.

The last three drives did not produce a great deal – $26^1/_2$, $25^1/_2$ and $28^1/_2$ brace respectively – and there were no tired birds. We shot virtually fresh birds all day, doing only one return drive. When Lord Walsingham shot more than a thousand grouse to his own gun in one day there were many return drives with many tired birds. That did not happen on our partridge day, as all those present could testify. Only one parcel of land was beaten twice for a return drive.

The views of my second loader, Bob Johnson, who worked for me for forty years and is now retired, are of some interest. He attributed much of the success of the day to the careful planning with flexibility for wind changes; the co-ordinated work of the beaters with so much ground being covered; the skill of the keeper, Archie Jacob, and the under-keepers in controlling the beaters in their approach to the guns as well as the flankers. We had no radio communication.

As soon as news of this achievement spread, people wanted to visit the shoot to see how we had done it. The late Lord Leicester, whose forebear had set the previous record of $835^1/_2$ brace, killed by eight guns at Holkham in 1905, telephoned me and fixed a visit.

Many others were surprised by the steep terrain, assuming that we must have been shooting hedge-hoppers. How wrong they were! We can ski at Rothwell and many fields can be combined only in one direction.

Lord Templewood (previously Sir Samuel Hoare), who had an estate in Norfolk, asked me to have tea with him at the House of Lords. I told him how we had built up the partridge population and, as we parted, he said, 'If I could do what you have done I should die happy.' This was a remarkable tribute from a man who had enjoyed such a long career at the peak of politics. But that is the way shooting grips some people, as it has gripped me.

On 1 October 1959 we again broke Lord Leicester's old record. The same six guns as on The Great Day, plus Guy Moreton, shot 1877 partridges out of a total bag of 2065 head of game. We had a fine warm day with a nice wind. Some time previously I had said to my keeper, Jacob, 'It would be very satisfying to kill one hundred brace of partridges over the same hedge in the same drive. If we ever do it I'll put up a commemorative stone with your name on it!' Well, in the first drive on that day in 1959 – over a nice little valley from Church Platts to Horse Walk – we killed 107 brace – a lifetime ambition for me then. The stone was duly erected and records the feat to this day.

Later, on my brother's shoot at North Ormsby Manor, where he followed my uncle, with eight guns, we shot 137 brace, all wild, in one drive. Again a stone was erected in honour of Ernest Turner, the keeper who had made it possible and who still comes out and picks up.

Since then we have killed 840 brace in a day twice, once with only four guns. On that day, 1 October 1960, the total bag was 1697 partridges, 46 pheasants, 127 mallard, 15 pigeons, 52 hares and 3 various – 1940 head with four guns.

These outstanding days have given rise to myths suggesting that the birds were driven about so many times that they could scarcely fly. Nothing could be further from the truth, as those who took part, including the keepers, beaters and loaders, can prove. As I have said about game-birds in general, partridges should be driven down wind whenever possible to make them even more difficult and that has always been done at Rothwell.

Our triumphs with partridges were not so much in the shooting as in having established conditions where so many wild birds could breed and survive. I had realized that a big stock of partridges did not require any real sacrifice of good farming practice. On the contrary, it was a sign of good husbandry because what was good for farming was good for these birds, which had always been common on well-managed land.

I shall describe, in some detail, how we improved the Rothwell estate to encourage the wild partridges in Chapter 10, which deals with shoot management. At this juncture a few general remarks may be apposite in the hope that, with major changes in farming practice in prospect and with increasing emphasis on the leisure use of land, the wild partridge will be given a chance to return, as it is already doing in a few areas.

Good cover, food and trained keepers for predation control are essential on partridge ground. There was a small stock of wild partridges after I had taken over the land and reduced the vermin, but forty brace was a good day's shoot. We shot very few immediately after the war to enable the stock to increase naturally, and set our minds to devising ways of assisting it.

I planted 1 acre of kale per 100 acres of ground in long narrow strips – 22 yards wide and 220 yards long. I used a frost-resistant strain that gives good cover for partridges, and if you let some of it go to seed it provides food in the summer in the form of the insects it harbours. The kale should be left standing throughout the second summer of growth. There is no doubt that kale is very helpful in maintaining a big stock of wild partridges. If you have an acre of kale to every hundred acres of other crops the partridges will fly to it and if there is food there they will stay contentedly out of sight.

In my view, shortage of adequate cover is a major cause of the decline of the partridge and this is linked with the timing of modern farming operations. When all the land work was done by horses it was completed much later in the spring. As a result, there was cover for partridges to get into, rough plough and more roots. Now everything is like a billiard table. The partridge sitting in a field then could not see other birds. Now he can and, when birds are pairing, they like to be out of sight of others. There is something in their psychological make-up which makes them dislike the sight of another pair at that time of the year. This is one reason why the prairies which have been created for mass cereal production are so inimical to partridges.

Grassland which was left to ripen for hay provided feeding ground and nesting sites for partridges which love to go on to grass, especially in January and February.

Now it is nearly all cut for silage several times and any nests are destroyed, often along with the tight-sitting hens.

Adult partridges like seeds – especially the seeds of plants classed as weeds, such as knot-grass, chickweed, scarlet pimpernel and fat hen, which are also hosts to insects. They are also partial to the buds and flowers of buttercups. The routine destruction of such weeds by modern farming methods has severely handicapped the bird. Even the cornflower, my favourite buttonhole flower, was once a weed of our cornfields until the drive for cereal seed purity, and weedkillers, made it a rarity.

I have proved to my satisfaction that partridges benefit greatly in the spring and winter months from additional feeding with wheat or cut maize regularly scattered into the cover by hand. A partridge needs about an ounce of food per day and this should be scattered into the cover every day from mid-September to mid-April, the amount being based on an estimate of the stock. Because some will be taken by the pigeons and smaller birds a little extra needs to be added.

We erected dusting shelters on the sunny side of the hedges – one about every hundred yards. These proved to be a great success. They should be properly constructed with a corrugated iron roof with a foot of soil and turf on top and dry sand and wood ashes inside. I could go round in my vehicle and see a covey fly from almost every shelter.

Like other seed-eating birds, partridges need grit and, as we are on chalk, we are short of it. So, occasionally, we sent a lorry to the local gravel pit to fill up with gravel washings. Then a couple of chaps would drive along the farm roads shovelling it into the hedge bottoms.

To improve partridge country you must have the co-operation of the farm workers. I used to put some suggestions in the wage packet each May. The following is an example, dated 13 May 1952, the year of The Great Day:

'The British record partridge bag stands at 835$\frac{1}{2}$ brace in one day. It was achieved in 1905 in Norfolk on the estate of Lord Leicester, who had forty-two gamekeepers. We are going to beat it if we can so I am going to make you all keepers for a few minutes each week. I want you to help me by regarding the game on the property as a crop.

'When working in the fields during the next eight weeks you can be of enormous help by being careful where you sit down to lunch, so as not to disturb nesting birds. Choose bare ground when possible. Go through recognized gateways, stick to tracks and do not cut corners.

'Please report all nests you may spot. Two shillings will be paid for every nest found which was previously unknown to us. The known nests will have been marked by a peg or some device. Please do not remove any markers.

'If you see any traces of rats let us know.

'Avoid putting any bags, fuel containers or implements near a nest. Do not leave bits of paper in the hedge bottom. When blown about they can disturb sitting birds.'

The whole staff co-operated enthusiastically with the results I have already described.

As regards nesting sites, some areas need to be set aside, and this can usually be done without much loss of usable land. Grey partridges do not like hedges with a lot of trees in them. They also prefer hedges growing on banks, probably because they are better drained. The more hedges you have, the more partridges you are likely to hold. The elimination of hedges to grow cereals prairie-style has made the return of the wild partridge in many counties almost impossible. The routine spraying of weeds has also deprived partridges of highly nutritious seeds and of the insects which lived on the weeds.

I fear that, unless there is a reversal of farming practices – conditioned, perhaps, by commercial factors – they will never come back in great numbers; but I devoutly hope that I am wrong and that the experience I have related here will, once again, be of practical use. It is up to individual farmers to decide whether they want to encourage partridges or not, though the Government could be very helpful, by offering grants for the maintenance of unsprayed headlands, for instance.

The reporting of nests to the keepers is all important. They cannot be expected to find every one. The nests need to be noted and marked but an over-zealous keeper who chases round the nests too often will cause birds to desert. Wild partridges are not stupid birds and their nests are sometimes difficult to find. The nest is usually sited to provide protection from the wind and catch the early morning sun, the worn entry pathways in the vegetation being the sign to look for.

Once a nest has been discovered the keeper should put a numbered peg about twelve feet from the nest, which should be recorded in a notebook. Later when the keeper does his rounds it is enough for him to see the cock bird somewhere near the nest to know that all is still well.

I believe that when a pair of partridges have safely occupied an area of ground for nesting and survive the shooting season they will return there, though I have no proof of that. We had an English cock-partridge paired with two hens and the latter nested almost touching one another for two consecutive years in the same place.

We rarely took away eggs for artificial incubation, doing this only if a hen had been killed.

Our records show that the rainfall in May, June and July is a crucial factor affecting the partridge stock. There is something in the adage that if it rains heavily during Ascot Week – the third week in June – there will be few partridges, but the weeks on either side are just as important. Prolonged wet kills the young chicks, especially if it is cold. They can manage to survive in wet or cold conditions, but not both. In dry weather partridges seem to take deliberate action to keep their nests damp by going off into the dew to feed each morning. Our experience shows that partridges need water and I shall deal with means of providing it in Chapter 10.

If undisturbed, the partridge is an excellent incubator and will usually bring off more than 90 per cent of her eggs. The chicks usually hatch in June, the 20th being, consistently, a big hatching day, according to our records.

On my well-keepered shoot there was an average loss of about
33 per cent of all nests due to vermin and to human disturbance,
including farm operations. This figure could not be reduced by all
the efforts we made and I have reason to believe that on some
shoots the loss was as high as 60 per cent or even higher – being
almost total on occasion.

Pheasants are another cause of ruined partridge nests because
they tend to lay eggs in them. They are bad news on a wild-partridge
shoot and it pays to kill all the pheasants off at the end of the season.

Grey partridge chicks up to ten days old rely almost entirely on
soft-bodied insects like springtails aphids, and small caterpillars.
During the second week tougher insects like weevils and ants are
eaten. During the third week there is rapid conversion to other
foods and very quickly they are eating the same food as their
parents, which includes only the occasional beetle or caterpillar.

The number of young birds available for shooting in the autumn
is directly related to the number of nutritious insects on the feeding
grounds. Further, this supply has to be within easy reach of the
nests. The spraying of weeds, on which these insects mainly live,
has been very deleterious. Crop spraying will have to continue
but if headlands are left where the weeds are not sprayed, the
partridges will take advantage of them. A large quantity of weeds
is not required. Even after several years of spraying, weeds will
regenerate if spraying is stopped. The seeds of many weeds can lie
dormant in the soil for long periods and they do not all germinate
in the same season.

There can be no doubt that to restore a partridge population the
prime requirement is to increase the supply of insects to the young
chicks. The chicks of redlegs are less dependent on insects and so
survive better. But it will all be to little avail unless predators,
especially foxes, are controlled.

As partridges have disappeared from so many areas the special
skills needed to drive them properly have also tended to disappear;
so it may be useful, should they ever return, to have a record of the
lessons we learned in that respect.

When flushed, a grey partridge's instinct is to get out of sight soonest. It therefore flies down hill or over any crest or big fence into any available cover. Partridges fly away from man so they should see the whole beating line together if they are to fly forwards. When a partridge sees a half-ring of danger approaching it will usually fly forwards but if it can see only one or two men it will fly anywhere. If there are any big gaps in the line birds will fly back through it so, when crossing a fence, the beating line must cross together, fanning out along the fence before proceeding.

There should be no talking in the beating line, signals to the guns in front that birds are coming being given by whistle, a horn not being so suitable, though it is sometimes used. The only time any other noise is allowable is when driving thick cover up into the wind so that the only quiet area is forward, where the guns should be waiting silently. Partridges have good hearing and silence before and during drives is mandatory. Chattering or laughing in the line can lose half the coveys in the drive and is infuriating for the host, the keeper and the other guns.

Good flanking, which is something of an art, is absolutely essential and, when expertly done, it should be possible to put 90 per cent of the birds from an 80-acre field over two or three guns. When badly done, however, it turns birds backwards. Partridges can be over-flanked and often are. If the flankers are too far forward of the beaters the birds may fly out through the side-gaps.

Guns should not grumble that they sometimes cannot shoot because the flankers are in the way, because if there were no flankers there would be a lot less to shoot at. Flankers should be prepared to run when necessary to hold birds in. The job of a flanker is often given to older men whose eyes and legs are not good enough.

The guns should be 40 yards apart when the birds are likely to come lowish, 45 yards when they are somewhat higher and 50 yards if the birds are very high. They should never be any further apart, unless the birds are exceptionally high, with a 60-yard maximum.

The further back the guns are from a hedge the better, as the birds will then tend to split down the line, but they cannot stand too far back if the birds are wanted for a return drive because too many of them will fly back or sideways.

Of course, the height of the hedge will govern how far the guns can stand back. If the hedge is low then it will be necessary to stand close to it to avoid being seen. This gives less time to deal with the birds by taking them in front, so high hedges make for easier and more interesting shooting.

Most guns who are not used to shooting partridges wait until they are very close, which makes the shot much more difficult. The easiest place to take an oncoming partridge is well in front.

A covey of grey partridges will appear to explode over a hedge when they see the guns, or are shot at, but they are probably flying considerably slower than a pheasant. This needs to be taken into account when engaging a high partridge.

Having chosen a bird stay with it: if you change to a different bird while you are mounting your gun, because it suddenly looks easier, the odds are that you will miss.

It is my experience that a gun that does well at wild partridges can shoot anything. I would rather shoot wild English partridges than any other game-birds, though grouse run them close as really challenging targets. I am convinced that such shooting ability as I may possess springs largely from my good fortune in being brought up on wild grey partridges. They present every kind of angle and demand quick and accurate shooting.

My observations over many years suggest that something happens, psychologically, to the wild grey partridge after the first fortnight of November. They fly more slowly and do not twist and turn so much, and so become much easier to hit. October and the first ten days or so of November therefore constitute the best time to shoot grey partridges. But whenever they are shot, they die like gentlemen.

By not shooting them after that you should leave a big enough stock for breeding. Leaving a brace to every five acres is enough in my opinion.

It is my view that unless seven good guns can kill a hundred brace in a day a shoot really has not enough stock and they are better left. There are very few places where that can be done today, though redleg partridges are providing sport on many shoots, but hardly of the same class.

There are very few shoots in Britain where reared redlegs can be shown properly. I have been asked to some where large numbers of them are shot but have always declined. I was on one shoot as a guest of a certain Lord Mayor and was delighted to see a whole covey of grey hand-reared partridges flying towards me but, when not quite within range, it suddenly veered and settled in a release pen!

Redlegs, which are not indigenous like the grey partridge, have survived in the wild since they were introduced late in the eighteenth century. They are, in fact, better fitted to survive our hard winters, probably because of their readiness to take to the woods, which grey partridges do not like as they always need to be able to see all around them.

Nevertheless, on a really good wild partridge shoot, redlegs rarely accounted for more than 5 per cent of the population because such a high percentage of them were shot. They come over the guns singly and few of them get through a good line. This also happens when redlegs fly out of the woods with the pheasants. As a result, a redleg stock is proportionately reduced every time a mixed population of partridges is driven. Further, reared redlegs tend to be shunned by any wild stock and have difficulty in breeding.

I am told that there are a few recently established shoots where redlegs are driven from high ground across valleys in huge numbers and provide challenging targets. I am also told, however, that the entire operation is ludicrously artificial. The birds are fed on pellets on the high ground, sometimes being released only a few days before each shoot, and in the winter, when it may be impossible to reach this ground, the very large numbers which remain at the end of the season are left to starve. This is an obscene situation, with which I would not wish to be associated, and seems guaranteed to bring the whole shooting fraternity into serious disrepute.

French partridges can become very tame. A member of my staff reported how one partridge came regularly to be fed, and chirped until it was. It learned to draw attention to itself by rattling the flap of the letter box, which was at the bottom of the door, and even walked into the house. Eventually the cock and his hen nested in the garden and reared eleven chicks.

In spite of my fascination with shooting, farming has always come first and the postwar revolution in farming practices spelled disaster

73

for the partridge. The old four-course rotation system was perfectly suited to the partridge's needs, but in the late fifties and onwards it became impossible to survive economically without major changes in the traditional methods. It was 'up corn, down horn', with more rapid turnover of the land to permit maximum crops and the greatly increased use of artificial fertilizers, herbicides, pesticides and other chemicals.

When I realized that these necessary changes meant the end for the English grey partridge populations, I knew that I could not be deprived of my partridge shooting, so I decided to switch that essential activity to Spain, where I have shot for the last twenty years. Eventually, eight years ago, I took over a shoot there, which I describe in Chapter 17.

We have some partridges, both English and French, at Rothwell but none are put down. We later tried rearing grey partridges and turning them out, but it proved to be hopeless. We managed to shoot only 5 per cent of the reared grey partridges for it proved very difficult to induce them to fly over the guns.

For me, the partridge remains the bird *par excellence* in every respect. I eat a lot of grouse in the late summer but when I taste my first young English partridge of the season I don't want to eat any more grouse.

I understand that I am sometimes referred to by people who do not know me personally as 'Partridge' Nickerson. I regard that as a compliment to which I would have aspired as a boy, had I thought of it. It is no coincidence that my armorial bearings bear a brace of wild grey English partridges as my personal salute to a splendid bird which is part of our heritage.

Chapter 6

Prime Target

Since the sad demise of the wild partridge on so many farms and estates, pheasants now account for the great bulk of the game-birds in Britain, representing more than 80 per cent of all those shot, according to various estimates. There is a substantial wild population, which must run into several millions, though these are mainly birds descended from reared pheasants which have managed to survive and breed naturally. Every year this population is being topped up by a huge number of newly reared birds which is probably as high as 15 million. So when the pheasant season opens in October, and for a couple of months before, the pheasant is, unquestionably, the commonest flying bird of any kind in Britain.

It can be said, with certainty, that the sight of so many magnificent birds in so many areas would not be there to be enjoyed by the public if there was no shooting. It is doubtful that such a large, conspicuous and highly edible bird could survive in this small island without active keepering and the topping up of numbers. It is more likely that it would have gone the same way as the bustard – to extinction – because, in my view, the pheasant is not an intelligent and resourceful bird like the grey partridge, which will always manage to survive, even if in small numbers.

There is one other way in which it differs from the grey partridge – it is not a natural inhabitant. On Christmas cards the cock pheasant seems to have ousted cock robin as the symbolic English winter resident but it is really an alien, though it has been here for centuries, possibly having been introduced by the Romans who imported it to Italy from its original home in Asia. So if a pheasant could speak it could not harangue the shooter, as the grey partridge or grouse legitimately could, by saying, 'Look, I was here first!'

We would all prefer to shoot completely wild pheasants and, until relatively recently, there were well-keepered, well-timbered shoots, usually of vast acreage, where substantial numbers of wild pheasants reared themselves, though, of course, to maintain and hold large numbers, extra food had to be provided. Without this assistance a pheasant needs a lot of territory to support itself, so a natural population tends to be thin on the ground. Natural mortality is also very heavy. The effects of modern farming practice have also been inimical to the wild birds and, on most shoots today, I doubt whether they contribute more than 10 per cent of the total bag. On the rolling cereal prairies, where the removal of nesting or roosting cover has been grossly overdone, pheasants have quickly become scarce.

The reared pheasant, when given time to adapt to its wild environment, offers a sporting target when sportingly pursued but far too many easy birds are shot for the good name of shooting. This is partly due to the fact that, on many shoots, pheasants are overfed and become too heavy, lazy and ponderous to fly in a challenging fashion. So, in the fifties when we realized that Rothwell might have to be changed from a wild partridge shoot to one dependent on reared pheasants, we set about producing a lighter, faster bird by the process of selection.

We had two lots of 500 eggs from two different sources, where no artificial rearing had ever taken place, and when they were hatched we weighed them all at six and at twenty-two weeks. At each weighing we selected the light-weight ones – 5 per cent of the total – for breeding, and kept doing this for generations. We also bred out the white ring round the neck, by selection, so that we would be able to recognize our birds instantly. The result was the Rothwell Pheasant, which are so much lighter and faster that some visitors find them difficult at first by underestimating their speed. They are now an established variety, the hens being particularly small and neat. Save for odd strays from other shoots there are no pheasants with white rings round their necks at Rothwell.

This breed lays a few less eggs than ordinary pheasants and one gets less for the birds from game-dealers, as they are not so large, but they provide substantially better sport. The strain remains peculiar to the estate.

It is very difficult to guess the weight of one's pheasants by sight and it is a mistake to let them get too heavy, as any pheasant will if it is overfed. When beginning to shoot the Rothwell Pheasants right at the end of November 1987, I found that they were heavier than I liked and the keepers were as surprised as I was. So, rather late in life I fear, I have decided that when the pheasant season opens I shall have a brace shot on every beat each week, and weighed. If they are getting too heavy the food will be reduced.

Just to show how difficult the Rothwell birds can be, here is a note from my records about the first pheasant shoot of the 1987–8 season held on 10 December 1987, a dull misty day with poor visibility and a light north-westerly wind:

We began at Tugdale, almost a ravine between fields and woods. We drove it differently with three drives all from the north and the guns facing in the same direction. I stood behind the line. After each drive the guns moved up the valley three or four pegs to the right. The total bag was 197. Tugdale provides my most difficult birds, high and curling.

The afternoon drive was Billy's Wood, with much land being blanked in during a leisurely lunch, for it takes an hour for this drive to be properly prepared. Again I stood behind the line. It lasted an hour and a half over a valley with 1453 cartridges fired.

I have never changed the strain of my pheasants any more than I did with the wild partridges, but on some shoots it becomes necessary to introduce new blood on occasion.

The essence of pheasant shoot management is to camouflage its artificiality and make the whole environment and the birds seem as natural as possible. I will consider those aspect in the chapter dealing with general shoot management.

I do not begin to shoot my pheasants, or anyone else's, until the last days of November and prefer them in December and January when they are really strong on the wing and there is usually good wind to make them curl. Since I do not like treating those guests I invite in January as second-class citizens, I put down enough birds to ensure that there are plenty left, and what Lady Sopwith used to call 'the dreaded cry of cocks only' does not ring out over my land, though if we are double banking I may require front guns to restrict themselves by shooting a cock each time before they shoot at a hen. Besides, the January birds are the best birds. If you haven't got many left you did not put enough down or you shot too many when they were easier.

The art of driving pheasants is to make them walk or run from where they want to be to some cover from which you can induce them to fly high over the guns. With game crops now being used on such a scale – as with partridges, I rate frost-resistant kale easily the best – their siting so that birds fly well out of them offers plenty of scope for imagination and is crucial to good sport. Obviously, they are likely to fly best if the cover crops are on high ground with the guns some distance away behind or just in front of high trees which the birds will be unable to clear unless they maintain their height or, better still, climb higher when they see the guns.

As I will explain later, when dealing with shoot management, Rothwell was bare of trees when I took it over so we had the advantage of being able to plant the woods and shelter belts where we wanted them. But on most estates the woods were originally sited with shooting in mind, very often on the higher ground which, of course, is why the landscape looks so attractive and delights all who pass it.

Presenting good pheasants is much more difficult on flat ground but it can be done by the siting of cover crops so that the driven birds can be induced to fly over tall trees with the guns placed on the other side. One often sees the strips of game crops sown too near the trees so that the birds have not enough room to gain height and simply fly or run through the trees.

Even the reared pheasant soon becomes a sensitive and wary bird, and when it feels it is in danger its first instinct is to run and keep running; so it has to be made to fly, which it would rather not do. Sewelling – strips of plastic on a string which can be pulled or which moves in the wind – can be used in woods to make the birds fly instead of running out at the end. The best place to position and operate the sewelling can only be found by trial and error in each wood. All too often, it is set in a position which allows the birds to flop down just at the end of the wood in front of the guns. The birds see the guns and then rarely come over them. Instead they fly back where they came from, over the beaters' heads.

In a wood that is being well beaten few of the birds will fly before their final emergence over the guns when they will still have all their flying strength. A pheasant is a bit like a lion: it can accelerate and move very fast over a few hundred yards but needs a rest before it can repeat the performance. So birds that have already flown during a drive through a long wood are likely to make poor targets. This is one of the main reasons why some birds fly higher out of a wood than others: they are on their first flight and their wing muscles are not fatigued. To discourage unnecessary flying there should be no frightening noises from the beaters. Only the tap of their sticks should be audible and dogs should not be in the line unless on leads.

For the best results the birds must *want* to fly in the direction where you have placed the guns. For preference, this should be accomplished by beating them away from 'home', usually the wood where they were released and are fed, and then driving them back in that desirable direction. If I think that birds will fly badly out of a wood because of weather conditions I have them walked up to a piece of kale or some other convenient cover on higher ground and they can almost always be driven over the line of guns, provided this has been re-sited on the path back to 'home'.

Surprisingly, in my experience a reared pheasant will often fly higher than a wild one if it sees a line of guns. The wild bird, being more wily, will slip out of the side if it can, but if the reared bird is going back 'home' it will fly high and keep climbing on a direct path.

Like the partridge, the pheasant has extremely acute hearing, as witness the way thunder or a distant explosion will set off the cock-birds crowing for miles around, often before it is audible to humans. Surely there is a lesson to be learned from that – don't make unnecessary noise by talking or laughing during pheasant drives.

While pheasants are obviously frightened by the sound of shooting, especially when they have heard it before, they will still fly over the guns if these are sited on the flight-path homewards.

If the birds cannot be driven back home the guns should be in line with some other attraction such as another wood, some scrub or at least some green cover. Many a fine drive has been destroyed when some area, to which pheasants flew from the high ground, has been felled or cleaned up over-zealously. With no cover to fly to, the birds have no option but to fly back over the beaters.

As the season progresses, pheasants soon learn that it is safer to turn back over the beaters rather than fly over the guns. They can be dealt with by having walking guns but it is possible to use flankers to deter or even turn them. We do this regularly at Rothwell, and I am surprised to see it so rarely done on other shoots. One flanker waving his arms will serve little purpose. What is needed is three or four flankers with big flags out in the open and walking abreast with the beaters. Pheasants will see them from inside the wood and it is surprising how many will fly forward or at least come out sideways in front of the flankers where a gun can be stationed. How often have you seen flankers with flags on a pheasant shoot? Yet the practice can make all the difference to a drive. Indeed I have so much confidence in it that I rarely, if ever, stand a back-gun in a wood. I do not think that birds should be shot at inside the woods. Some birds will fly quite high over a back-gun but the majority are likely to be dropping birds.

The main problem with pheasants as the season progresses is their tendency to flush, so that the majority of the birds in a drive may fly over the guns in one or more clouds. A really skilful keeper will keep this to a minimum in his woods by reducing noise from the beaters and keeping dogs out of the beating line. He will move his line slowly and if there is a fox or hare in the drive he will see that the beaters let it out. Flushing the pheasants is the chief damage a fox is likely to do and a hare can put the birds up in a cloud if it is rushing, frightened, through cover. When game-cover, like maize, has become very thin through weathering it is almost impossible to prevent flushing, which is why I prefer frost-resistant kale.

For pheasant shooting I like a good wind – though not a gale – and a dull, grey day. The birds rarely fly so well on sunny days – even away from the sun.

I site the guns, often four or five and never more than seven, well apart and if the presenting front is narrow I double bank them rather than have them close together.

I have largely dealt with the technique of shooting pheasants in Chapter 4 but would make a few general points here, at the risk of being repetitive, because they are so important.

Low pheasants presenting from the front are a bore and should be left, but if you are the end gun then a lowish bird at a long distance, say forty yards, is a testing target and may be taken, provided it is safe to do so.

Many high pheasants are missed because they are fired at when too far away, while other guns leave them too long and have a difficult shot behind their heads. In my opinion, the place to take them is a few degrees in front of the vertical.

When shooting at very high pheasants, as at Helmsley in North Yorkshire or in the Tugdale valley on my own shoot, it is the last flick of the wrist that brings them down – the final extra movement of your swing through the bird.

Perhaps the most difficult pheasant is the glider, the bird which is put up on high ground, gathers enough speed to plane down and comes over the guns at deceptively high speed and, usually, twisting or turning. The best way to deal with such a bird is to snap at it, with little barrel movement as soon as it is within range.

The number of pheasants which makes a good driven day is a matter of personal preference. The average on most shoots would seem to be between one and two hundred. Many people, used to shooting that number of birds, decry larger numbers, claiming that they would not like to shoot so many. However, I usually find that such critics have never had the opportunity to shoot large numbers of good birds and, if given it, enjoy it as much as anyone and do not refuse a repeat invitation. On a well-populated pheasant shoot where the birds are excitingly presented, as we believe they are at Rothwell, it is surprising how easily and quickly a good team, using two guns, can reach a high number.

Numbers are not the objective. It is the challenge presented by each individual bird that matters. One of the best days I can remember on the last day of the season – 1 February 1985 in a gale – produced few birds but of the highest quality. Having a lot of birds left and nothing planned, I decided to have a shoot on my own at Tealby, an estate near Rothwell which I used to own and where I now rent the shooting. I left the house at 10.10 and was back at 1.10 – three hours flat. I had shot just seventy birds but every one had been curling and a cracker. I know it sounds indulgent but I feel I have earned the right to a solo effort on days when, having made no prior arrangements, I suddenly decide that I want to shoot. The results are often more memorable than an organized day and my diary records another such an occasion for 30 January, almost the last day of the 1986 season:

It was very cloudy with a cold north-east wind, the kind which makes the birds fly at Rothwell, and such sporting days should not be wasted. I went out at 10.15 with the keepers and about twenty beaters, with Teal, a labrador, and Will Jacob loading my 28 bores for me. We drove the Old Rookery and I killed a few drakes, a few pheasants and a very good snipe. Then we shot Charles's Plantation (named after my son and planted when he was four) and brought back Diana Wood (named after my daughter). I was in heaven: the birds were dancing about in the side wind and very difficult.

Then we drove the House Wood over the garden while I stood near the road sign to Rothwell. I went in for lunch and went to bed for forty minutes while the beaters drove everything into Plover Walk. This turned out to be one of the most exciting drives of my whole life. I claimed 71 birds and they picked up 77. Then we took everything directly over the house, taking 40 beautiful birds there. We then brought Lincoln Hill down and finished at the Ram Pond with 1 teal and 9 mallards. The keeper's card showed that for the day I had 267 pheasants, 20 mallards, 1 snipe and 1 teal – 289 head. What an indulgence? Yes, but absolutely thrilling: and which shooting man would not love to experience it – on a 30th of January once or so in a lifetime?

Some days with few birds remain just as pleasantly memorable.

On an occasion in Gloucestershire, in 1984, eight guns shot thirty-seven pheasants. We were required to shoot a cock before we could shoot a hen, a device I have tried myself sometimes. I shot six pheasants and a jay and it was most enjoyable in lovely steep valleys and woods providing difficult wild birds.

Chapter 7

A Bird out of this World

Wherever I am shooting I feel remote from the mundane, but a grouse moor is truly out of this world. And the grouse is a fitting resident, wonderfully adapted to the conditions, which can so quickly change from benign and breathtakingly beautiful to bleak and cruelly harsh. I have often thought, when standing in my butt, that if the nation decided to adopt a bird as its emblem, as the Americans have, then the grouse would be a splendid choice, not only because it is indigenous and thrives well only in Britain but because of its hardiness and resilience. The partridge is my first and greatest love but the grouse is the most exciting bird in the world.

I would rate the grouse as intelligent. It has the advantage of being entirely wild, has not been softened by coddling and, without its wits about it, could not survive in such a tough and unforgiving environment. I never cease to admire the leading cock-grouse of a covey when he settles just out of shot from the butts, surveys the scene from a rock and eventually takes himself and his companions away to safety.

It is the grouse's peculiar movements coupled with its speed downwind which make it, for most shots, the greatest sporting bird in the world. It is a great leveller for the shooting fraternity because every bird is different from the one before. You get a few beating up against the wind, some sidling along side winds, some flat out down wind, some crossing, some angling, some low, some high. Always they seem to be moving in several planes of space at the same time, lifting up and down, sliding along the contours, shifting from side to side. Winged magic on the wild moor! That is why over the door at my moorland home, at Middleton-in-Teesdale, there is a Latin quotation – *Humilis jacet ipse ruina* – warning the guns that they are about to be humbled. And invariably we are, to some degree or other.

The oldest ways of shooting grouse are walking them up and dogging, which both involve strenuous exercise, marching through heather and peat bog and reacting rapidly as the grouse fly away. These methods are becoming more widely used again with the surge in the popularity of physical fitness and also because they are the cheapest forms of grouse shooting and can be practised on moors where there are rarely enough birds for driving. Such grouse are often far from easy to hit but a few competent guns can wipe out whole coveys when they rise a few at a time, something that rarely happens when the grouse are driven. As with pheasants and partridges, the cream of grouse shooting is provided by driving the birds over the guns who are usually concealed in butts, normally built of stone and turf.

The driving of grouse is a special art and, while I have devoted many years to studying it, I am still learning. On most large moors, especially early in the season, one needs between twenty and thirty fit beaters, including the flankers and keepers in support. Later in the season, in October for instance, when the birds are wilder, one can do with many less. Flankers make or break the drive and the difference between good and bad flanking is mirrored in the bag. They must be close to the end guns and should not move without advising the guns that they are going to do so. There are rare occasions when flankers and even beaters have to be behind the line of butts at one end. There is, of course, a special onus then on the guns concerned regarding safety. (Some men will not flank near enough to the butts because they have been peppered. When in the end butts always keep an eye on the flankers.)

I am a believer in big flags for the flankers, especially for the end men. Flankers need to be taught to give the birds a touch of the flag at just the right moment so that the birds go over the butts and down the line, providing shooting for as many of the guns as possible, not just one or two. The flankers need to keep out of sight until the last minute and then pop up. It is the surprise which makes the birds turn.

Each beater should carry a white flag, and I like the keeper to indicate his presence by carrying a distinctively coloured flag. The outside men should carry red flags and must be the only ones to do so. This is explained to the guns who know that they can shoot safely beyond the red flags. Having two men together carrying red flags – which I have often seen – is a recipe for disaster.

When only one set of beaters is being used the keeper should walk with them, his flag letting the others know where he is. The other beat-keepers should be in the line to keep it orderly – one keeper carrying a green flag to, say, every six to eight beaters.

My team of beaters and flankers can put grouse over three butts in almost any line. Most flankers have never been trained, beyond getting a few words from the keepers. I have had sand tables put in the garage, drawn in butts with my thumb-stick and then shown the people where they ought to be and how they ought to move. Flankers are usually chosen from beaters who have become too old to walk the distances required for beating. They need to be retrained then and will become enthusiastic.

When a drive has put a lot of grouse to one end of a moor and lunch intervenes before the return drive it pays to stick a row of flags on the butts to deter the birds from returning until you want them.

The beaters should be lined up and ready to start by the time the guns are in the butts and they should be quiet until they begin to move, as chatter can empty a drive later in the season. It is the host who should place the guns in the butts, provided he is fit enough, and they, too, should be quiet. It is, of course, equally a mistake to have the beaters out too early, for then birds may fly over empty butts. The commonest fault is to have the beaters out too late so that the guns are kept waiting too long.

There is considerable skill in knowing which butts to fill and which to leave out when there are more butts than guns, as is always the case with my shoots. There is also enormous satisfaction at the end of a drive when you know that you got it right.

Of course the grouse must be driven in such a way that they are kept on the moor and not driven off it. The birds will want to stay on the moor where they were hatched and most will be inclined to return if driven off, but some may not.

The packing of grouse into large flocks all tending to get up and fly together is an infuriating problem which happens as each season develops, and seems to be insoluble. It means that the whole stock in the drive can fly over the butts in a few seconds, giving very little chance of much shooting. Presumably, packing began as a natural reaction to attack by predators, limiting the damage they can do to grouse in flight, but it also happens to be a brilliant solution to avoid being shot.

Grouse packs can be enormous and they can come over in one cloud or in a long trailing mass – what I call a 'river of grouse', which can be almost a mile in length in a big grouse year. I once managed to fire fourteen shots at one pack of grouse. Squatting grouse join a pack flying over them, and so it grows.

I have noticed a few things about packing. The more grouse are shot at the more they will pack: leaving them quiet reduces the tendency. The more persistent the wind the more they will pack. The more it rains the more they will pack. The warmer it is the less they will pack.

I believe that the females have a tendency to pack earlier and more readily than the cocks. Towards the third week of September one sees packs of about twenty hens. I have often shot four grouse out of such a pack and they have always all been hens. Others have noticed hen packs.

It is my experience that grouse tend to pack more on some moors than on others. On some of the Cleveland moors they hardly seem to pack at all.

I suppose that the best answer to packing is to shoot as many birds as possible before packing begins. Unfortunately October, when packing is most likely to be in full swing, is the most sporting time to shoot grouse. The birds are well grown and there is strong likelihood of a good wind. The grouse are easiest to shoot in August, especially when the weather is warm and there is little wind. Under such conditions I am inclined to cancel the last drive rather than have too many easy birds killed when they will fly so much better on another day. However, there were days in August of 1988 when the Wemmergill and Swaledale grouse flew so fast in the very high winds that they did not need to be any more difficult – either to drive or shoot.

87

Like most game-birds, grouse do not fly unless they need to or are forced to, being very content to squat in the long heather looking up in the air from time to time to check what is going on and to look for raptors. However, if a grouse sees others flying it is inclined to join them, especially if it happens to be sitting in short heather. This is one reason why uniformly short heather is a disadvantage on a moor – it encourages the grouse to pack and come over the butts simultaneously in large numbers when small coveys would provide better shooting. Flying grouse are disinclined to settle in short heather which is why it is important to have some really long heather about 300 yards in front of the butts. The term 'settling ground' seems to be out of use these days but it is an essential adjunct to inducing the birds to fly over the guns the way you want them.

Though bigger than a partridge, the grouse is not a large target. An average cock-grouse measures 14–15 in. and weighs 1 lb 8 oz while the hen measures 13–14 in. and weighs about 1 lb 4 oz. So, because of the bird's excellent camouflage, it is easy to miss seeing a single bird or even a small covey coming low, and a quiet whistle from someone in the next butt with sharper eyes may be your first warning.

Quick shooting with the gun always moving is essential for dealing effectively with grouse. You must be able to move your body quickly and pull the trigger the moment the gun comes into the shoulder. I am sure that light-weight guns like the 28 bore help in this. What you may lose in spread of shot you gain through speed of movement.

You should not move, however, until you intend to shoot. Grouse can spot movement from a long distance and are likely to veer away from it. You can stand up in the butt so long as you – and your loader if you have one – stay still. What I call 'bobbers in the butt' scare a lot of grouse away from them and I have often benefited when I have had a bobber or two next to me.

You must be deliberate with a grouse – pick out one bird, ignore the rest, and shoot it. If you are thinking about your second bird you will probably miss both. Have enough confidence in your first aim to pull the trigger as the gun comes into the shoulder. This is the real secret of all successful shooting but is specially important with grouse. Lining up a bird is the surest way of securing a miss. So is shooting 'into the brown', which is cruel because it can wound birds but rarely kills them: you must pick out a particular bird and concentrate on it.

When a covey is moving sideways a fair way off it is best to select the first or last bird: otherwise you will just shoot into the brown and kill nothing, though possibly wounding several. With a crossing bird you should be swinging before the gun comes into the shoulder. Try to get two shots off in front – pop-pop – as often as possible.

It is surprising how grouse are so often missed behind, the reason being that once they have passed the butt they are easily missed over the top. You need to shoot low – at the legs – bringing the left hand down, if you are a right-handed shot. An aimed shot with a stationary gun looks a certainty but nearly always results in a miss. You have to raise the gun for safety purposes as you turn round, so bring it down on to the bird and shoot just below. That way the gun is bound to be moving. I cannot stress too often the maxim that shotgun shooting is about *movement* – your movement.

Downing a grouse a long way out in front can look very spec- tacular but such a bird is almost always a runner and very hard to pick. How often one hears, 'Did you see that bird George shot so far in front? A marvellous shot – and now he can't find it.' Some pundits advise engaging the birds at the maximum possible distance but I believe one should resist such shots because the poor bird is likely to provide a meal for a fox or die a lingering death. Let them come just far enough so that you can shoot two in front.

With a big covey, or a pack coming, it is often a good idea to fire a shot over them when they are still far out, if they are about to settle out of range in front. It is unlikely to turn them back but, instead, splits them up and they may then go over several butts instead of over one. It can also stop them from settling a short distance in front of the butts but out of shot for, having then been close enough to size up the situation, they may fly back to where they came from; and if a covey is settled there, others may join them. This is one aspect of shooting as a team, which is particularly important on a grouse moor, where any competitiveness can be really dangerous.

Accuracy is more important on a grouse moor than anywhere else because it is so essential to get a high proportion of the birds shot. If too many are left, serious overcrowding when the food supply becomes short is inevitable and this is almost invariably followed by an epidemic of disease and a poor stock in the following season. One of the problems faced by owners of grouse moors in a big year is getting a really good team of guns with the capacity to cull a heavy stock. They are in such demand that they are hard to come by because so many people want their services.

Adult grouse are essentially herbivorous, feeding on the shoots, flowers and seed heads of heather with additional sustenance from bilberries, grasses, rushes and other plants. Their main food – probably more than 80 per cent of it – is ling (*Calluna*), which they much prefer to the more beautiful bell-heather (*Erica*). The more acceptable food there is on the moor the more grouse it can hold. The food supply depends on the weather, which can be very rough on a high moor, so the grouse is a very weather-dependent bird. The season of 1987, which saw a welcome increase in grouse populations in both Scotland and England, was evidence of this. The previous winter had been mild and there was some warm weather in early spring which encouraged plant growth.

Like all herbivorous creatures, the grouse has to eat a great deal every day because its food has comparatively poor nutritive value. It tends to pack its crop with heather in the evening to see it through the night.

A great deal of research has been carried out on the grouse and, coupled with my own observations over many years, it has left me in no doubt whatever that the major factor affecting grouse populations is food supply and that the general decline over the years has been due mainly to deterioration in the amount and quality of the heather which, in turn, is linked with poor or non-existent moor management. As I shall discuss in some detail later, the lack of management is, to some extent, due to the reduction in the number of keepers but, even where keepers exist, the management often leaves much to be desired.

In my experience the food supply in the vital weeks – the spring – depends far more on the wind than on rain or snow. Grouse are very hardy birds, so long as they can get food, and they tread snow as it falls, and easily escape being smothered. They can also burrow into snow. But a cold north-east wind, day after day, will dry out the heather, giving it an almost burned appearance and reducing its nutrient value when the birds need it most. This is when worms and parasites do so much damage to birds weakened through hunger. March is the danger month and it can seem to be very long to the grouse waiting for some warmth and sunshine to plump up the heather shoots.

A hen-grouse usually lays between six and eleven eggs in late April or early May, in a nest which is not much more than a scrape. The eggs can withstand severe weather and the hens will continue to sit in snow. It is the well-fed birds which lay the most eggs. When heather is scarce or of poor quality most of the clutches will be small, as though the birds can sense that there is no point in laying many when few of the young are likely to survive. I had never seen such large clutches laid or coveys so big as in the 1987 season. This must have been due to an abundance of the right kind of food at the right time, including insects for the chicks. I prefer to thank the Almighty for this rather than attribute it to good husbandry alone, though that is a most important contributory factor.

The birds are generally monogamous in a season, but not for life, though an aggressive cock-bird with a large territory may have two hens both nesting in it, almost side by side.

I strongly recommend that owners of grouse moors should visit their territories during breeding time and not just turn up on 12 August hoping for the best. The same rules apply as to any other shoot. To get results from a satisfied keepering staff you must keep in personal touch with them.

As is well known, grouse populations can be seriously affected by strongylosis (grouse disease). Experiments in which grouse have been caught up, treated and released show, not surprisingly, that birds heavily infected with the strongyle worm lay fewer eggs and rear fewer chicks. The damage is minor when grouse numbers are small but becomes epidemic when populations get too high. The eggs of the parasite pass out in the grouse's droppings and the birds then eat an infected shoot up which the hatched worm has crawled. The parasite cannot multiply in the bird. Each has to be ingested separately. A couple of weeks of unbroken dry weather is helpful because the parasite will only move up a wet stalk.

Some keepers have tried administering anti-worm pills to individual birds at night, when they can be approached and caught. The operation involves driving across a moor in a four-wheel-drive vehicle with a spotlight. The birds can be seen by their eyeshine and provided the Land-Rover engine is not stopped – or a tape-recording of the engine noise is maintained – the birds can be netted, dosed with an antihelminthic, such as fenbendazole, and released with little difficulty. It is said that if about 25 per cent of the birds are treated, the overall worm challenge can be reduced to an acceptable level, though I have my doubts. In fact, I consider the whole process to be hopelessly impractical and the publication of the method of catching the bird at night is an invitation to poachers. I am appalled to see that there are now even special lamps on sale and advertised in the shooting papers for this purpose. It is now possible to buy quartz grit coated with the anti-worm material, which saves catching up the birds, but on a moor rich in grit, how can the birds be induced to select the medicated variety, which is expensive? To repeat, the best precaution against grouse disease is heavy shooting, and heather-burning to provide enough food later.

Grouse are also susceptible to the disease called louping ill, which is carried by the sheep-tick. In Scotland the sheep-tick has inflicted damage on grouse populations which was quite unnecessary. Some years ago the Scottish hill farmers stopped dipping their sheep with the result that the sheep-tick increased so enormously that it infected the deer and the hares as well as the grouse. Happily this did not happen on the moors in the North of England, where I do most of my grouse shooting. The tick seems to favour bracken, so bracken control, which is necessary to prevent the invasion of heather-ground, helps to reduce the tick population too.

Sheep – and cattle – compete with the grouse for food, and overstocking makes appalling inroads into the heather which is grazed so heavily that it dies, being replaced by coarse grasses and bracken. Many thousands of acres of heather have been lost this way in recent years and I shall give my views on that distressing problem in Chapter 11.

Grouse populations are very susceptible to attacks by predators and on most moors there are too many foxes and crows because of inadequate or inefficient keepering and the invasion of the ground by coniferous trees, which provide havens for both. Sitting grouse and their eggs are easy prey.

There is no doubt that, for these various reasons, the quality of grouse shooting has declined but in many areas it has remained good and, possibly, the general decline has been exaggerated. Most of the books about Big Shots and Great Shoots refer, in nostalgic wonderment, to the bags achieved by Lord Ripon, who is said to have shot 97,503 grouse in his long lifetime. That was at a time when grouse moors were at their best with plenty of keepers and no other expense spared, yet my records show that in the last fifteen years I have shot more grouse than Lord Ripon did in his last fifteen – and he continued until his death which occurred on a grouse moor. My best-ever year was as recent as 1988 when I shot 3390, while I had accounted for over 3000 in the previous season, as I also had in 1982. Lord Ripon killed 3435 grouse to his own guns in his best season, using 12 bores, while I used 28 bores.

On 15 August 1988 I was in a team of eight guns which shot 550 brace of grouse. The grouse that were there all flew and mostly over the butts, whereas, usually in August only about two-thirds come over. It was an outstanding day.

I give these comparative figures to show that the grouse populations cannot have been so bad in recent years on moors which have been well managed.

The record for the number of grouse shot in one day by one gun belongs to Lord Walsingham, the renowned shot who spent so much time thinking about shooting that he neglected his personal affairs, grossly overspent and lost the fortune he had inherited. On 30 August 1888 he killed 1070 to his own gun on Blubberhouse Moor in Yorkshire, which he then owned. All the birds were driven over him in twenty drives while he stood in a narrow waist of the moor. Two lines of beaters drove the birds backwards and forwards all day.

I have never tried to compete with that record but I have, occasionally, indulged in the luxury of a shoot on my own on

93

the odd day when I had not organized a shoot with guests but felt like shooting and had a lot of grouse which needed thinning. I wanted to try each butt which provided the most difficult birds – the fastest and the highest – on my moor at Reeth and my diary records the result:

I was in the first butt and shot my first grouse at five past ten. They were very difficult and I shot ten birds. I then stood in a paddock where an old lady from the farm used to milk her cows and carry the milk miles down into Reeth. I killed another ten grouse there. Then I shot eight standing in the open in another grass field. Then they brought the whole of Kearton pasture off to me and I had eleven fantastic grouse with my spaniel, Sweep, and my labrador, Teal, sitting there without a lead and never moving during the drive. The dogs picked all the birds up and I had thirty-nine by lunch. After a bite I went down to the low moor and killed twenty grouse there. Then I turned round and they brought it back to me. I killed a right and left out of each covey that came and killed a lone pair. That made a dozen birds – seventy-one in all and every one picked. It was highly satisfactory and very exciting.

On another occasion, in late September 1988, my son Charles and I had a day's shooting at Reeth to ourselves on a windy day when the grouse were very sporting. Father and son had $73\frac{1}{2}$ brace. Charles shot extremely well and memorable moments occurred when a flanker swished a big pack over me and, through very quick action by my loader, George Graham, I managed to thin it out by seven birds. Some other wonderful days have been spent: alone with my elder son Robert as a companion, or my second son Charles; with my son-in-law Ian and his wife Diana; with my other daughters Louise, Eugenie and Rosémarie, who all use their own dogs to pick up; or, alone with my wife, just the two of us, when we've regularly killed over 100 brace of partridges in Spain. Of course I often shot with my brother Sam before his terrible illness – which he is bearing with such great courage. There have also been some happy days in the field with my younger brother Ben.

One is only the short-term tenant of one's property so it makes sound sense to enjoy it while you can.

94

Because of the difficulties of the terrain and the position of some butts it is usually grouse which the shooting man has to give up first because of the ravages of age. With modern four-wheel drive and caterpillar transport, however, the reasonably fit shot can continue for much longer. I reached seventy-three during the 1987 grouse season and never enjoyed a season more. However, one cannot spend a day on a high moor without admiring the strength and endurance of our forebears who walked from drive to drive before the days of motorized transport. It is tough enough just walking to the top butts on many drives and it is fun to watch the struggling guns turning round at intervals, ostensibly to admire the view, but really to recover their breath! I have heard of some overweight guests being helicoptered up to the top butts on some shoots. Apparently the grouse were surprisingly unaffected, as they also seem to be by low-flying aeroplanes.

Since heather is the key to good grouse stocks I decided that, having enjoyed myself on the moors so much over so many years, I would show my gratitude by setting up a Foundation for Heather Research, a project which is now well under way and which I describe in Chapter 11. If I can be the means of helping to regenerate heather, not only for the grouse and the wild life, but for all who enjoy the rolling, purple landscape, I can think of no memorial that I would prefer.

Chapter 8

The Delights of Wildfowling

I have been a wildfowler all my life – it has been a passion with me. Waiting for duck in a hide is more exciting for me than waiting for grouse in a butt or partridges behind a hedge.

To illustrate how keen I am, my diary records that after travelling down from the grouse moor at Middleton-in-Teesdale early on 20 September 1975 I was on my way across to Read's Island in the Humber Estuary by 9 a.m. to stay there for two days and nights: 'It was wonderful to have seen the sun rise over the moors just after leaving Middleton and to see it set over the Humber Estuary and to see the full moon rise all in the same day. I was very pleased that at my age I was getting a few lefts and rights when it was very dark.'

If you are creating a flight pond, as I have done at Rothwell and various other places, I would advise planting trees round it in such a way that there are entry and escape routes between them, and site these so that they face the hide. That way you can see the ducks when it gets quite dark because they have to enter and go out that way. If the pond is already encircled by trees it may be necessary to cut some down to create one or more of these funnels. They will greatly increase the number of birds coming within shot and you will see them better.

A hide must give you plenty of room to swing your gun, and some wildfowlers, being overly concerned with camouflage, handicap themselves in this respect. Some camouflage is necessary and one should always wear a hat. A glove on the left hand conceals the whiteness of the skin which ducks can detect from a long distance with their quite remarkable eyesight. It is also advantageous, if inconvenient, to wear a mask which is more comfortable if stitched round an old spectacle frame with the lenses removed. While sitting in duck hides in warm weather I have sometimes been eaten alive by midges, so a stock of effective fly-repellent is essential.

I don't bother with duck-callers but often throw a dozen or so rubber decoys – mallard, wigeon or teal – on to the water, according to where I happen to be shooting. It is difficult to know whether they do much good. Some days the ducks seem to avoid them. Until we can talk to a wild duck we shall never really know.

There should be two hides on every flight pond and only one person should shoot a pond at one time. With two guns on a pond one of them is likely to shoot too early before the birds are properly within range. The siting of the hide is paramount. In some situations it needs to be a little way out over the water with access that permits safe departure in the dark.

The water on a flight pond must not be too deep if ducks are to patronize it regularly, and some shallows are essential. The teal, for instance, cannot get very far down for its food. If you can have two ponds about a mile apart, then feed one before dawn for the morning flight and the other in the early afternoon for the evening flight.

When flighting a longish piece of water at night, say a drain some five yards wide, I like a piece of string stretched across carrying two or three plastic bags so that the ducks will try to fly on past me instead of settling in front.

It is my belief that a wild duck can remember where it was shot at for about three weeks, so three weeks is a good time to leave a flighting pond quiet.

Occasionally one is tempted to let a few ducks come in and settle in the hope that they will attract others, but my motto is 'first come first served', and I shoot the first duck that shows in range. But be sure that it is in range. Most people find it difficult to resist the temptation to shoot too early. If two or more duck are coming in make sure that both are in range before you fire your first barrel to make sure that you have a chance of a right and left. When a pair of wigeon come in to feed, the drake is usually in front. So shoot the duck first then the drake – a case of 'Ladies first!'

Shooting mallard successfully is difficult: the easier they look the more often they are missed. Like all ducks, mallard should be shot in the head, for a wounded duck is a sorry sight. If shot in the right place, a mallard should put his head back.

In general you need to shoot *at* mallard, with a moving gun, and the majority of experienced pheasant shots miss them in front. For a very high bird a flick of the wrist is usually enough. With a really distant crossing duck, however, you need to give a big, deliberate lead – seeing daylight in front of the bird. It is then surprising how far away you can bring down such a challenging target.

I suspect that duck can detect in advance when it is going to be foggy, presumably from the general weather conditions. I have noticed many times that duck will not move in advance of fog, perhaps realizing that they will have navigation difficulties. One is waiting, excitedly, for the evening flight, nothing arrives then, shortly, fog descends.

I have also noticed some odd behaviour about single ducks and geese which I have often put to good use when I have been in a hide with the wind strong and blowing towards me. If such a bird is crossing and likely to remain out of range it can be brought nearer by firing a shot in the air, while remaining fully concealed. The bird tends to lift and then allow itself to be carried by the wind to what it believes is safety. This ruse has rarely failed for me with a single goose.

At the end of the season I like to shoot mallard drakes only. It is exciting to pick a drake out of a fast-moving group and bring him down. Reducing the drakes gives the ducks a less harassing time in the mating season.

A wounded duck is such a pitiful sight – maybe it is the special affection for the toy ducks of childhood, though it is an endearing bird anyway – and since it is not easy to dispatch it is sensible to carry a priest as anglers do for knocking their quarry smartly and quickly on the head. This is even more necessary for dispatching a wounded goose, and I seldom shoot at a goose now.

Normal guns are perfectly adequate for most wildfowling and many wildfowlers handicap themselves by using guns which are too heavy and difficult to swing. I find my 20 bores and 28 bores can bring down anything that is really shootable. Bigger and heavier weapons also encourage a gun to shoot at extreme ranges, wounding birds which cannot be picked. They also reduce the chance of getting the rights and lefts which are so satisfying.

The delights of duck shooting are so unique that even when I have been shooting grouse or pheasants for days on end I still cannot resist having a go at the ducks if time is available. Here is a short note which I tape-recorded on 4 October 1987:

I am home from the grouse moor for the first time since 11 August – and I am in a hide at 6.15 p.m. with Will Jacob to load my 28 bores with American Remington cartridges – 7½ shot, equivalent to English 6. I have a few mallard decoys out and the ducks have been fed here. It is the first time ducks have been shot here this season.

I had 21 ducks by 7 p.m. By 21 minutes past I had 45, the majority mallard and a few teal. By 7.30 it was too dark to shoot. A truly marvellous evening – very mild, no wind and almost a full moon. Billy Jacob told me that the pickers-up had accounted for 42.

When teal are coming towards you into a wind it is most important to let them get past you before shooting them. The instinctive move is to shoot one in front when they are about thirty yards out, when the rest will then turn away. If you take them when they have just passed, you should certainly get two and, with a good loader, you might get three or even four, which is extremely satisfying. I shoot a lot of teal every year and, almost invariably, find that there are substantially more drakes than ducks. I wonder if this is a common experience.

I like teal to eat and find that they are never shot in the body – indicating that when they are missed it is in front. My wife serves them as hors d'oeuvres and, on one occasion, after hearing so many guests remark that there were no pellets in the birds – I always try to shoot duck in the head – she tried to take me down a peg by surreptitiously opening a cartridge and sprinkling a few shot on to the plates. The joke succeeded, to my surprise and dismay.

Read's Island – some 100 acres, with thousands surrounding – in the Humber Estuary about mid-way between Barton-upon-Humber and the mouth of the River Trent and reachable only by boat, has been a wonderful investment in pleasure. It was probably in 1934 when I first shot there, paying 10 shillings a day – the equivalent of 50 pence – to the shepherd who was employed by the tenants and lived on the island. Later, my friend, Fred Davy, DFC, AFC, and I became tenants and in 1957 I bought it outright from the Humber Conservancy Board. The way I acquired it may be of some interest. Fred and I had managed to instal 300 Irish bullocks on the island – in a hilarious operation involving old landing craft – and as one of the banks looked like collapsing against the sea we were in danger of losing them. We put in a claim to the board and, at a big meeting in Hull, I suggested that since the board was insisting that the island always lost them money they would be better off giving it to me. Finding that impossible, as I expected they would, they offered to sell it. I proposed to take it off their hands provided they repaired the bank, which they agreed to do.

I have been wildfowling on the Humber Estuary since I was a child, and since 1934, every season on Reads Island. In those fifty-four years there have been many days when one only shot the odd duck or two, and there have been a few days when they never seemed to stop coming. I think that it is the unknown that has a tremendous attraction in flighting and in wildfowling in general. It is usually a dawn and dusk affair – the sunrises and sunsets – and the moon can be as splendid as the sun on rising. It is the cream of all shooting for me. Outwitting these wild birds in their own environment gives one an enormous sense of satisfaction. Without the help of beaters, on the tide edge in a barrel, or in a hide on the sea bank, or in the rushes, or in the sea asters, in the open under a part moon lying on the banks, or shooting from your knees, the variety is infinite compared with game shooting.

During those fifty-four years on Reads Island I have had bags from zero and two or three to twenty, thirty, forty, and, exceptionally, fifty. Once in my life the ducks never stopped coming for almost ten hours from before sunrise till after sunset and I was shooting almost continuously; it was unbelievable. This happened to me on 2 December 1983 after four good pheasant days that week – two at Helmsley, two at Rothwell, and all high birds. I was waiting for the dawn on the Friday morning. Using over-and-under 20 bores, I was kept busy from dawn until after dark and never went into the house, managing with sandwiches which were brought out to me. It was easily the best wildfowling day of my life. The many blank days – or days where there were very few birds – helped to make this day even more enjoyable. It is worth thinking that if you never have a little day, you never have a big day – and I've had plenty of little days at wildfowling.

I then returned home to shoot pheasants the next day on a friend's estate in Lincolnshire. A six-day shooting week in my seventieth year! Fanatical? Perhaps, but for me, the spice of life.

Looking through my records of these memorable days spent remote from cares, I would rate my most satisfying encounter with wildfowl as a right and left – at a wigeon and a pink-foot goose. I have never liked to shoot a lot of geese, but the noise, the clamour, the moon, and the excitement together make the pursuit for the odd bird or two very thrilling. I have shot them in the Marissma in Spain and on the lochs in Scotland. It is the wonderful places that one visits to see and hear these birds, that makes it exciting – not the numbers shot.

I have spent many nights on Read's Island waiting for the geese to flight off the mud-bank in the hope of shooting them under the moon. Geese talk to each other while sitting in an estuary. Then suddenly they go quiet about five minutes in advance of flighting towards the land. They need more than half a moon to feed at night.

Goose shooting can be extraordinarily exhilarating, particularly under the moon. I have shot them in many positions – even lying on my back. Number three shot is quite big enough for a goose and it is cruel to shoot them further away than number three can deal with them. BB shot are unnecessary.

My most memorable goose shooting has been done elsewhere.

Chapter 9

Various

The wood pigeon could be properly described as 'a bird for all seasons' because, being a very damaging farm pest often present in enormous numbers, it can provide a challenging target the whole year round. I love shooting pigeons. Here is a tape-recording I made at Rothwell on 1 June 1981 after rising at 5 a.m.

I am in my pigeon hide. I can see many species of wild birds and can hear the cuckoo almost all the time. The hawthorn is in wonderful bloom, especially those bushes which have not been trimmed. Quite a few pigeons have come but there seems to be something they don't like and I am so well camouflaged that I don't think it can be me. I get so excited by pigeons: every one is so different. I have just fetched a high one down. The sun is half breaking through the mist and the pigeons have started to come more frequently. I am enjoying myself shooting at everything – not just the easy ones. These pigeons do an enormous amount of damage, especially to peas, and it is important to reduce their numbers. I have to go to London later today for the Agricultural Forum tomorrow. On the journey down I will be thinking about these pigeons.

Pigeons are marvellous practice for pheasant and duck shooting but provide excellent sport in their own right. They can gain height and jink more quickly than any game-bird and can fly faster. They are shot in very large numbers all over Britain yet nobody complains about it as they do about game-birds, even though they are, truly, wildlife. Could the reason be that, by and large, it is not the so-called 'privileged' who shoot them?

Some people have made a speciality of shooting very large numbers of pigeons as a means of pest control. They generally achieve this by waiting in hides until the birds are very low and almost unmissable. That is proper under those circumstances but I restrict my pigeon shooting to the challenging birds and I would recommend those who want practice for other game to do the same.

When shooting pigeons on your own make a hide, preferably close to a single tree next to some standing corn or other crop. The tree should have a bare top if possible because pigeons prefer that. Feed the area once or twice a day with half a bucket of small beans. Put down a dozen decoys fairly close together – three yards apart – head to wind with a couple lofted on to the dead branches of the tree. Those on the ground should be well away from the hide – at least thirty-five yards. A few fertilizer bags on sticks in the ground help to keep the pigeons off the rest of the field. (In Spain they use live decoys – tame pigeons tethered to little see-saws which are placed about eight feet high up small oak trees. When a pigeon is sighted the keeper pulls a string and the see-saw unbalances the bird which makes it flap its wings. I do not know if this would be legal in Britain but it works like a charm.)

One should have several hides in different places and, though pigeons have such huge appetites that they seem to be capable of feeding all day long, it pays not to overshoot them under normal circumstances. In hard weather, however, when food is scarce, it is astonishing how pigeons will continue to come and come to a field of greenstuff though shooting is almost continuous. Most of these pigeons will be immigrants which arrive in the autumn, sometimes in enormous numbers.

I usually use a 20 bore gun with number six shot though I am now so wedded to my 28 bores that I use them too. I wear a camouflage jacket, a face mask and gloves, as for duck shooting. (I had it made in 1947 and it was never washed until 1982 when the smell was getting a little unbearable!)

One can start shooting in the spring – a couple of hours between tea and dinner – and carry on until harvest with wonderful sport – with down-wind, up-wind and side-wind birds. Then, of course, one can continue through the autumn and winter. And pigeons make good eating.

Wood pigeons can be driven like pheasants and, at Rothwell in July we beat through several woods with up to five guns in a line of straw-bale butts about twenty yards back from the cover. The butts make an immense difference to the bag. Driving pigeons this way does no harm to the pheasant poults provided you have no dogs with the beaters. They like to leave cover down-wind and come in up-wind. The male pigeons come out first and the sitting hens last. It might be thought unsporting to shoot these hens but the wood pigeon is a most damaging farm pest with an appetite for almost anything.

It is an expression of my love of shooting that after a succession of big pheasant drives I have often gone on to shoot pigeons and enjoyed some of the best birds of the day. And, of course, on almost every pheasant drive some of the most difficult birds that come over the guns are the odd pigeons which chance to present themselves. As I have already said, these birds should be shot at whether the pheasants have started showing or not. The noise will not make the smallest difference.

My advice for dealing with pigeons is essentially the same as for pheasants but the target is substantially smaller and it is even more important that the gun be fired as it comes into the shoulder because, unlike the pheasant, the pigeon will take evasive action as soon as it spots the movement of the gun. You must shoot *at* the pigeons coming in towards you and not in front of them, as one tends to do early in the season. For the very high pigeon the final flick of the wrist is all-important. And for the really long-distance crosser you need to see daylight between the gun and the bird.

On most game-cards the few pigeons which tend to be shot during the day are listed among the other additional kills as Various. So this is a convenient place to consider the various in general.

The most welcome and most exciting of all is the woodcock, a most delightful wild bird which does breed in Britain but is not present in shootable quantities until large numbers of migrants fly in from Europe – mainly from Scandinavia, North Germany and Russia – mostly in October and November.

They are quite slow fliers but because their twisting flight is so erratic they tend to be missed behind. They are very adept at changing speed. The trick is to get the gun up, blot them out and fire as fast as possible. Lining them up is a sure way of missing them.

There is a growing school of thought that woodcock should not be shot at all, being a beautiful form of wildlife which harms nothing. There is also the danger element, for the woodcock is a low flier. We have all heard the story of Tom Turner, who was a keeper who decided to retire when he reached ninety-five. When asked to what he attributed his long life he replied, 'The speed with which I ducked when somebody shouted "Woodcock".' Many people are so keen to shoot a woodcock that they become over-excited when one appears and take risks which they would not do with any other bird in their determination to shoot it.

An increasing number of shoots now bar the killing of woodcock, partly for safety reasons but also because they are truly wild life. We all deplore the appalling behaviour of the Italians and Maltese who shoot our migrant songbirds so, perhaps, it would not be unreasonable if the Scandinavians objected to our shooting their woodcock. Being close to the east coast at Rothwell, we get a good share of the migrant woodcock but, now, I tend to shoot them only when I want one or two to eat. I fear that I am very fond of a woodcock – cold or hot, provided it has not been kept hot very long, when it tends to go hard.

A right and left at woodcock is regarded as a major achievement if only because the opportunity for it arises so rarely. Having done so much shooting I have managed to bring it off three times and missed one other chance. I have seen three woodcock so close that they could have been shot by someone with two guns but I have witnessed this only once in my life, in 1983.

My best personal performance against this elusive quarry was at a shoot at Bawdsey on 7 December 1962. Six woodcock came over me singly while I was standing in a rather wide ride. I killed each one with the first barrel. Then a couple came over and I dropped them with a right and left – eight woodcock in eight shots, something I have never done since or am ever likely to do again.

Many people have seen a woodcock carrying a chick, as though deliberately moving it. I surmise that when this happens it may sometimes be an accident. A woodcock has long thin legs and the chick has a large head so when the bird is disturbed from brooding it may jump with a young one between the legs. On the other hand, a woodcock has been seen to deposit such a chick in a safe place and then return for another, so the behaviour must be deliberate on occasion.

Another long-beaked various which has given me great enjoyment in the past is the snipe of which there are three varieties, though only one, the common snipe, is regularly shot.

I had the pleasure of shooting snipe with my old friend, Guy Moreton, now sadly no longer with us, at Tyree in the Hebrides, where we shot over a hundred snipe between us each day. The accommodation was a bit primitive. When I complained to my landlady that rain was coming through the ceiling in my room her response was, 'Well, its nae dropping on your bed, is it?' But the shooting was worth the discomfort.

A snipe is a tiny target, very fast and adept at zig-zagging its way to safety. The moment to shoot is when the bird turns for the first time, though longer distances offer more challenging targets. It is a rising shot and one needs to shoot slightly *over* the bird, swinging fast and shooting without delay as the gun comes into the shoulder.

Snipe spend most of the day resting in cover and feed mainly at night but especially during the full moon, so it is wise to book snipe shooting when the moon will be full. The snipe will also be full and they then sit a bit tighter, giving the gun a better chance.

As an experiment, at Tyree, we took some men from Rothwell and some flags and they were able to drive the snipe to the two of us. They are easier to shoot that way so we reverted to walking them up.

There has been a definite decline in the snipe population and I think that, on some estates at least, snipe should not be shot for at least two seasons from the time of writing. There can be little doubt that the decline has some connection with the widespread drainage of land but, rather mysteriously, there are also substantially fewer snipe in areas which remain as before. Perhaps a ban on shooting after the end of October for a few seasons would help the population.

This would be a considerable sacrifice on my part. In my view, the snipe, when in good condition, is probably the tastiest bird that flies.

Another wading bird which is superb eating is the golden plover which frequents moors and peat-mosses in the breeding season but likes pastures and arable land at other times. On our Wolds, where they are not far from the shore, which they also visit, flocks of golden plovers come on to the cleared pea stubbles and on to the old airfields. Their flight is very rapid with quick wingbeats and the whole flock wheels and wavers as though flying to a single command.

When you have fired a first shot the rest of the flock or a single companion bird, if there is just a pair, dives to the ground with great speed, making a second shot very difficult. This almost reflex behaviour can be exploited if you spot a golden plover flying high when you are in a hide. A shot into the air will cause it to dive down and bring it within range. Another trick, when walking fields where there are likely to be golden plover, is to send your dog out in front. As often as not, the plovers will mob it, giving you a chance to shoot several of them as their mobbing continues.

Golden plover can also be driven, rather like grouse, when they are feeding on grass fields, and we have done that regularly, with success, on Read's Island.

On the table the golden plover is a .very close second to a snipe. When we were honoured by a visit from HRH The Duke of Edinburgh, who came to shoot at Rothwell, we gave him a golden plover pie, a tremendous delicacy which he had never had before. It was quite a coup, I felt, to have been able to provide something novel for a man who attends so many dinners in so many lands that there can be little in the food line that is new to him.

Before the days of myxomatosis rabbits were so plentiful that they made up a large part of the bag on every shoot and there was a special place on every game-card for them. Several hundred might be shot in the course of a day's pheasant driving and rabbit shooting was a sport in its own right. Today, the few rabbits accounted for in a day's shooting are usually knocked down by the beaters or seized by the dogs and end up among the various.

It is surprising how many good pheasant shots cannot get to grips with rabbits because the basic principle is the same – to kill a running rabbit cleanly you need to concentrate on the head, as you should with a flying pheasant. Look at the rabbit's head and try to ignore the rest of it. This means that, if it is running away, you must fire well over the top of it and not at its hind quarters. And your gun should be moving – as always – when you fire. If you are shooting at a sitting rabbit – which is not very sporting but sometimes necessary in areas where rabbits are doing damage – be sure to shoot low, almost at the ground in front.

Young people can have no notion of the quantities of rabbits there used to be prior to myxomatosis. They were in plague proportions. Whole fields were lifting with them and they inflicted enormous damage on crops. But what fun and what practice they gave us! A group of us – the six who shot the record partridge bag – once killed 602 rabbits at Rothwell in just over 20 acres of kale in a day. It was 25 January 1950 with the ground frozen like brick. The keepers had ferreted all round the area and as it was the only piece of available cover the rabbits made use of it. We had previously cut rides in the kale to force the rabbits to bolt across and shot them – with our backs to the beaters and no dogs allowed – as they ran.

I had experimented on a small scale beforehand and had found that the rides should not be more than about five yards wide otherwise the rabbits would not race across them. If a ride is more than five yards the rabbits poke their noses out and look up and down but don't bolt across to give a really good sporting shot. If it is less than five the rabbit may be across before you have proper time for a shot.

We stood the guns so that everyone shot to his left and nowhere else. That way the rabbits were shared out and guns were not shooting at the same one.

It was a wonderful day's sport and made useful economic inroads into the rabbits. Six weeks previously four of us had killed 421 rabbits on a different area on the estate.

Before such a shoot it pays to 'stink' the rabbits out of their burrows. This can be done by soaking small potatoes in creosote or paraffin and rolling them well down into the occupied holes.

It was also enormous fun to get a call from a neighbour to help him clean up his rabbits when corn was being cut. The last half acre or so would be literally moving with rabbits and we would knock them off as they bolted. I remember shooting eighty-eight couple of rabbits myself out of a piece of corn. We had to send for a cart to get them home after we had gutted them in the field, as we always did in those days. I can recall the smell now. Not pleasant but nostalgic!

Rabbit shooting is always hazardous and shooting them out of corn, with the cutter still going, was usually accompanied by extra dangers. My neighbour would be on a tractor with a hammer-gun fully cocked and a whippet in his arms. He either let the whippet go or had a shot!

Hares too are sadly depleted these days, again, I believe, mainly through changes in farming practice, though disease may be a factor in some areas. A few hares can eat as much as a sheep so, when they were plentiful, they had to be thinned out, usually in great drives involving a very long line of beaters and as many as fifty guns, who would account for several hundreds in a day. As a rule, the woods would not be driven during these shoots to thin down excessive numbers, so those taking refuge there provided a big enough breeding stock for future seasons. The hares were a useful extra crop, most of those sold to game-dealers going for export to the Continent.

The hare is a large animal and about thirty yards is the maximum distance at which it should be engaged. One needs to be able to see its eyes before shooting at it with the certainty of a clean kill. Far too many hares are shot at from long distances, which results in much unnecessary suffering. If two hares are running towards you, shoot the furthest first, then shoot the other as it runs away.

An increasing number of seasoned shots are declining to shoot hares, which is a good trend in the interests of safety alone. With hare or rabbit shooting the danger of ricochet on flinty or frozen ground is always present. 'We don't shoot ground game' is figuring more and more in the opening instructions given to the guns when assembling for the day.

I am sure that it is true to say that the best old-fashioned farming practice was as good for hares as it was for partridges. While a lot of rabbits were a sign of bad husbandry, a lot of hares indicated that the land was in good heart. The hare needs a varied diet, so huge tracts of cereals, grassland or rape, like we see today, do not favour it. The widespread cutting of grass for silage kills thousands of leverets. Stubble-burning with immediate ploughing, and weed-spraying, all militate against the hare. Some chemical sprays can kill hares if they lick their coats after being contaminated, as they are pretty sure to do. The numbers of hares killed by motorists – almost certainly far greater than those shot by sportsmen – must also have made substantial inroads into their numbers.

It has been calculated that the country-wide hare population has halved in the last twenty years. I would rate the loss much higher.

Chapter 10

Shoot Management

An entire book could be written about the management of shoots but I will endeavour to distil into one chapter the main lessons I have learned – and am still learning – in a lifetime of running them. One cannot really write in general terms about running 'a shoot' since all shoots differ, but there are some golden rules.

The essence of management is knowing what you want to do and motivating reliable people to do it, the choosing of those people being a crucial factor. This is just as true in running a shoot as in running a business.

Of course, many shoots today are run almost entirely as businesses, and I cannot offer much detailed advice in that specialized direction because I run my shoots essentially for the pleasure of my family, my friends and myself. Rothwell is one of a dwindling number of big shoots in which no days or guns are sold. I sell a few days on my grouse moors but that is only because I cannot find time to shoot them all myself. The locations of the moors in Teesdale, Swaledale, Allendale and Nidderdale give a good geographical spread: it is most unlikely that they will all be poor in any one season.

It is a commonplace that 'the master's eye' – the constant and critical observation by the owner of everything that is going on – is essential on the farm. It is equally essential, perhaps more so, on a shoot. There are some people who take shoots, hire a keeper and never go near him except when they turn up with their friends to fire their guns. They are almost invariably disappointed and quickly lose a good keeper. They are also likely to get rooked.

On my shoots I watch everything like a hawk. I want to know

how everything is done and why things are not done. I have a pocket tape-recorder and record everything of which I need to take note so that I can translate it into action without delay. I recommend the tape-recorder: too many good ideas are forgotten and wasted through failure to record them when they flash into the mind, especially as one gets older, for it is the short-term memory that fades.

I set the greatest store by human relations. The right atmosphere on a shoot, as on a farm, is everything and that depends on good relations with staff. When I am moving round my shoots in my vehicle I stop and speak to everybody, as I do when moving round the farms. I learn a great deal that way and all the staff know that I care. Naturally, I always thank the beaters and the keepers if the day has been to my satisfaction. If it has not I let them know why, but never in front of anybody else.

The costs of running a shoot are rising to such an extent that, for many, they have become prohibitive. In 1983 the total annual expenditure on shoots was estimated by the Standing Conference on Countryside Sports at more than £36 million, probably much too low a figure in my view, and must now be much higher, with inflation and other factors affecting all the main items. So the careful watching of costs is vital to the continuation of the sport and costs certainly can be cut if the owner keeps them under scrutiny.

On most shoots much money is wasted through the feeding system. Most keepers put down far too much food in the hope of preventing their pheasants from straying, but this has the reverse effect in my experience. The more food that is easily available, the quicker the pheasants fill their crops and, with nothing much else to think about, they wander. On many shoots, perhaps most, hoppers are filled up as a matter of course, and are regularly raided by rats, pigeons and other birds. The pheasants become over-fed and excessively heavy. I have already mentioned the value of occasionally weighing some of the shot pheasants in this regard. Food should be scattered thinly under litter or on strawed rides to keep the birds busy looking for it. Wheat is the best all-round food for pheasants. I think that they get too fat when fed on maize but they certainly like it.

There is no doubt that pheasants love beans, and some unscrupulous people grow them to attract birds from neighbouring ground. The only solution, in self-defence, if this is happening, is to buy some beans and feed them instead of wheat.

In winter a partridge needs about an ounce of food a day and now that sprays have killed off so many weeds one has to provide it. Feed-wheat is the best but, obviously, cannot be used on land which is to be used for growing seed-wheat. In that circumstance, which we faced in many areas of Rothwell, cut maize should be used. The partridges must be fed every day in thick enough cover to hide them from human view. Feeding should start in mid-September and continue until mid-April. The food should be scattered by hand in the kale strips rather than presented in hoppers. The birds will then stay in the cover.

There are some shoots where the keeper negotiates with local farmers for grain supplies without any oversight, and this is a recipe for fiddles.

Shoot management is about creating a suitable environment for game, usually in farmland conditions. A shoot with a heavy concentration of birds is, of course, highly artificial because the natural stock which land can carry without artificial aids is remarkably small. But there is an art in making a shoot appear to be as natural as possible. There are some, which shall be nameless here, where the artificiality is preposterous. Huge numbers of pheasants and partridges are fed on high ground which could never sustain even a small population and are released at intervals to be driven over guns. On some such shoots the winter mortality is appalling because they are not fed once the season ends and they die of starvation. Such practices, while commercially rewarding, give shooting a bad name.

It is, of course, grossly uneconomic to leave too many birds unshot but this is commonly done in spite of heroic efforts at the end of the season. For various reasons few shoots manage to account for 45 per cent of the birds that are put out so there is usually little danger of failing to leave enough for breeding. At Rothwell, including the birds caught up for laying pens, we usually attain a recovery rate of about 58 per cent of what is released at six weeks of age. Though pheasant shooting does not begin at Rothwell until late November or early December, about 45 per cent are shot and picked and the rest are caught up. I attribute this to the devotion to duty of the keepers in preventing them straying – driving them in every day before mid-December – putting them over the guns and protecting them against poachers.

I have already dealt with the particular danger of leaving too many grouse and encouraging disease.

As this is not a handbook I do not propose to go into the details of rearing birds and will limit my comments to a few general observations.

We have tried every possible form of hand-rearing grey partridges and, since we have never been able to kill more than 5 per cent of the total reared, I am firmly of the opinion that they are not worth rearing on my ground. As I have already said, I do not bother with hand-reared redlegs because my experience with wild greys spoiled me for such an easy target and I can shoot wild redlegs in Spain.

The practice of releasing partridges from pens a few days before shooting is becoming perilously close to the immediately released caged pigeon, which is illegal, and plays into the hands of the anti-shooting lobby.

Pheasants are now being bred like poultry and gamekeepers are becoming more and more like poultrykeepers. A good poultry handbook will, therefore, give sound general advice. To reduce the risk of disease, for instance, game-birds, like poultry, must be kept on clean land. In my experience of rearing many thousands of pheasants and millions of domestic ducks, hygiene is of paramount importance. If young birds are reared on the same ground year after year disease is almost inevitable. Yet one sees young pheasants being pushed through the same unit three times in succession. The whole rearing operation is so expensive that it is not sensible to economize on land. The site of the rearing field needs to be changed regularly.

The fresh ground for the birds should be flat and rolled after a shower before being trimmed to the right length. It should have some clover in the bottom for preference.

When starting a stock of pheasants always inspect the adults and buy a strain which looks as though it will produce strong fliers.

I like to catch up half the hens that I need for breeding in November so that I know they are safely penned. Then I can afford to wait until the end of January to catch up the rest. We collect conifer tops from the Forestry Commission for the laying pens.

Stress is of great significance to young, hand-reared birds and it needs to be reduced as much as possible when, for example, birds are being moved. With rearing costs being so heavy, losses must be kept to the minimum.

The number to be reared is entirely a matter of personal or syndicate preference. If you happen to shoot a lot of birds on particular days, keep quiet about it. Otherwise you may find you draw the attention not only of the critics but of saboteurs. If you rent the land you may also embarrass your landlord.

Shooting and farming are often in conflict. The game, inevitably, does some damage to crops and the shooting interest may require the siting of cover crops where the farm manager does not want them. At Rothwell, when there is direct conflict, farming gets priority because my farms have always been run as commercial enterprises and I am a farmer first and a game-shot second. This would seem to be only common sense in such a competitive industry but there are still some shoots where farming takes second place, as it regularly did in the past. I believe this to be generally unnecessary because good farming and good shooting practice can coexist and I believe that they do at Rothwell.

As I have said, we are very fortunate at Rothwell in having a major share of the only high ground in Lincolnshire – the Wolds. I have already mentioned that we changed the whole area and created an environment where wild partridges and later pheasants could live with intensified farming, but some further detail of how we did it is relevant regarding my ideas on management.

When I took over Rothwell it was almost derelict. I had become the head of our quite large family on the death of my greatly revered father at the early age of sixty-two. He had owned Thoresway next to Rothwell. For the previous ten years I had been helping with the management. With the imminent approach of the Second World

War, the Chairman of the local Emergency Agricultural Committee invited me to farm Rothwell, being unable to find anyone else to take on the tenancy. Many of these high Wold farms could not be let because they were so infertile. I agreed, somewhat reluctantly, to take it on at a rent of half a crown (now 12½p) an acre. There were 5 ewes and 7 lambs in what is now my dining room and 200 chickens on the third floor!

The fields were swarming with rabbits, rats and rooks and infested with carrion crows and other predators. The rabbits had eaten all the hedge bottoms and there was not a hawthorn hedge of any size because they had been barked and the roots had been exposed by the burrows. Apart from that, the land – very thin soil on chalk – was too poor to grow good thorn: the hedges averaged no more than three feet in height.

There were virtually no trees on the estate. There were no shelter belts. No wonder that Rothwell had a reputation as being one of the worst parishes in the whole area! As for game, forty brace of partridges was a big day on what should have been excellent partridge land. There were literally no pheasants, mainly because of the absence of cover, but also showing what happens when they are not cared for and keepered.

We improved the soil by deep ploughing and, with some courage, I suppose, looking back on it, we changed the old, established Wold practice. In those days, the Wold farms cropped in a four-course rotation – a quarter turnips and swedes; a quarter clover; a half corn – spring barley, wheat and oats. We set about improving the general fertility and introduced the re-seeding and fertilizing of grass leys. From my earliest days I have been fascinated by scientific research and have been something of a pioneer in applying it to agriculture. The way Rothwell soon became a world centre for plant breeding, especially cereals, is a story which will have to be told elsewhere. I continue my plant breeding and seed growing.

We laid on miles of water pipes over the shoot and the birds immediately benefited (water being necessary for both partridges and pheasants). In places where no water was handy we put sloping strips of old corrugated iron bent at the bottom to provide a gully into which condensed dew could run. Partridges need plenty of water and in a dry season will suffer without it. I am convinced that a *major* reason for the high recovery rate of the pheasants we rear is due to the fact that we have good supplies of water.

I have already mentioned the importance of dusting shelters and grit for partridges. Grit is, perhaps, even more important for pheasants, as can be seen from their habit of pecking about on roads. I have often wondered whether the appalling carnage of pheasants on the roads could be effectively reduced by greater supplies of grit in areas away from traffic.

Over the years we have planted over a quarter of a million trees – conifers as a nurse crop but enough beeches to make a deciduous stand that should last 150 years. One belt is 1 $1/_2$ miles long. The trees were mainly to protect the land from cold winds but they' served as obstacles over which the partridges could be made to fly and later as cover for pheasants. Starting from scratch offered one big advantage – we could plant the woods where we wanted them and make them the optimum length and width. By and large, shelter belts are better than big woods, which are sometimes difficult to drive and need more beaters.

There is skill in planting woods in the right places and a good forester is invaluable. Deep thought needs to be given to the shape, size and direction of belts. The width should be gauged so that a relatively small number of beaters can cover them and, if necessary, can walk the pheasants to some high ground from which they can be sent back to their home, climbing high over the guns. Narrow belts also mean they can be successfully shot with only a few guns, which is what I like – four or five or even less.

It has been a special pleasure to be able to name woods after my children – Robert's Wood, Charles's Plantation, Diana Wood, John's Wood, Louises's Plantation, Rosie's Copse, and Jennie's Wood. They all provide excellent sport. (My youngest son, John William, was accidentally killed when a Land-Rover he was driving turned over. I have commemorated him, additionally, on the estate with a sixty-foot-high fountain in the parkland in front of the house and which I can turn on and illuminate from my study.)

I have also named a wood – Billy's Wood – after my former keeper, now shoot manager, Billy Jacob, who has given me a lifetime of devoted service – forty-seven wonderful years.

Equally satisfying is the extent to which other farmers in the area have since planted trees.

We steadily planted hedges, trimmed in profile like a letter A, to reduce the cooling and erosive effect of the wind in exposed places, and are now maintaining more than twenty-two miles of hedges which are trimmed every year to an average height of twelve feet. The surface area to be trimmed amounts to about seventy-four acres but, besides looking beautiful, they provide many acres of habitat for wild life, enabling birds to nest in and under them. They provide berries for the autumn and winter, and are an important contribution to conservation in the area. I will not have hedges subjected to flail cutting which, while cheaper, bruises them and makes them bleed. Like all things in Nature hedges should be treated with respect, and flailing savages them.

The hedges enabled us to stand back for the partridges without being seen instead of standing on the hedgerow, which was what had happened generally in Lincolnshire previously. Of course, this greatly improved the quality of the birds as well as the numbers coming over the guns.

I have planted hedges to link up woods so that birds can be blanked in from one to the other without forcing them to fly. My showpieces are double hawthorn hedges – each with a ten-foot-wide alley between two thick hedges up to 400 yards long. They work beautifully. The pheasants trot through the alley obligingly. Each hedge looks splendid when it is all in blossom, and the heavy crop of berries nourishes birds.

We have planted additional trees to hide farm buildings. We have also bought woods which marched with as are close to the estate as these became available, to provide coverts for the hunt. These are not shot and have been left as wild life sanctuaries. I have indulged myself by planting a few ornamental flowering trees on the edges of my woods because they give me and my guests pleasure. I love my trees and if, and when, I have to stop shooting and active farming, they will be one of the reasons why I could never 'up sticks' and live abroad.

It is important on a shoot, as well as on a farm, that there should be good, trustworthy stiles and gates which open and shut easily. If barbed wire has to be crossed there should be places where it is covered with plastic bags so that legs can be lifted over without damage or injury. There are some shoots where it is difficult for elderly people to reach their pegs without crawling under wire. There is no excuse for this and the keeper should have his tip reduced and his attention drawn to the matter.

The whole parish of Rothwell, with neighbouring land which I have purchased as it became available, has become one agricultural operation providing a great deal of local employment. The fields vary in size from a six-acre paddock near the old Saxon-Norman church to eighty acres, the average being in excess of forty acres. The ground is so steep that the ploughing on more than a third of my acreage has to be done by caterpillar tractor or four-wheel drive tractor but this, of course, provides terrain from which high and difficult birds can be presented.

I also rent from friends slightly more than 2500 acres nearby for shooting, again Wold land providing challenging birds. On land which I have rented for shooting for a long time, if the young farmer wants it back to shoot it himself I try to do a deal whereby he has the pheasant and ground-game shooting while I keep the wild partridge shooting, if this still exists. In return we do the keepering and I sometimes supply some pheasant poults for release. I have been the shooting tenant of a lot of land for over fifty consecutive years at various locations in Lincolnshire.

The disposition of game-crops on a shoot is crucial to the holding of birds and to their presentation. I still prefer frost-resistant marrow-stem kale, which can be folded for sheep. In my view, the special seed mixtures offer no advantage over frost-resistant kale for wild partridges or reared pheasants. What we did, for many seasons, was to harvest seed from those kale plants which had best withstood the winter, showing that they must have been frost-resistant. So over the years we were selecting for hardier and hardier kale which has stood us in very good stead in the toughest winters.

The way we sow some of the kale may be of interest. We use a six-row drill but fill the container for the sixth drill with turnip or swede seed. This means that when the drill turns round at the end of the field there will be two rows of turnips or swedes between wide strips of kale. These rows gave the beaters somewhere to walk and tap without getting wet through or knocking the kale down.

Maize has become very popular and, while I do not have much experience of it, I am told that it is almost essential for holding reared redleg partridges, but once it is thinned out or laid by frost birds tend to flush out of it. It also encourages rats and I understand it is held to be mainly responsible for the huge increase in the farmland rat population in counties like Hampshire.

Artichokes are good and are perennial but they soon become thin and are easily knocked down by frost. Rape, which is now so widely grown, is no good as cover for partridges or pheasants because it tends to get too wet and to hold the wet. In fact game does not seem to like going into rape whether it is wet or dry.

Neighbours who plant game crops near boundaries with the obvious intention of attracting other people's birds are a great nuisance and a disgrace to shooting. Such people tend to shoot everything they can entice, creating a vacuum in the hope of sucking in more game which, of course, happens. Nature abhors any vacuum but especially one with food in it.

On any shoot it is essential to spend time dealing with the boundaries. This, in my opinion, is one of the most important duties of the keeper. Straying birds must be driven back towards the centre.

To have neighbours who are strongly anti-shooting is, of course, no help whatever. For many years I was consulted over the choice of the vicar for the delightful church at Rothwell and, since my shoot surrounded the church, there was no way that I could have entertained the appointment of a parson who was opposed to shooting. It would have been unpopular with all those members of the local community who take part in the shoots or otherwise benefit from them. So every candidate was carefully vetted by me and I ensured that they had no objections, usually by taking them out on a shoot and watching their reactions before appointment. Shooting parsons are uncommon these days but a militant anti-bloodsporter would be a menace in the countryside, and a wise bishop should appreciate that. A shoot can make a substantial contribution not only to the local economy but to the local community spirit.

The kind of problem an anti-shooting parson can cause is demonstrated by a story which a certain shooting man, now deceased, delighted in telling. His peg at a shoot at which he was a guest was near the vicarage garden and he shot a bird which fell into it. At the end of the drive he opened the gate to ask permission to retrieve the bird but was beaten to it by the parson's wife who rushed out, picked it up, ran into the house and slammed the door!

After cover, food and sympathetic neighbours, the most important factor in game conservation is what is generally known as vermin, which can have such devastating effects that I will devote a special chapter to it.

Like everything else in life, a shoot is changing all the time. Crops vary in position; trees grow higher or have to be felled, having had their day. So the management cannot be static but needs to move with the changes. One should never be completely satisfied with a shoot but should be experimenting with possible new stands or devices to make the birds more challenging. Succeeding is very satisfying.

When a shoot is rented, the co-operation of the farming tenant is essential. If he is hostile the shoot will be hopeless. Always meet the farmers involved before renting a shoot, and discover their attitude. If they don't like shooting or look as though your presence will not be welcome, you will be well advised to search elsewhere. Farmers are more likely to co-operate in the planting of game-cover and the suspension of farming operations in sensitive areas on shooting days if they are offered an occasional day's sport.

Where there is much woodland it is also essential to discover the landlord's attitude to forestry. There is nothing worse than to arrive at a wood to find tree-fellers at work inside it.

It is always easier and more rewarding to run a shoot when you own it. Landlords are keen to have the shooting rent but some are not prepared to put themselves out in return. When the tenant improves the shoot they are also prone to increase the rent accordingly though they may have contributed nothing, on the grounds that the shoot is now much more lettable. On one grouse moor, by dint of enormous and costly endeavour, in burning, draining, road-making and concreting the butts I brought the bag up and all I got, eventually, was a kick in the pants. Any owner is entitled to run his property the way he thinks fit but that does not make such treatment any easier to bear. The improvements which I initiated and paid for greatly increased the yield of grouse and enhanced the capital value of the moor by at least seven figures, such value now being based on the average annual bag.

There should be encouragement for tenants to improve a shoot by knowing that they will not be penalized by a rent increase. As things stand, there is no tenant right, as there is in farming, so that a shooting tenant has a share of the value of the improvements he has made. I believe that this is one of the reasons for the general decline in the quality of grouse moors.

In fairness, the responsibility should cut both ways and there should be a dilapidation clause to penalize a tenant who has failed to maintain the shoot or moor properly.

With the increasing demand for pheasant shooting and the decline in standard agriculture, more small farmers should consider the feasibility of putting their land together and letting the shooting rights. Five neighbouring farmers with say 200 acres each could form a co-operative to provide a 1000-acre shoot, putting in say eight strips of kale, an acre each, to provide cover. They could rent out the land to an individual or a syndicate which then does the rest. I shall have more to say about this opportunity in the following chapter with special reference to hill farms.

The general relationship between the owners or tenants of a shoot and the rural community is all-important. The community will usually supply the beaters and flankers and they are unlikely to oblige, with all the effort they should, if they are ignored and not treated with the respect and consideration they deserve. Like a ship, a happy shoot is a good shoot and on a good shoot the same beaters, loaders and pickers-up will turn up in all weathers year after year. True, they are paid but they do not come just for the money. They come for a sporting day out in good company. At Rothwell I have always been extremely fortunate because everyone in the area is a friend and I have established similar situations on my grouse moors.

There is a growing problem with respect to access to the countryside now being demanded by town-dwellers. Nothing can be done about rights of way except to ensure that ramblers keep to the paths and keep out of the woodlands during the breeding and rearing season. They tend not to interfere with pheasant and partridge shooting days because the rambling season tends to be over then, but they can be a problem on the grouse moor, though they have not been to me. For some reason town-dwellers fail to appreciate that most moors are as privately owned as farms are and that rates are paid on let moors. (In England and Wales land is rated if let for sporting use while in Scotland it is rated if shooting can be practised on it whether it is let or not.) Nor do many walkers appreciate that heather is a *crop* which has to be tended and on which they have no particular right to walk.

A major management challenge which I have had to face is the continual erosion of Read's Island, my wildfowl area in the Humber Estuary. An earthen embankment encloses about 100 acres, which form the heart of the island, and this area is comparatively secure; but outside that the shores are eroded by the tides and shipping. Banks are washed away, and in some places built up, by the natural currents, but more seriously by the wash of big ships sailing too closely. Some natural erosion is inevitable as the island has been formed by silt brought down by the Yorkshire and Midland rivers which flow into the estuary. Trying to reduce the damage and restore the situation is a constant problem.

To assist with the maintenance costs, I decided in 1976 to devote the grazing on the island to deer farming and introduced a herd of fallow deer bred for venison. I have a warden on the island and the herd has increased to 300 head. We had previously introduced a small population of hares for shooting and used to have to change the blood every five years or so but they eventually disappeared. They are excellent swimmers. (Rabbits too can swim when forced to do so.)

An important and regular item of management on all shoots is the quick and assured disposal of the game, usually to game-dealers. The game needs to be stored in fly-proof larders until it is collected, which in the warmer weather must be pretty quickly. The master's eye needs to be kept on game prices.

Game dealing, like game production, is big business, enormous numbers of pheasants being shot each year with many of them going to the Continent because of saturation of the home market. The main problem with sales occurs after 31 December because, for some legal reason, none can be imported into European countries after that date. The residue then has to go into cold storage at high cost.

I am told that in strict legal terms it is unlawful for anyone to have game-birds in store after the middle of February. This, apparently, is an old law brought in to discourage the killing and sale of game during the closed season. Nobody seems to take much notice of it, however.

It is, of course, a great convenience to own a house on or near one's shoot, not only for oneself and family but for one's guests, and I have been very fortunate in this respect. My house at Rothwell is our comfortable family home. There is simple but adequate accommodation on Read's Island, where I have been well served by a resident couple. For many years now I have owned Middleton House, in Middleton-in-Teesdale overlooking Wemmergill.

It is a great advantage not to have a long journey after a day on the grouse moor. The air may be bracing but grouse shooting is physically exacting. It is, however, worth all the effort one can make to have the pleasure and privilege of being surrounded by miles of well-kept heather on a sunny day, facing the wind and watching in anticipation as the grouse hurtle towards the butts.

I now propose to describe the special aspects of moor management which make such a wonderful experience possible.

Chapter 11

Grouse Moors – a Heritage in our Trust

The demand for paying guns on grouse moors, especially from abroad, is growing year by year with the steady increase in general prosperity and leisure time. Only an increase in the availability of well-managed heather moorland can satisfy this demand. Botanical studies have shown that without management, in the shooting interest, the heather moors would degenerate. A quite small, well-keepered moor in Scotland or North Yorkshire can hold many thousands of grouse but on a moor which has never been keepered, one can walk for a day without seeing a grouse, though a few would probably persist there. Why such a difference? One word answers the question – management.

There is no doubt in the minds of those researching into the subject that, while there is no single cause for the decline of the grouse, it does all stem from poor management practices. The progressive diminution of grouse in Scotland can be laid firmly at the door of lack of heather management. Where the heather has been properly managed, providing a patchwork of short heather for feeding and long heather for cover and nesting, the grouse have survived well, in spite of ticks and other problems, and are currently on the increase. Changes in attitude towards the value of grouse and their needs are required, and this will take time.

Heather is food for both grouse and for sheep and, in the interests of the economy of hillside farms and estates, should be treated like any other crop. Instead, over hundreds of square miles, it has been largely neglected and where there used to be a complete canopy of

125

heather there is now only patchy heather or none at all. Cumbria has lost three quarters of its purpled moorland since 1945 and in the whole of Wales there are less than 100,000 acres left. What is needed is a change of attitude from the all too common belief that heather is 'natural' vegetation needing little assistance.

Burning is the usual means of clearing old heather so that it is replaced, in patches, by more nutritious young growth. It is a crude device but effective, and other methods such as cutting or flailing by machinery, though they are used, tend to be prohibitively expensive or physically impossible in so many places.

For obvious reasons burning needs careful supervision and burned places should not cover a large area, the fire being controlled so that it does not get out of hand or set the peat underneath alight. It is best done in long strips not more than thirty yards wide and at right angles to the drive, so there is old heather, a foot long and more, nearby for cover and nesting on the edges when the young heather sprouts and the grouse begin to feed on it. The strips can be as long as is practicable provided they remain no wider than about thirty yards.

A poorly controlled fire can cause severe damage to wild life and to property by burning fences and woodland. It can also spread to a neighbouring moor with serious legal consequences. The heat of the heather-burns can lift the peat underneath and this may delay the germination of new heather seeds for a year or two. This can be observed where a vehicle has crossed recently burned ground and consolidated it. The new heather germinates first on the wheel tracks. Further evidence of the lack of soil compaction is the extent to which sheep simply pull heather shoots right out of the ground. I have little doubt that rolling would greatly aid germination on burned ground, but is impractical.

A badly controlled fire can set the peat alight, burning away the organic matter, destroying the heather roots and delaying re-growth for a long time. When all the roots are lost on a steep slope the soil has nothing to hold it together and serious erosion can follow.

The great problem with burning is finding the right number of days when weather conditions allow it to be done. Under the Hill Farming Acts heather can be burned only between 1 October and 31 March in England and Wales. In Scotland, where the practice is called muirburn, the period is extended to 15 April for moors below 1500 feet and to 30 April for higher land. Sometimes special extensions may be granted, depending on weather conditions. Notice also has to be given to landlords and neighbours.

On average there are only about twenty suitable days in a good burning season so advantage must be taken of every reasonably dry day or half day. Burning cannot be left 'until later' because enough more dry days may never occur. In the Dales they say, 'We have six months winter and six months bad weather.' It is by no means as bad as that but dry days in the period permitted for burning need to be exploited. Winter is the safest time because in the early spring, when most burning seems to be done on many moors, conditions can quickly become dangerously dry.

It is also necessary to have the right tools so that the fire can be stopped where required. The old-fashioned home-made birch brushes are not as effective as long-handled aluminium brushes, which are almost indestructible, enable the operator to stand further away from the fire and are less exhausting to use. An old farm sprayer converted to provide water can be valuable in an emergency.

A burn must be carefully planned to take advantage of natural firebreaks like streams, roads and previously burned ground. The wind, of course, is a crucial factor and fires should never be allowed to burn out at night with nobody watching.

Other things can be done to improve prospects for a good crop of grouse but the fundamental problem on most moors is overgrazing of heather by sheep, which can slowly graze it to extinction. The main food of sheep on a moor, alternative to heather, should be grass, particularly the species known as sheep's fescue (*Festuca*) which grows well on the steep slopes. On a badly managed moor where this and the other nutritious grasses are overgrazed, the grassland is invaded by rough grasses, mainly the mat-grass (*Nardus*) and the blue-moor grass (*Molinia*). Mat-grass is particularly obnoxious because it is not only unpalatable but turns the ground into shaggy 'white moor' which is dull to look at and useless to grouse or sheep. The sheep then spend more time grazing the young heather shoots so heavily that the heather ground is invaded by the mat-grass too. Enormous acreages of good grass and heatherland have been overrun by mat-grass in recent years, entirely as a result of bad practice.

Once established, mat-grass and the other rough grasses are difficult to eradicate but they are weeds which should be eliminated, and farmers and shoot owners should set about them. Ways of doing this using a herbicide called Dalapon are being investigated. When the rough grasses are effectively controlled by spraying, bilberry and then heather can gradually take over. (I suspect that the importance of bilberry (blaeberry in Scotland) in the grouse's diet is underestimated. There is a lot on my moor at Reeth in Yorkshire, one of the reasons why the moor is generally so good.)

Patches of the moor-rush (*Juncus*) should not be sprayed because grouse eat the flowers and seed-heads, as they do of a number of other moorland plants.

Bracken (*Pteridium*) is another invasive weed of moorland where the soil is more than nine inches deep, meaning that it thrives on the best moors, and it is increasing its hold in many areas. Its fronds and dead leaves smother the grasses and, while cattle eat young bracken, given the chance – which they should not be – sheep do not. Bracken harbours sheep-ticks which can not only kill grouse but pass on a virus to human beings, especially children, causing a rash and flu-like symptoms. There is also some evidence that if ingested, bracken can cause cancer. Repeated mowing will eventually kill it but is costly. Chemical treatment, usually from aircraft, is also expensive but some owners, including myself, have found it worthwhile.

We spray Asulox mixed with water and a wetting agent, called Agral, applied by a helicopter flying six feet or so above the bracken. The spraying needs to be carried out one week either side of 1 August when the fronds tend to be fully extended. We have found this to be the only period when the spray is effective. Given a twelve-hour dry period after the spraying, so that the agent is not washed off, there should be a near-total kill.

For follow-up in the year after spraying, or for the treatment of small patches of bracken, we adminster the same chemical by hand in knapsack sprays or some similar method.

Young heather shoots provide about 90 per cent of the adult grouse's diet while the older plants give them cover and nesting sites. So it is obvious that the only way to stop birds from leaving a moor, and of maintaining an on-going population, is to ensure that there is plenty of heather to eat there. Yet on most moors the total mass of sheep has been allowed to increase steadily over the past forty years. For understandable reasons, serious overgrazing began during the last war and has continued since. A very large estate in Durham has lost 75 per cent of its heather moorland through overgrazing. (Incidentally, in Scotland red deer and hares, when they are present in profusion, can make serious inroads into the supply of heather. Research has shown that heavy grazing of heather by rabbits can also be damaging.)

So, what can be done about the sheep problem? Whatever is done needs to be done gently, so that livelihoods are not threatened and the local community is not alienated. Sheep are necessary for the local community but it will often pay an owner of a grouse moor to reduce the number on his moor by compensating the tenant farmers proportionately. He will reap the benefit in sport for himself or in the increased rent he can charge for his let days. But measures need to be taken to ensure that the number of sheep really has been reduced. I take steps to have a close watch kept on the sheep-grazing on my moors to ensure that tenants are not overdoing the stocking. It is not difficult to count the sheep after clipping when they stand out on the hill. Also, during the winter, when most of the sheep damage is inflicted, I send someone to do a sheep count. When this was first pointed out to the graziers they tended to be surprised, if not startled. We take a tough attitude to those graziers whom we know to be bending the rules. We warn them that we will continue to monitor the situation, but try to keep as friendly an atmosphere as possible because conflict will benefit nobody.

On hill farms where sheep have been removed during the winter and then restored briefly in the summer it has been noted that the ewes and lambs browse the heather quite hard even when there is plenty of palatable grass. So it will usually be a worthwhile investment for an owner to buy any lower ground marching with a grouse moor which comes on the market so that he can move some of the sheep down on to it. I have done that with some of the grouse moors I have bought, to the satisfaction of the sheep-farmers.

It is my belief that, in many areas, sheep farming alone cannot sustain the economic viability of the heather uplands. Forestry can help in certain places but I believe that the development of grouse shooting, with the extra money it brings into the area, can halt the current economic decline of the hill farms.

Under changes in the Agricultural Grants which came into effect in October 1985, Heather Regeneration attracts grant. Grants are available for the regeneration of heather by cutting and burning. There is also a grant for the fencing of the land to control grazing by stock. But still more positive inducement is needed.

According to consultants, hill sheep farmers can double their income by careful management of the heather for grouse shooting. A 5000-acre block of heather moorland should produce 1000 to 2500 lambs for sale annually, worth between £30,000 and £90,000, and give employment to one or two men. This should yield an annual trading profit of £12,000 to £30,000 inclusive of subsidy and other Government support. The same area should also be able to carry 800 breeding pairs of grouse, providing full-time employment for a gamekeeper and a ten-year annual average bag of about 1500 birds. On such moorland, well managed, shooting rights should bring between £30,000 and £40,000 with a net income of £15,000 to £20,000. This would add a very helpful extra profit of £3 to £4 per acre.

This prospect offers an opportunity for hill farmers who own the shooting rights on their land to join together to form co-operatives which could let the combined grouse shooting and share the assured income on an agreed basis. Such co-operatives ought to be eligible for a grant from the EEC.

When sheep have to be reduced in the interests of the grouse, trading 10 per cent of the winter grazing for a population of grouse of, say, 150 per square kilometre yielding 20–40 brace shot, can be cost-effective when grouse bring £50–£60 a brace or more for shooting, with £70 not being uncommon.

Currently, the rating and the VAT charged on shooting interests are serious disincentives to hill-farm shooting co-operatives, and if the Government really wants less intensive farming, more rural employment and an improved environment, it should take some legislative action to reduce these burdens.

The result of failing to re-establish the grouse will be an increase in the rate of unemployment and depopulation, and I have made this point as strongly as I can to the Ministry of Agriculture here and to the European Economic Commission. I recommended the setting up of a special small department in the Ministry of Agriculture to encourage the formation of co-operative ventures by small farmers and to provide technical advice and training. In response, the current Minister of Agriculture, John MacGregor, has assured me that the Government is very keen to promote the vitality of rural areas through the contribution which well-managed game facilities can provide. A 'band of knowledgeable and enthusiastic experts' is being established to act as advisers to farmers and landowners on game as a profitable sideline. The EEC is said to be increasingly aware of the value of field sports as an alternative land use. This is promising but it is deeds that matter and the pressure needs to be maintained. I will continue to apply it wherever I can. In Spain entire village communities of small farmers put their land together most effectively for wild partridge shooting, letting the rights in a block while continuing to farm in the usual way. It brings a great deal of money into the communities and the same could happen here with grouse co-operatives on the hills and pheasant co-operatives lower down.

Next to excessive numbers of sheep, the major threat to the grouse moors is afforestation by coniferous trees. Until recently it has been subsidized through tax relief. As a result, numerous hill farms have disappeared, probably for ever, under enormous blankets of conifers. Timber is a necessary commodity but not at the expense of heather-land. In my view, heather moorland is every bit as worthy of subsidy and, in many areas, more so, in the public interest as well as the hill farmer's. The purple heather is what people like to see, not endless square miles of timber. It is not generally appreciated, as it needs to be, that it is grouse shooting which was originally responsible for the development of the heather moors in the quantity and quality which observers believe to be natural. And only grouse shooting will keep them in being.

On moorland, spruce trees, which are the most commonly planted, qualify for description as weeds – plants which are totally out of place. The march of these serried ranks of boring and alien trees over moors once gloriously covered by purple heather is an indictment of our time. They quickly become huge areas of semi-darkness in which nothing else can flourish and are death to many forms of wild life. The cry that grouse shooting should be banned to save wild life is the cry of the ignorant, mainly town-dwellers who know next to nothing about wild life but need a cause in which they can be vocal. The truth is that many forms of wild life, especially birds, as I have said in a previous chapter, depend on the good management of moorland. Without that they lose their environment and depart or perish.

The threat is, at last, being taken so seriously that the Nature Conservancy is even using an American sky satellite to observe grouse moors in the Grampians and North Pennines – to note how habitat changes, including afforestation, are affecting grouse and other birds like curlew, merlin and golden plover. The vegetation patterns show up clearly on satellite photographs.

Sheep farming, on its own, is unlikely to be able to stem the advance of the conifers. Coupled with grouse farming it could. A farmer can get as much, and probably more, from grouse as from sheep and he gets it every year. On some hillsides grouse will always be a minority interest but a very useful one in the farm accounts.

As with other forms of shooting, a well-run grouse moor brings a lot of useful money into the community living near it. Many of the guests stay at hotels and their wives buy in the shops. Local hill farmers and their staff serve as loaders and beaters and the keepers are usually local people, or become so.

For grouse farming – for that is what the management of most good heather-land is about – drainage is of the greatest importance on wet moors. I have established to my satisfaction that grouse drink a lot of water, so springs are needed to provide this in a dry season while the dampness around springs also encourages insects on which the grouse can feed. Drains, however, can be a source of considerable loss in a very wet season when young grouse, in particular, can easily be drowned in them. Heavy drainage in a wet year, with a quick run-off of water which would otherwise have been absorbed by the peat, can also cause problems by making it difficult for vehicles and beaters to cross swollen streams.

At this point I should, perhaps, briefly describe my personal grouse-shooting interests and experience with them. I suppose that I brought a farmer's eye to the moors which I shoot, and look at a hillside of heather as I would look at a crop of wheat.

I own several moors, having decided that, with increasing interest in leisure they would be a sounder investment than agricultural land, with capital values which would increase, especially as I intended to improve them. (People who own grouse moors tend to be popular, since so many want to shoot there. I understand that, in their address books, some individuals put PWAG after the names of certain people they have met. It means Person With A Grouse-moor!)

Stublick Moor in Allendale, Northumberland was bought in 1979. It covers 5600 acres, has excellent heather, and we have planted a shelter belt there.

The heather was in poor condition when the 3500 acres of Stean Moor in Nidderdale, North Yorkshire were first taken over in 1978. We drained the whole place, sprayed every bit of bracken, and fenced a lot of land to keep off the sheep and let the heather grow. It was astonishing how quickly the heather returned and the grouse with it. We had an excellent season in 1988.

As a simple experiment I fenced off a patch of heather and excluded sheep entirely for six years. The difference between the food available for grouse inside the fence compared with that outside was truly enormous – 500 times! Of course, total fencing off on a large scale for such a long period is impractical so we began rotational grazing for sheep, fencing off areas of moor to give them three or four years of respite from grazing. The effects have been remarkable. The feed value of the heather for the grouse, and eventually for the sheep when they are allowed on it, can be increased up to forty fold!

This should surprise nobody because it is obvious that no crop can be grazed all the year round, especially when greed and the Government's sheep policy encourage overgrazing. Where practicable, heather should be grazed rotationally like any other crop.

This fencing off of sheep-free areas has been called – by others – the Nickerson System and I shall have more to say about it later. Suffice it to say here that it is most important to mark wire fencing on moors with pieces of shiny metal or corks, otherwise many grouse may be killed by colliding with them. An unmarked fence sited on a skyline or running down a shoulder can be a deathtrap.

We have attempted to resuscitate bare areas by implanting turfs of heather – plugs we call them – taken from moorland which can spare them. The idea is to put the plugs in some distance apart hoping that they will take root and then join up. It has been only moderately successful but we shall persevere with it.

When I bought Reeth Moor, comprising 8000 acres in Swaledale, there was fierce competition for it because of its consistently high merit and its accessibility. It is particularly beautiful, there is a plentiful supply of natural grit, the heather is excellent and is noted for the speed with which grouse recover after a poor year. Some of the ground is high – over 2000 feet. There are four different days' driving, each traditionally of five drives. Annual bags have been as high as 4400 brace in the past and have been over 2000 on several occasions in recent years. With improvements in management we hope to increase the regularity of such seasons. The tenants and local people have been most helpful.

From 1952 I had the shooting on the 17,000 splendid acres of Wemmergill Moor, in Teesdale, which belong to the Strathmores, and invested in it heavily because, though I could not buy the moor, I had a long lease on it. Wemmergill has been famous over many years.

One area of the moor, the Shipka pass, provides perhaps the best grouse drives in the world. It is a wide, deep ghyll with a stream running through it and, with careful planning, it is possible to enjoy four marvellous drives without moving out of it – all testing birds, especially on a windy day. It is best with a south-southwest wind. It still houses The Kaiser's Butt where, before the First World War, Kaiser Bill stood when he was a guest of Lord Lonsdale, the Yellow Earl, so-called because of the colour of his carriages.

In the twenty years before I took over Wemmergill not a yard of burning or draining had been done. I introduced carefully controlled burning to ensure a regular supply of young heather and put in thousands of miles of drains. The result was an improvement in the grouse population and in the bags.

Wemmergill does not recover from a poor grouse year as quickly as some other moors; the rainfall is much higher, but in a season when everything goes right Wemmergill has a greater power of producing grouse than any moor I know.

I WAS A TENANT OF WEMMERGILL FOR THIRTY-SIX CONSECUTIVE YEARS. It gave immense fulfilment to me and joy to my family and many guests. In September 1978 a party, which included the Prince of Wales, who shot like a tiger, killed 380 brace in a day. It will always remain my favourite moor and I continue to shoot there, though less frequently.

On all my moors I made a deal with the sheep farmers to dip their sheep four times a year, before it became compulsory, in the interests of reducing the tick problem.

Never buy or rent a grouse moor that is all the same height. Birds like to get on cooler, high ground in warm weather and may go in search of it if none is handy. On many moors the weather varies considerably between the high and low ground. Low ground may be fogged off while high ground is in sunshine or vice versa. The wind may be so strong as to make shooting on high ground almost impossible while it is practicable on low ground. Sometimes, in winter and early spring, the birds do better on ground of one height than on another. So with a choice of high and low ground you stand a better chance of a decent stock and of retaining it. On several counts, therefore, a moor offering alternative heights is worth more money.

An 'island' moor, which does not march with other moors, should always be a good prospect if it is big enough because there is no worry of disease caused by neighbours leaving too large a stock of grouse.

As grouse need quartz grit to digest their food a good moor should have a plentiful natural supply of it, and most do. Where it is scarce it pays to put grit down for, otherwise, birds will travel a long way to find it.

Another tip – if you have a VIP coming to shoot it may pay to leave part of the moor unshot for a week or two, for the grouse will collect there. On one occasion I wanted to give Prince Charles, The Prince of Wales, a specially good day at Wemmergill and rested one beat for a month. As we set out I remarked that if we could have had a west wind for the beat which I had in mind – the one I had rested – we could expect to shoot 300 brace in the day. We had 120 brace by lunch and then the wind changed to where I wanted it. 'You are under test now!' His Royal Highness remarked. I had indeed stuck my neck out.

We shot the rested beat and killed 260 brace in the afternoon, the total bag being probably the biggest in Britain that year. It was also the Prince's biggest personal bag up to that date.

In the management of any grouse moor the location of butts is all-important and on some old moors many of them are in the wrong place because the heather has changed, yet they go on being used simply because they are there. Some butts have never been re-sited in more than a century. Experience will show where the butts ought to be for best advantage, and new ones should be constructed during the off-season.

In some places butts have been set ridiculously far apart – as much as seventy yards – to ensure that at least some of the birds will pass over the line. This is quite unnecessary with good beating and flanking skills. Forty to forty-five yards between most butts is enough but they can be set fifty-five to sixty yards apart where the birds come very high.

While most butts are circular it would be better if they were square in front. In a round butt it is sometimes difficult, in the heat of action, to be exactly sure of one's orientation and this can increase the risk of a dangerous shot. If the front of the butt is square it is much easier to know where one is in relation to the other guns. Of course, if the butt is to be used for return drives the back should be square as well.

Butts need far more attention than they usually get. On one moor of my acquaintance the butts have boarded floors which are dangerously slippery. Boarded floors should always have chicken wire or slats nailed to them for safety's sake. Otherwise, it is unsafe to have a loader in the butt and it is possible to slip and shoot somebody in the next one. The first thing I do when I acquire a moor is to rough-concrete the butt floors so that guns and loaders are not slipping about on mud or wet boards. I also ensure that the butts are well drained. In some, one is standing in stagnant water!

A butt should also be big enough so that the loader can operate in comfort and safety, and the whole floor should be level. The worst kind of butt has a ledge on which the loader has to step. He can fall off and, as I have said before, the person most likely to *kill* you in the shooting field is your loader.

Frankly, in my experience as a guest, some butts are so dangerous that if the owners – and their insurers – gave them more thought they would do something about them.

A good butt should also be big enough to accommodate a spectator. A few extra well-cut turfs can form a temporary platform for the young so that they can see and shoot over the top.

Some butts have been made with entrances which are narrow enough to exclude a sheep but this makes difficulty for the older and more corpulent guns, and it is the guns for whom the butts are primarily provided. A roll of wire can be used to block the entrance and in the winter can be put right round the butt to protect it.

I do not like numbers on grouse butts because so often one is not filling the first or even the first few butts in a line because of wind conditions. Telling the guns to add numbers to the number they have drawn or been given seems to be too much of a mathematical exertion for even the chairmen of some of our largest companies. Indecision about who is in which butt can lead to unnecessary climbs up stiff gradients and even to arguments. So another of the first things I do on a new moor is to paint the numbers out.

All butts should have a dog peg, painted white and positioned towards the back where a tethered dog can lie down out of the way and will not cause a hazard.

Some keepers do so little to keep the butts in order that last year's spent cartridges are still there when a new season starts. That is disgusting and should never be tolerated. The least that keepers should do is to clean up the butts and re-turf them, when necessary, the tops being fastened down with pegs or twine. Butts are expensive and time-consuming to build and the neglect in maintaining them, which is so common, is uneconomic as well as disgraceful.

Good access is essential on a moor – not only to make more butts possible but to facilitate burning and the control of predators. Road construction on moorland is very expensive but can substantially increase the capital value. The consequent snag is that it makes the moor accessible to tourists, but that can usually be controlled if the roads are not suitable for ordinary cars. Private roads can be controlled by having lockable gates and these can be of great value in foiling the activities of the anti-shooting mobs, who do not seem to like walking.

When new roads are being planned their visual impact from long distances needs careful thought. One does not want to scar the landscape unnecessarily or arouse objections from 'environmental groups'.

There is no doubt whatsoever that when grouse stocks are high it is absolutely essential to shoot them hard in the interests of the years to come. A big grouse population is the result of artificial interference with Nature and can be controlled only by the artificial aid of shooting. This, of course, is best achieved by putting in as many days' shooting as practicable and by inviting a sufficient number of experienced shots who can deal with the birds effectively. If a large stock is left a great percentage of it will die either on the moor or on some other moor, to which excess grouse have migrated in search of food and found themselves driven off by the residents. As I have pointed out in a previous chapter, it is a rule of Nature that overcrowding leads to a population crash for one reason or another, and grouse are no exception. On the contrary they have proved that rule down all the years that records have been kept. It is an illusion to believe that by leaving a large stock another good season will be ensured. In my experience the following spring after a big year with too many left is a particularly dangerous time. Later when the heather has grown and flowered there is usually plenty of food until a hard winter knocks it back.

In the early eighties I decided that, having had a lifetime's pleasure out of the moors, I would like to give something permanent back to them. Moorland is like any other land – you can't go on getting more out of it than you put in. I had put a fair lot back, particularly at Wemmergill, but felt I should do more. My long-term aim was, and remains, a million more acres of pure heather in Britain. In the short term it would be fun to have some thoughts and theories of mine put to the test by professionals.

Since good heather management is the main secret of success with grouse, I had long thought that, like any other crop, heather should be susceptible to improvement through new varieties. So, after some success with the breeding of plants I set up the Joseph Nickerson Heather Improvement Foundation with a personal endowment in 1985. (Registered as a charity.) In summary, its objectives are to conserve and protect the natural environment of the United Kingdom by promoting and encouraging the improvement of moorland and other upland areas, through the development of skills and techniques, and by research into developing improved strains of heather and improved methods of husbandry with, of course, the publication of all useful results. In short, its objectives are to find means of recovering the lost heather-land and to preserve and improve what currently remains, the current slogan being 'To encourage the farming of heather as a crop. To strengthen the viability of communities in heather uplands by the effective management of sheep and grouse.'

My partially retired colleague, John Denton OBE, who was chief executive of Nickerson Seeds and the plant breeding work for more than forty years, agreed to oversee the project and I could not have found a better man to do it. It transpired, as I had long believed, that the most immediate problem is one of management and that overgrazing and general poor management are the main causes of heather erosion.

We decided that we should sponsor research on heather erosion through various existing bodies which had the facilities. At the time of writing there are five main projects which are already producing promising results. They are:

1. An economic survey of income from heather moors in Northern England and Southern Scotland by the Department of Agricultural Economics at the University of Newcastle-on-Tyne. Computers are being used to determine the most favourable economic scenarios.

2. The Zoology Department of Durham University is making a small study of the effects of the insects and other invertebrates on heather moorland. Initially, it is a survey to examine the effects on the insect population of sheep-grazing due to the presence of sheep-dung and what happens if it is not there.

3. The Macaulay Land Use Research Institute (formerly the Hill Farming Research Institute) is carrying out a research project on the regeneration of heather by seed on moors where heather has been lost or is likely to be lost. (Heather produces enormous numbers of very tiny seeds which are easily blown about during dry periods.) Interesting results were obtained in the first year and the work is to continue on a larger scale.

4. A study of the effects of mechanical defoliation of heather as opposed to burning, since the former may do less damage. This three-year project is being carried out on Dartmoor by ADAS. A site was selected on Dartmoor and plots were laid out in 1987. Cutting techniques and flailing by tractor are being compared with burning as means of heather management. The early results indicate that while regeneration of the heather on plots which have been flailed is not as good as on burned plots, it is substantially better than no management at all. And, of course, flailing is less dependent on the weather. Perhaps flailing will prove to be a useful adjunct at times when keepers have not been able to complete their burning programmes.

5. A large-scale experiment to compare controlled sheep-grazing with free grazing is being carried out in Scotland by the Reconciliation Project which is concerned with demonstrating the importance

and economic advantage of implementing better management practice on heather uplands. It has been given that name because its
purpose is to reconcile the conflict between grazing and grouse
interests and between shepherds and keepers in particular. As
a token of gratitude the project has been named The Joseph
Nickerson Reconciliation Project. (This may sound as though I
have fallen out with somebody but I appreciate the kind thought.)

The Reconciliation staff are also pursuing research into what they
call the Nickerson System of heather grazing because I initiated it
through my private experiments in fencing off land to keep the
sheep out, as I have already mentioned. Plots were laid out at four
centres in Scotland in 1986. Each plot, of one hectare, replicated
three times, is fenced to enable sheep-grazing to be controlled,
winter grazing from November to May being eliminated. When
sheep were kept off in the crucial months from 1 October until 1
May the improvements in growth were very obvious: the effects
on heather and grouse populations will be evaluated over several
years.

These and other experiments have already shown that when
badly depleted ground is fenced off the heather will regenerate
spontaneously and is well able to compete with grasses if not eaten.
Given two growing seasons without winter grazing, the heather
reasserts itself and then recovery accelerates annually. Over three
to five years it can re-establish dominance over the coarse grasses
and once it reaches a mean length of about six inches one can
expect to find cock-grouse competing for space in it.

The Reconciliation Project is also examining the effects of a
large local fox population on grouse moors which are bordered
by large blocks of forestry, where the foxes cannot be dealt with.
Blocks of timber are inimical to grouse because they fragment the
environment – vast expanses of heather being the ideal situation –
but they do additional damage by serving as strongholds for furred
and feathered vermin in which foresters have little interest.

Apart from the foundation work as a private experiment on Stean
Moor, I had about nineteen acres of heather planted by hand on
heatherless land and fenced it off excluding sheep. The results were
fantastic. It worked but was too costly for large-scale application.

141

Through the Heather Foundation we are now considering the sowing of heather seed, which should be a much cheaper process. In addition, the Foundation has given a grant to the National Trust to enable it to examine the possibility of grass-seeding land which has been laid bare to the peat by erosion, as a step in re-establishing heather later.

I also have in mind the possible creation of new varieties of heather using the plant-breeding knowledge gleaned from the improvement of cereals and other crops. In theory, at least, it should be possible to produce more nutritious varieties or, perhaps, more frost-resistant strains. Heavy frost accompanied by biting wind can be very damaging to heather shoots, cold dry winds in February being especially injurious.

In most winters a covering of snow keeps the heather green and protects it from frost. Provided the snow is soft the grouse can get down to their food with no difficulty, but if it freezes solid they are in trouble. This is when some long heather serves such a useful purpose. Its tips may not be as nutritious as young heather but they provide a bite when nothing else is available. Grouse cannot compete, however, with a thick covering of ice which can blanket a moor when continuous drizzle freezes solid. If there is nowhere lower down for them to feed they die of starvation.

In the winter of 1985–6 it was so cold on Reeth Moor that the snow froze solid and I was informed that the grouse had left the moor in droves for the valleys. I sent up a powerful tractor with a man walking in front to watch for big holes and, with my men from Lincolnshire working in shifts, we cleared a lot of the heather. Within forty-eight hours literally thousands of grouse were feeding on it. It was another costly experiment but an interesting one.

To intensify general interest, the Heather Foundation launched an award scheme in 1988 – The Joseph Nickerson Heather Award – with a prize fund of £10,000 'to recognize endeavour, calculated to strengthen the viability of rural communities in the heather uplands by the effective management and integration of sheep and grouse farming enterprises'. The large number of entries has been most encouraging. The foundation as a whole has helped to encourage greater interest in the heather moorlands and many centres of research are becoming involved, with the Ministry of Agriculture giving support.

The 1988 winner, who received the trophy and £7000, was Sir Anthony Milbank who has the 4000-acre Barningham and Holgate estates near Richmond in Yorkshire.

The Ministries of Agriculture and the Environment have now become aware of the importance of the heather situation and are lending their weight wholeheartedly to a change. They have provided £50 million for grant aid in the uplands where heather is so important. Half the cost of burning can be recouped.

Experiments conducted mainly in Scotland over many years now have shown that it is possible to hatch grouse under broody hens and rear them under broodies or artificial brooders and then put them out on the moor. In several years between 1957 and 1969 the late Lord Rank reared up to 700 grouse on the Cawdor Estate, using picked-up wild eggs. Though he proved that they can be reared, the weakness of the system lies in the fate and behaviour of the birds after their release. Most of them die within a year while, if kept in captivity, they live longer. Lacking the territorial drive, the reared birds tend to wander off the moor and disappear.

As soon as the entire shooting season is over, there is a shoot management meeting at Rothwell to assess the whole game season, detect any lessons to be learned and plan the next one. Routinely during the season I have received information about the game situation on the several shoots along with the weekly report about the farming enterprises.

In my shoot management ventures I have written my signature across several square miles of England, as I have with my farming, and I hope that it will still be legible for many years after I have gone. But, in spite of all that one can do by way of management, it is the Almighty who finally disposes, particularly regarding wild birds like grouse. He does this mainly through the weather over which no man is ever likely to have control. After the remarkable regeneration of the grouse in the season of 1987 I wrote a letter to the *Daily Telegraph* and several other journals attributing our good fortune to God and was, perhaps, surprised by the number of sportsmen who wrote in agreement, expressing thankfulness for this blessing from above.

143

Chapter 12

The True Conservers

The shooting fraternity is constantly under critical attack from people who claim to be conservationists yet there is no body which does more for conservation. I am certain from my records that, on balance, I am a creator of bird life in spite of my shooting tally, for I have established environments for game and wild life which would not otherwise exist. And there are thousands like me. Every well-keepered estate is a conservation area and usually a place of natural beauty.

As I have already pointed out, it would seem certain that during the autumn and winter, and possibly at all times, the pheasant is the most numerous bird in Britain, entirely because of shooting, without which there would be very few and probably none.

It was not shooting which caused the crash of the country's wild partridge populations but the economic necessity to change farming practices in ways inimical to that bird. It is shooting, however, which has brought the partridge back in many areas through artificial rearing, especially of redlegs.

I hope I have made it clear that, without keepering and shooting, the grouse and the other wild moorland birds would become rare. As Prince Philip is reported to have stated recently, 'The grouse are in absolutely no danger from people who shoot grouse.' (I know what he meant but the literal interpretation would also be true of some people I have watched.)

Much of the heather on which the grouse feeds would disappear and, eventually, so would the moorland as a whole, as it has in most of Wales – through forestry. The once-famous Llanbrynmair

Moor is a prime example. The heather was not managed, the grouse shooting fell away and so did the sheep farming as coarse grasses took over. It is now a forest with the total decline of moorland birds. The Royal Society for the Protection of Birds is greatly perturbed by the general loss of grouse moors.

Forestry is very important but we should afforest in the right places and with the right trees. The grouse-shooting interest is in the van of the campaign to halt the march of the alien conifers over the face of the moorlands, especially in Scotland. The recent ending of the tax concessions for commercial tree planting should slow the march but the Government still seems to be prepared to see 100,000 further acres a year blanketed by conifers – dense, dark forests which are so inimical to wild life and any other form of vegetation.

Without the moorland much wild life would disappear. On my Stublick Moor, for example, there is a nice population of merlins, those delightful falcons little bigger than mistlethrushes. They are ground nesters and very subject to predation by foxes, which we keep in check. On one of my grouse moors the old keeper liked fox-hunting and even encouraged a few foxes without my knowledge. When he was in command we had no merlins, but when a new young keeper set about the foxes the merlins returned and the merlin population rose to six pairs. On Wemmergill, in 1988, eight pairs nested. It greatly pleased me when scientists recently surveyed our merlin nests on Stublick and reported that, perhaps, they were at their highest practicable density – a pair per 1000 acres. And they are spreading out from us: we have recently had one recovered more than 100 miles away.

Choices have to be made between a common species like the fox and rare species like the merlin. The Royal Society for the Protection of Birds has to remain neutral, vocally, on the matter of field sports by the nature of its Royal Charter, but it acknowledges that, but for the shooting interest, many upland habitats for wild life would have disappeared.

Golden plovers are also specially susceptible to foxes. I know when I see young golden plovers on the grouse moor that the foxes are being controlled. It is important that protected birds like peregrine falcons, merlins, owls, eagles and others which hunt on grouse moors should never be shot or harried. For owners to encourage or allow their keepers to do that gives ammunition to the anti-shooting fraternity which is, otherwise, driven to base its case on ignorance. It is only the predators which prey seriously on the breeding stock that need eliminating – mainly foxes, crows, jackdaws, rats and stoats.

The racing pigeon enthusiasts have a case against the peregrine and under one new eyrie on our grouse moor we found seventy-four aluminium rings. However, we are prepared to lose a few grouse to keep the peregrines going and the fanciers should be prepared to lose some pigeons, which can be bred more easily than falcons. After all, it is the tame pigeons which are intruding into the falcons' natural habitat, not vice versa. The peregrine is a marvellous creation. I remember shooting a pigeon in a wood at Thoresway many years ago and accidentally downing a peregrine falcon which had been close on its tail but which I had not seen. Sadly he received enough pellets out of the pattern which had killed the pigeon to bring him down and I had to dispatch him, to my great regret.

Perhaps the best advertisement for lowland shooting is the enormous number of songbirds on a well-keepered shoot. They come out of the crops and woods in their hundreds because some of them partake of the feed provided for the game but, mainly, because of the reduction of predators like magpies and jays, which kill them. Both factors are extremely important in winter when many wild birds normally die of starvation and predators are driven to take anything that is available. People who come to stay at Rothwell in the spring find it hard to sleep in the early morning because of the volume of the dawn chorus.

Because of the great extent of the rearing and artificial feeding of the mallard, this bird is probably commoner than it has ever been.

It has to be conceded that much of the wild life legally classed as vermin suffers in the interests of game but, happily, in the enlightened era in which we live, such inroads can be minimized and many birds and creatures which were persecuted in the past can now be preserved. Compromises can be made. Sparrow-hawks are death to partridges but, when Rothwell ceased to be mainly a partridge shoot, we encouraged the return of these birds and they are becoming quite common. My keepers are forbidden to destroy them and I will not now permit an inexperienced shot to shoot at pigeons during a pheasant drive because he may shoot a sparrow-hawk in error.

Sparrow-hawks had become almost extinct in Lincolnshire, not so much from shooting but because of the cumulative poisons like dieldrin and aldrin. When these were in regular use as seed dressing they were eaten by the wood pigeons and some of these were killed by sparrow-hawks before they died, since being weakened they were easy prey. The hawks were poisoned in turn. Quite a few of us have taken steps to re-establish sparrow-hawks on those estates where these dressings were once widely used on winter wheat. Now they come and take tits and greenfinches feeding on the bird-table outside my study window. It is all part of the country scene, as God intended, and exciting to witness, tough as it may be for the prey.

As regards foxes on my pheasant shoot I ensure that when the local hounds hunt over my land there will always be foxes for them to find because hunting has given me some of the happiest days of my life. Until I was fifty I hunted regularly – once six days in one week and five days in the following week, with fourteen different packs of foxhounds, including Brocklesby, Southworld, Burton, Blankney, West Norfolk, Grove and Rufford, Derwent, Pytchley, Quorn, Belvoir and Cottesmore over my lifetime.

The greatest service to wild life and to the human community made by the shooting interest is undoubtedly the siting and preservation of Britain's deciduous woodlands. It is the pheasant coverts deliberately planted on the hillsides years ago which have made the British landscape so uniquely attractive. And it is mainly the shooting interest which keeps them as they are. Most people seem to be unaware that on many estates and farmland it would be uneconomic to keep woodland going and preferable, commercially, to clear and plough it. This is not done, either because owners need the woodland for pheasant shooting or farmers gain considerable income by letting it for that purpose. Surveys have shown that farmers interested in game shooting spend substantially more on landscape improvement than others.

I – and others – deliberately leave the odd dead tree in a prominent positon so that the woodpeckers can enjoy themselves and my family and I can enjoy them. We put up boxes in barns and other places for owls. Many of us also leave enough nettle beds so that we can enjoy the butterflies.

There are several areas at Rothwell which I have set aside as sanctuaries and are available for study by professional naturalists.

Every estate owner, farmer and shooting syndicate can contribute a great deal to conservation and we should all do so. The most direct effort we can make is to plant trees and hedges, and leave wild, undisturbed corners in fields where partridges and other birds can nest. We can make ponds for waterfowl. I have planted huge numbers of daffodils on the roadsides of North Lincolnshire and sown many wild flowers – not just because I love to see them, but because I owe the countryside so much and because they will be there long after I have gone.

It would be illuminating to know the total annual sum which the shooting interest spends on conservation, deliberately and consequentially. It must run into many millions of pounds.

There is a great deal of senseless prejudice by those dedicated to ending what they call blood sports, which these days even include fishing, where there is very little blood about. Shooting is widely misrepresented in the media through ignorance and spite, usually by town-dwelling writers who know nothing about it.

We should do all we can to dispel the idea that we are sadists who shoot birds for the sake of killing – the result of some bloodlust. Reared game-birds should be regarded as a crop – a crop that will die if it is not harvested, just as a field of wheat will rot if it is not gar-nered. A farmer can be fond of his sheep, cattle and pigs but cannot get emotional about selling them for slaughter, which is the reason why they exist. A similar situation exists regarding game-birds.

Many of those who are anti-shooting do not object to the killing: they object to the fact that so many enjoy the process. It reminds me of the advice: 'Next time you commit adultery don't enjoy it and then it will be permissible.'

Anyone who keeps his eyes open on the roads will see that the motor car is a great slaughterer of wild life – hares, rabbits, foxes, badgers, hedgehogs, pheasants, squirrels, songbirds. I travel so far each year by motor vehicle that I should be the last to class motorists with vermin, but there can be no doubt that they kill an enormous amount of wild life. Much of the slaughter is unavoidable but, all too often, one sees no effort being made to avoid pheasants and hares. Indeed some seem to take pleasure in creating a cloud of feathers or knocking down a hare caught in headlights, though the result is inedible. Some drivers have so little consideration that they will drive through a pheasant with chicks for the fun of seeing them massacred. There is more roadside carrion for the magpies than there was in the days of the gibbets. Yet this sickening situation is usually ignored by the loud-mouthed 'antis'.

Perhaps the most glaring expression of the ignorance of the antis has been the deliberate liberation of mink, from mink fur farms, into the British countryside. Still, one wonders if the sight of what these ferocious foreign pests do to the indigenous wild life on river banks would deter such fanatics, who are the terrorists of the animal world.

Which 'saboteur' ever saved a hedge or saved a tree? They are really wild-life saboteurs.

As I write, the shooting fraternity is under further pressure from the anti-gun lobby, which includes some police officials who should be better informed. The opposition to the ownership of shotguns flares up whenever there is a murder carried out by such weapons. There was particular outcry following the massacre in Hungerford, though the individual concerned used a pistol and rifle for his appalling purpose. The circumstances behove us all to ensure that our sporting guns are kept under the most secure conditions possible but, whatever we do, determined villains will still gain access to shotguns.

I suspect that many of the antis are more concerned with opposing their idea of privilege than promoting the welfare of wild life. They should take careful note of what has happened to some estates in northern Italy where shooting fell under the edicts of local municipalities which happened to be controlled by Communists. One typical municipality brought in two decrees. The first declared that nobody should be allowed to shoot more than three pheasants or other game-birds in one day. The second ruled that this privilege should belong to anybody who cared to make use of it, access to all previously private sporting land being everybody's right.

The results were inevitable. Everything was shot off including the songbirds, which had previously been spared the attention of Italian 'sportsmen'. The owners declined to rear any birds or spend any money on keepering. So these estates are now game and wild-life deserts and their owners come to Britain to shoot.

Banning shooting in Britain would inflict enormous damage on the countryside, yet that, or something near it, has been debated in the European Parliament with an overwhelming majority of MEPs in favour. In October 1988 the Parliament voted for a complete ban on shooting throughout the Community except in specially permitted areas which would, no doubt, be specified by the Parliamentarians, most of whom know nothing about shooting.

Further, if the European Parliament's wishes ever became law all forms of shooting would have to be carried out to strict bag limits, with 'inspectorates' ensuring that the limits were observed.

All this should make the shooting fraternity highly apprehensive of what might happen after 1992 but, even without EEC restrictions, something similar could, conceivably, occur in Britain under a left-wing Labour government in view of the threats issued by some 'hard-left' MPs, who tend to be townsmen, ignorant of country lore and intent on attacking any form of privilege, whether earned or not. Left-wingers are always banging on about 'the community'. They fail, totally, to appreciate the extent to which shooting has been, and still is, a powerful force in country communities, not only by providing employment but in providing a common interest. In Rothwell, for instance, there is no doubt that shooting helps to bind the local community together.

Shooting also serves as an important link between town and country, promoting a better understanding of rural life and problems. The Standing Conference on Country Sports estimated that 55 per cent of shotgun owners live in towns.

Left:
The king's feather – a badge pinned on the author by the King of Spain

Below:
The best wild-fowl shoot of the author's life – 2 December 1983 on Read's Island in the Humber Estuary. Shooting alone, with no beaters, Will Jacob loading, all wild with no reared birds

Aerial view of the village of Rothwell with the author's home on the right. The circular object is a fountain to commemorate the author's third son, John William, who was killed in a motor accident

Read's Island in the Humber Estuary – the author's wild-fowl shoot

Middleton House, Teesdale, County Durham, the author's home during the grouse season

His Majesty King Juan Carlos and the King's aide, Spain, 1981

The author and Lady Nickerson seated behind a typical Nombela partridge butt

The guns on the north side of Wemmergill, 26 August 1974

A 'shoulder' of wild partridges (plus one pigeon) shot during one drive at Guedea in Spain

The author with his Spanish keepers at Nombela

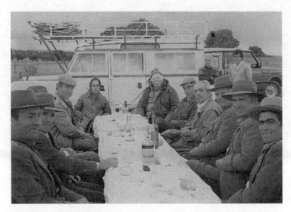

With the keepers after lunch

The author at Los Quintos, Spain, as a guest of Pepe and Carmen Mora-Figuero

Guests at Rothwell, 1960

Guests at Rothwell, 1981

The author in the park at Rothwell in 1972 with, from left to right, Charles Nickerson, Lord Forte and his son, Rocco

After a cock-drive at Rothwell. From left to right: Claude Foussier, the author, Valerie Giscard d'Estaing, Lord Whitelaw 18 January 1986

In a true democracy, in which we are fortunate to live, we can do no more than counter the grim prospect of the political assassination of our sport with convincing argument. It will be a continuing struggle. Meanwhile, those of us fortunate enough to possess shoots must plan to leave behind us a good, on-going situation, preferably better than we found it, so that future generations will, at least, have the option of continuing with it and experiencing the joys of the countryside, as we have. Too many farmers think that they have the right to exploit the land any way they like for profit.

It is my personal belief that for both economic and social reasons connected with the increase in leisure, the sport of shooting will prosper rather than decline. Hunting in its various forms is not inhuman but, in fact, very human indeed, being part of the instrinsic nature of many men and women. It is, of course, more highly developed in some people than in others and I seem to have been born with more than my fair share of it. It has been a bonus and I thank God for it.

Chapter 13

Creatures Called 'Vermin'

Frankly, I dislike the word vermin, which seems to be defined as 'offensive creatures so damaging to various interests that it is legal to destroy them'. I would rather compare them with weeds, which are no more than plants in the wrong places. They are God's creatures which happen to be out of place in certain areas where they conflict with man's interest. To dismiss them as vermin is an arrogant attitude on man's part, especially since, as species, most of them were here long before us, and I frequently remind myself that it is we who have usurped them.

Some of these creatures are marvellous works of creation, as the word creature implies, being wonderfully adapted to survive. Yet nobody doubts that the rat or mouse is out of place in the home and, by the same token, the rabbit and wood pigeon are out of place to the farmer, and the carrion crow, magpie and fox to the keeper. To those extremists who say that nothing should be killed I would respond – 'Have you ever swatted a fly?' Frederick the Great was right in his advice to his generals when he said, 'He who would preserve everything preserves nothing.'

Where vermin are not out of place they should be treated with consideration and respect, and on my land they are.

The prime example of vermin is, of course, the fox. I hunted regularly for over thirty years and, like Mr Jorrocks, grew fond of the fox. I have yet to shoot my first fox but, when Rothwell was a partridge shoot, my keepers had to destroy many because wild grey partridges cannot co-exist with foxes from April to July. I have proved, beyond question, that one of the factors responsible for the decline in the wild partridge population has been the reduced control of predators, like the fox, through lack of proper keepering, the other factors being the reduction of natural chick food by agro-chemicals and the loss of hedgerows and other nesting cover. As I have described in Chapter 5, we lost many nests to foxes and other predators at Rothwell, in spite of all the precautions we took.

You can have foxes on a pheasant shoot, provided that they cannot get into the laying or release pens, where they will kill for pleasure, or hysteria, especially if they are well-grown cubs, but not where you are hoping to have wild partridges. At the time when hen-pheasants are vulnerable, while laying or incubating on their nests, fox cubs are quite small and one bird will make a meal for the litter but, a month or so later, when partridges are sitting, the cubs are much bigger and a vixen may need to take six or seven hen-partridges in a night to feed them. No shoot can tolerate such losses.

The nests cannot be adequately protected by naphthalene flakes, which we tried, or by any other available repellent. Indeed a fox or badger is probably astute enough to learn to associate the smell with sitting birds or eggs, and go searching for it.

Though every bit as cunning as they are famed to be, foxes can be lured by the right bait. There is nothing they like better than a dead hare or duck. They seem to prefer a diet with a strong flavour, which explains why they also like fish. They are also partial to a rat and, to some extent, they pay for their keep on a pheasant shoot by the number of rats they kill.

A common practice in Lincolnshire for dealing with foxes was to plough a furrow fourteen inches deep round a field. Foxes would always run down it because they could not be seen, and it was the easiest thing to set snares in it.

We did not control foxes after the end of July, when the partridges and pheasants are finished nesting, and foxes can then be tolerated in the hunting interest, though most keepers dislike them, not only because they take game but because they can so easily spoil a drive, in a wood or in kale, by rushing up and down, putting up the birds too early and making them fly in all directions in large flushes. Foxes are useful for taking any wounded birds not recovered on a shooting day.

153

In my experience there need to be about six foxes in a parish for a pack of hounds to be reasonably sure of finding one above ground and even then earth-stopping has to be well done.

Incidentally, while shooting people do a lot for hunts in this way, the hunting fraternity does *nothing* for shooting. The few foxes they kill could be disposed of more certainly in other ways and a hunt can cause a lot of disruption on a shoot, especially on the boundaries. I say this as a man who enjoyed hunting even more than shooting when I was doing both. There is room for both hunting and shooting with reasonable give and take from both sides.

Sensible precautions are, of course, essential on a pheasant shoot. The wire around the pens must be sunk deep enough to deter a fox from digging under it and, preferably, with an additional protective stretch of buried wire in front of it. Trails of straw from the combines put down for pheasants when they have been turned out can be dangerous if young pheasants start jugging in them, as they will, for the foxes will easily snap them up.

Considering the number of foxes killed each year by keepers and local authorities – it can run into hundreds on one big estate heavily stocked with game – it is an attribute to this splendid clever animal that it still keeps its population high.

The Reconciliation Project, which I mentioned in Chapter 11, is trying to quantify the effect of large fox populations on grouse: there is no doubt that it is catastrophic. Once a grouse population has been allowed to fall below a certain level it is very difficult to resuscitate it under the pressure created by foxes and other vermin. Unfortunately, many moors now have the additional problem of nearby coniferous plantations, from which sanctuary foxes are inclined to roam for miles. Unkeepered areas of moorland offer similar haven. In the spring and summer, when fewer sheep die, the foxes turn to live lambs; and the grouse, when the hens are sitting and there are fledglings about, provide easy pickings.

For many people a fox is too much like a dog for them to be able to bring themselves to shoot it. Nobody is likely to blame you for declining to shoot a fox if, like me, you explain that you never shoot them under any circumstances. If you are a guest on an estate which wants foxes shot and you do not like doing that it is better to let your loader shoot them – he will usually oblige but if he declines you must respect his wishes too. (I never allow my loader to shoot a fox because I hate to witness it.)

Never let your loader shoot a fox unless it is at very close range and absolutely safe. Nothing is worse than seeing a wounded fox limp away to die slowly in agony. There is a common misbelief that if you get one or two pellets into a fox it will eventually die of lead poisoning. This is not true of a dog or a human being and it is not true of a fox either. A fox can be crippled and forced to continue to try to survive in a handicapped condition. It can also die a slow and lingering death – not from lead poisoning but from its septic and gangrenous wounds.

I do not accept invitations from shoots where foxes are destroyed during drives. I will never go to a shoot again where this happens and it is many years since I witnessed such an event.

I am told that shooting foxes by lamping them at night is an exciting sport for those who enjoy such an activity, but it is not effective if relied on alone; it can only be an adjunct to other methods.

Among ground vermin I rate the rat as almost as damaging as the fox on lowland shoots and possibly even more so because of the great increase in their numbers. My observations convince me that it is the worst enemy of the partridge. One bitch rat suckling young in a dry June is capable of eating every partridge egg on a half-mile run of a hedge. Rats love eggs of any kind and all ground-nesters may suffer as a result. On one property of mine, Read's Island, where rats are kept under tight control, I had a minimum of nine pairs of short-eared owls nesting and a maximum of twelve pairs.

I have noticed that, for some reason, rats seem to thrive especially well in wet seasons. They are thirsty creatures and that may be the reason.

The rat population explosion recorded in counties like Hampshire and Surrey seems to be linked with the increased growth of maize as an animal feeding crop and as game cover. The rats love it. Another factor is the demise of the barn owl, which did such a valuable service in feeding on rats. The British population of this once common bird has fallen by 70 per cent since 1932 to only about 5000 breeding pairs. Apparently, there has been a surprising climatic factor – prolonged snow cover. This deprives the owls of their food and they cannot stand more than a few days of starvation; while in the first forty years of this century only one winter had more than twenty days of snow cover, since then twenty-one winters have reached that level in many parts of the country. Intensive farming has also reduced the owl's hunting grounds, old barns which housed them have been pulled down and large numbers have been killed by traffic. A national campaign to reverse the trend has been launched, and it may succeed. One thing which farmers can do to help is to fit a tea-chest or some similar box inside the roof of modern barns to encourage the owls to nest there.

Sadly, poisoning is the only effective way of reducing the rat population. Preparations based on warfarin can be distributed in hedgerows in sealed plastic packets and the rats will eat their way in. With older poisons we used to have to change them regularly. This may have been due to acquired immunity but I have a feeling that when the rats died quickly, as they did with the old poisons, their fellows sensed that it was the result of what they had eaten and avoided it. Warfarin takes some time to kill and that may be why it has continued to be successful.

Warfarin also carries the advantage that there is an antidote to it should a dog eat it. Some of the stronger rat poisons are deadly to dogs and to be avoided on that score alone.

Nobody seems to disagree with killing rats, yet they are engaging and highly intelligent animals. They are so successful that they do enormous damage to other wild life apart from game. Their numbers in a poorly keepered area can be guessed at by the number now seen dead on the roads.

Rats do, of course, have a part to play in the balance of Nature. Where they have been largely exterminated, their place is taken by voles which are normally kept under control by the rats. This is no bad thing for the shooting interest because voles do not harm game, but provide food for the owls and other predators which might otherwise attack chicks.

The stoat is a wonderful hunter and a family will hunt like a pack of hounds, capable of wiping out a whole covey of young partridges. In the spring they follow the fences and watercourses but when the corn gets high they will hunt in it. Trapping boxes for such creatures should be placed in every 200 yards of hedge or fence.

I had a pet stoat which lived in the rockery under my study window at Rothwell and used to hunt the mice. One morning before breakfast one of my house guests, the late Guy Moreton, shot it, thinking he was doing me a good turn.

Feral cats, those which were domestic and have run wild or are descended from such stock, are great enemies of the partridge as well as of the pheasant. So are domestic cats which hunt on the edges of shoots. A cat usually leaves a trade-mark on a plundered nest in the form of scattered feathers and intact eggs while a fox is much neater in dealing with the bird but may leave a few half-eaten eggs. A report on 'feline delinquency' published in 1988 claimed that Britain's six million cats kill 100 million birds and mammals a year. Many of the mammals, of course, were mice and field voles and while many of the birds were house sparrows, other species including songbirds were regularly taken. Cats learn to lie in wait round bird-tables early in the morning. Young birds which have just left the nest and cannot fly or fully appreciate danger are particularly vulnerable.

Of course one cannot blame the cats, which are behaving as Nature intended. In the case of domestic cats it is the owners who are at fault for failing to keep them under control. At Rothwell my keepers used to catch the parson's cat repeatedly about once a fortnight – and let it go. Then when anyone complained that my keepers must have killed their cat we could always say, 'Look at the parson's cat. It is eleven years old. You should look after your cat like the parson does.'

A keeper should never shoot a cat within half a mile of a dwelling as it may well be somebody's pet.

All I am prepared to say about dogs, as predators – as about cats – is that if people live near a pheasant or partridge shoot they should not allow their pets to roam loose and unaccompanied.

We kept records of how partridge nests had been destroyed by predators over several years. The average lost over a ten-year period was 30 per cent and the chief culprits were foxes, dogs and cats. Rats had not done so much damage because we had really gone after them. These losses occurred even though the ground was being intensively keepered. On areas where less care was taken they must have been very much higher.

I count moles as creatures to be controlled because they have the habit of surfacing under partridge nests and tipping them over, probably because the damp there attracts worms. On a well-keepered shoot where the stoats and weasels are under control, the mole population increases enormously. We discourage the moles by putting naphthalene flakes under the nests. Our experience suggests, however, that the smell rouses the curiosity of badgers and an old, toothless badger will eat eggs. One such creature had accounted for more than seventy nests before she was caught by my keeper, Monty Christopher, who later went to Sandringham, where he has been so happy.

Grey squirrels are probably of little importance to game, devoting their attention to songbirds and their young. They certainly damage young trees, especially sycamores, which seem like caviare to them.

Hedgehogs are also occasional egg-eaters, consuming those of any ground-nesting birds which they come across. They also eat a lot of noxious insects, however, and are attractive animals. In any case, so many hedgehogs are slaughtered on the roads.

The extent to which crows, magpies, jays and jackdaws prey on eggs of all kinds is illustrated by the number of wild birds on a well-keepered shoot. Hundreds of blackbirds and other songbirds will come out of a wood on well-keepered land as the beaters go through. I am very proud of the numbers at Rothwell which, fortuitously, serve another purpose. If large numbers of wild birds do not come out during a drive I know that the game-birds are not being fed properly.

Carrion crows are a perennial problem, especially on grouse

moors where they have increased and do great damage to eggs and chicks. They will even eat the young leverets which, I believe, is why the doe spreads them about and suckles each in turn. Ravens, which are protected birds, will peck the eyes and tongue out of a sheep while it is incapacitated when lambing or stranded on its back.

One way to deal with carrion crows is when they are nesting. It is my experience that a carrion crow can count up to three. If two of you go to a tree with a nest in it and one walks away the crow will rarely come back to its eggs but if four do it and three walk away, while the other remains hidden, it will fly back within twenty minutes before the eggs get cold, when it can be shot. Three with two walking away may do the trick but four is more certain.

If the hen carrion crow is shot the cock will brood the eggs for a couple of days or so and will then weary of the task and eat the eggs.

Rooks are not usually regarded as vermin on a shoot but, in my view, they are very bad because they carry gapes and can be responsible for big losses if they are roosting in woods where there are pheasant release pens. Though it is not well known, they also eat eggs and young chicks, especially in hard or very dry weather when their more regular diet of cereals, worms and insects is hard to come by. They will also take the eggs of game-birds, ducks and any other ground-nesters like plovers and pipits. I have noticed that when young rooks are learning to fly they follow a hedge from tree to tree and spot game-birds' nests in the process.

In any case, rook shooting is great fun, especially when one is young and just starting to shoot. At one of the rookeries we patronized, Johnson's Wood near Rothwell, there were a certain number of brown birds year after year. This, presumably, was the result of some mutation in feather colour. It must be uncommon though I recently saw a single brown rook near Reeth in North Yorkshire.

The magpie is an inveterate egg-eater and killer of chicks and small birds. It hunts hedgerows and will tear a thrush's or black-bird's nest apart to get at the young. Magpies have been known to attack sickly or injured stock and even a donkey! I fear that, handsome as they are, I give them no quarter. With the outlawing of the pole trap and the general disapproval of poisoning, except for rats and mice, magpies are best controlled by shooting.

159

My Spanish keeper plucked a magpie as food for his tame owl and I was astonished how small the body was, though the head is big. So you need to be accurate to kill one. Because magpies are so damaging to the Spanish partridges, my wife and I have improved our accuracy at shooting them. The secret, for those at long distance, which they usually are, is to line them up and just move slightly with them as you pull the trigger. If you make your usual swing you will probably miss it in front, though, as always, some movement of the gun is necessary.

Here, from my diary, is how magpies are controlled in Spain, where they are very numerous:

> A keeper and I set off at 8.30 a.m. for a mountainous area where the magpies were doing no good to the partridge nests. The keeper (whose name was Jesus, common enough in Spain) climbed a solitary dead tree and placed a live, tethered, tame owl to a branch so that it was highly visible, while we remained in hides. After about half an hour magpies arrived to mob the owl, which seem unconcerned: I killed six and two jays. We then packed up and moved to another area where the owl was set up on a large rock. We killed four magpies there.

This trick can be played with a stuffed owl but it does not work nearly so well. I once set up a stuffed owl in my garden near the tree where I feed the birds on peanuts in several dispensers. It took just one and a quarter hours for the birds to realize that the owl could be safely ignored!

In Spain magpies are kept in some check by the greater spotted cuckoo which lays its eggs in their nests, usually removing a magpie's egg each time it does so. It may lay several eggs in each nest but if any magpie eggs remain the cuckoos make no effort to throw them or the young out, and they are reared together. A pity that the greater spotted cuckoo cannot be encouraged to come here!

The jay, which is even more beautiful than the magpie, has equally intolerable habits, raiding nests for eggs. It has to be afforded the same treatment. There are plenty of unkeepered areas where both

160

jays and magpies, as well as crows, can flourish. And there is plenty of carrion on the roads for them.

The jackdaw is probably underrated as a snatcher of eggs and a killer of chicks and young ducklings. It is adept at raiding laying pens early in the morning and, surprisingly, in view of their impudence, they are difficult to catch.

Huge flocks of starlings have done enormous damage to the trees at Rothwell by the vast weight of their droppings on the boughs and foliage. By their sheer numbers they defeated our efforts to counter them. They also defeated the RAF, practice flights of the Lightning fighter planes from the local airfield at Binbrook often being delayed for as long as two hours a day – in the morning and evening when the birds moved out and in – because of the danger of ingestion of the birds into the engines. My staff, helped by several RAF men, did all they could to frighten the birds off but to no avail. We eventually solved the problem by setting aside an area of thickets, called Roman Holes, where the starlings were allowed to roost, being scared away from everywhere else. They soon learned to go there and still winter there, year after year, because we actively discourage them from going anywhere else.

Chapter 14

A Thief by any other Name . . .

'Oh 'tis my delight on a shiny night in the season of the year.'
The Lincolnshire poacher is famed in story and in song but, as
throughout the rest of the country, he is not what he used to be.
The romantic view of the poacher is no longer justified, if indeed
it ever was. Poaching, especially of the reared bird, has always
been a form of theft but the poaching of pheasants, and especially
of deer, has become a highly organized industry operated by gangs
of up to ten – often desperate – men, who may all be equipped
with guns and prepared to use force if confronted by keepers and
even by police. Such poachers are persistent criminals involved in
a lucrative branch of organized crime. They qualify for the title
vermin and it is a pity that they cannot be treated accordingly.
However, the shooting fraternity must always stay within the law,
whatever advantages this gives to the poachers.

As my old keeper, Father Jacob, points out, poachers are so
mobile today with their four-wheel-drive vehicles that they are
very difficult to catch. In years past poachers needed to walk
miles to get into the middle of a big estate. Some of the modern
poachers have pressed their wives into service as drivers. They
drop the men at various places and return later to pick them
up with their loot. A woman seen driving is less likely to attract
suspicion. Formerly, women were not associated with poaching,
but they are into everything these days.

The modern poachers also make use of the available technology
like silencers, walkie-talkie radios, infra-red binoculars, night sights
and specially made lamps.

It is unfortunate that the pheasant, which is the most numerous game-bird, should be the easiest to poach because of its habit of roosting in trees.

Usually one or two of the gang are trained to use a silenced rifle, a .22, and the pheasants are bagged, about twenty to a sack, and hidden to be picked up later. Because of the sheer weight and the limit on time, about 200 seems to be the usual haul for a gang but, on occasion, many more can be taken from a really big shoot.

It is, perhaps, fortunate that shot pheasants bring such a low price, because there are so many of them. If they brought £4 or £5 a brace the temptation to poach them would be even greater.

The beater who puts a pheasant under his coat or hides it during a drive is common enough but does not pose much of a problem because the keeper usually hears about it and can get rid of him. One really needs to know one's beaters, as I have the good fortune to do at Rothwell. In some areas, however, all sorts of people have to be pressed into the service and at one shoot in Sussex, youths from a reform school were employed. At the end of the day most of them were found to have pheasants concealed on their persons!

It is obviously essential to ensure that dubious characters are not employed as beaters because they can use the occasion to reconnoitre the estate, see where release pens and feeding areas are and spot the best ways in to return at night with their friends.

Poachers have always been adept at using their local knowledge to outwit the keepers but on one shoot in Buckinghamshire – and no doubt on others – they have excelled themselves. A main railway line passes through this estate and the poachers used to position themselves with their .410s under the trees where pheasants were roosting and wait for an express to hurtle by before firing their fusillades. Their guns could not be heard above the din from the rails. The owner solved the problem only by abandoning the shoot.

On many shoots men chasing hares with lurchers, for sport as much as for game, do damage through the disturbance they cause and some of them, who believe they have a right to hunt wherever they want, can be aggressive.

Only constant vigilance by a devoted staff can prevent poaching and it is the keeper's main duty to deter poachers rather than to catch them. Regular night-watching is the best answer and keepers should vary their routine. Like generals, poachers know that time spent on reconnaissance is rarely wasted and will note the times when keepers are on the watch or at home or in the pub. Poachers soon learn which shoots are well watched and tend to avoid them, though some may regard them as a challenge.

It is a good idea for keepers to take the numbers of any cars or vans parked near shoots and to do it ostentatiously so that the drivers can see it being done. If drivers object, the keeper can simply say that those are his instructions.

Keepers should make use of the available technology. Walkie-talkies are very helpful, especially if linked up with the police networks, and enable a keeper to get in touch with others on neighbouring shoots.

Infra-red beams linked with alarms and other electronic devices can be used to protect pens. Tripwires which set off alarms or fire blank cartridges can also be effective.

On my pheasant shoot we operate a duty timetable and all the staff participate. We have at least two people watching for poachers all night and every night during vulnerable periods. We have a few surprises for them and they tend to go where things are easier.

It is an enormous help to have the support of the community. If the local people are on your side because so many of them have a stake in the shooting interest they will report on any suspicious-looking strangers and inform on any local poachers.

Collaboration with the police is all-important. In these days when so many poachers are armed villains, prepared to resort to violence, it is unsafe for keepers to tackle them alone. The well-known lines 'All the pheasants ever bred, won't repay for one man dead' apply to keepers as much as to anyone else. Some police forces will co-operate but others will not on the grounds that they think they have more important work to do. Our experience is that they are keen to do so. It pays them because they often secure information about other unrelated crimes and even make arrests for them when questioning poachers.

Sadly, when poachers are caught with the necessary evidence of their crime, which is not always easy to prove, the penalties imposed by magistrates are usually far too lenient. This is especially true when poachers claim to be unemployed when in fact, in addition to drawing the dole, they are self-employed in the poaching industry and paying no tax.

Under the law poachers can lose their vehicles, which is the heaviest penalty they are likely to suffer, but all too often they claim that without transport they won't be able to continue in work or to look for it if they have none, and magistrates usually buy this sob story. The result is that the vehicles continue to be used for poaching forays.

In our area, some of the poachers take their suits or working overalls with them, change in some barn after their night's foray and go straight to work in Lincoln or wherever.

It must be a mistake to encourage poachers but this is sometimes done. I know of one shoot where they let the keepers invite friends in to shoot the wood pigeons, on the grounds that it will stop them from poaching. This inevitably enables poachers to see the lie of the land – where the pens are and the big roosting areas. One cannot expect gratitude from the man who believes that all game is fair game.

Something else which encourages poachers is too much game on the boundaries, especially if these are near public roads, as they often are. For that reason, the regular and resolute driving in of pheasants pays dividends as it does to the shooting in general.

Chapter 15

A Race Apart

A retired admiral of great charm and who had demonstrated outstanding administrative ability was brought in to run a large shoot which went steadily down. One of the guests, who had drawn an excellent position, asked his loader why there was so little to shoot at. The loader, who was a keeper on a nearby estate, made a telling reply: 'Would you have appointed a gamekeeper to fight the Battle of the Armada?'

Keepering is a specialized and highly professional business, requiring knowledge, dedication and never-ending application. In view of the large amounts of money invested in shoots, and the extent to which many are run as commercial enterprises, it is remarkable that there are so few institutions offering training courses on gamekeeping. The Standing Conference on Countryside Sports estimated, in 1983, that there were about 5000 full-time and part-time gamekeepers in Great Britain. Yet without any certificate of training it is difficult to know whether a man who applies for a keeper's post has even the minimum qualifications.

A keeper who comes for interview usually knows what he wants in the way of wages, clothing, accommodation, fuel, light and telephone, holidays – he is entitled to a month a year, though few take it all – transport and assistance from the farm. So what should the prospective employer know about him? He should come from a well-run shoot and it is essential to be able to find out the real reason why he has left or wants to leave it. Some owners are prepared to give a keeper a resounding reference to get rid of him. If you do not know much about running a shoot yourself you will be wise to have a candidate interviewed by an agent who does.

It is most important to find out the man's attitude to time. If he seems overly inclined to talk about his time off and his right to attend other shoots, to load or pick up, in what is really your time, then you need to be wary. A keeper must be prepared to work very long hours, unstintingly, especially at certain times such as the rearing season. That is why gamekeeping is more a way of life, rather than just a job. The keeper who is in the pub every night is no good.

A prospective keeper must have a real feel and love for the countryside and be interested in the woodland, the hedges and wild life. The concept of a gamekeeper as a conservationist may raise guffaws among the ignorant but that is what the good modern keeper is required to be in the interest of the good name of shooting, on which the continuation of his profession depends.

A keeper must be physically strong and be prepared to work outdoors in rough weather. In short, he must love his work. A lazy keeper is hopeless and there are some about, especially on grouse moors with absentee owners, where they are induced to do little once the short season is over.

Perhaps the most important characteristic on which you will have to make a judgement is the man's capacity to get on well with others, and especially with your farm staff. A difficult or evil-tempered individual can cause havoc to the whole community. On the other hand it may pay to have a keeper with a reputation for standing no nonsense. I remember interviewing a prospective grouse-moor keeper and knew that he had been up before magistrates for hitting two young men who had been walking, away from a path, on his moor. I questioned him about it and the two men had said that they were policemen on their day off. They were very impudent and refused to leave so he 'saw them both off' by putting his stick across them. He was fined two pounds.

He sounded just like the man I wanted. I took a chance and engaged him, and he has turned out to be a topper.

If married, a keeper must have a wife with a matching temperament and it is important to interview her at the same time. It pays to be able to offer her some extra work, perhaps even assisting her husband, to sustain her interest and give her a little extra money.

For a shoot to be a success it is absolutely essential to have full control of the keeper. This would seem obvious but there are some syndicate shoots where the owner of the land or his agent pays the keeper and is able to give him orders. This carries the advantage that in the event of the keeper having to be fired for some misdemeanour he cannot sue the syndicate for unfair dismissal, and getting a dismissed keeper out of an estate cottage is also then the responsibility of the owner. Nevertheless, failing to have total control over the keeper carries major disadvantages, especially when the owner's ideas about shooting differ from the syndicate's. This is particularly true when the owner's own shoot marches with the let land.

There must be a really close relationship between keeper and employer. If you take no interest, except when you turn up to shoot on your own ground, you are going to be disappointed and you will find the keeper doing what *he* wants, with your interests second. Lord Sefton was once asked how many keepers he employed and replied, 'You had better ask my agent.'

If the employer is readily available, then the keeper should be responsible to him, with direct access. Otherwise, I think that he should come under the farm manager, with his game being treated as one of the crops. There should certainly be a laid-down chain of command because the keeper who is allowed to be a law unto himself invariably causes trouble. Where the judgement of Solomon is needed in a serious conflict of interests, say between the forestry and the shoot, the employer must play that role and let his decision be known, firmly, to all concerned so that there can be no further argument about it. (When possible, it pays to involve forestry workers in the shoot and so capture their interest in its welfare. For instance, my head forester, George Graham, is now my loader for the grouse season, and loves it.)

When there is a good estate agent he can be designated as the arbitrator of conflicts but while, in my experience, many estate agents love to shoot, they are not that adept at either shoot or farm management.

When there is continuing 'needle' between the keeper and the farm manager one of them will eventually have to go – or want to go – unless the conflict can be resolved with good will, as it often can. Continuing conflict generates a hopeless situation for a shoot.

A good keeper will be the hardest worker on an estate, putting in a prodigious number of hours in all weather and often at night. So he is worthy of all assistance and appreciation. Above all, he must be clear in his mind what you want him to do. Keepers tend not to be highly educated, in the general sense, and with some you need to take time to get your ideas across. It is time well spent.

As I have said, some grouse-moor keepers are among the laziest. They have to work hard during the short season and then some tend to do very little or nothing. There are those, however, who do their job conscientiously throughout the year, burning and draining being very hard work. Such men are rare and should be rewarded.

All keepers need to be kept in check to some degree. Mine must do what I want and not what they want and if they go against my orders they know about it. A keeper who is full of excuses when you want to change a drive is no good to you. Make time for discussion and listen to the voice of experience, by all means – a good keeper's view should always command respect – but do not let the keeper make the main decisions.

A good beat-keeper will know how many birds he has to show on a drive, will be able to show them in a challenging way and show as many as the owner wants to be shown. The control of numbers of birds is extremely important on let days when it is essential to provide enough birds, but not too many. Sometimes one marvels at the skill with which keepers can judge the number of birds to put over the guns. Usually they have spotted the ability of the guns to kill them from the pick-up on the early drives.

Honesty is all-important in a keeper because the position offers such opportunities to make money on the side by selling eggs and birds, and fiddling on the feed. For the right reward, he may even turn a blind eye to poachers. (Hence the line in the Lincolnshire Poacher's song: 'Bad luck to every gamekeeper who will not sell his deer.') The keeper who is badly in debt is always a danger because of the pressure on him to resolve his problem by some fiddle or other. Fortunately it quickly gets around a country community when a keeper is bent, but an absentee owner may be the last to hear of it.

I owe an enormous debt to good gamekeepers for a lifetime of magnificent sport and in particular I am indebted to one man, now eighty-five years old, who has been called a 'King amongst Keepers' (in the *Sporting Gun*). His name is Archie Jacob and, apart from his personal service to me, he produced a whole family of sons and grandsons who continue to give me service and pleasure from their skills. It was a lucky day for me when he answered my advertisement for someone to clear out my rabbits.

Archie Jacob came to Rothwell forty-seven years ago. He was then aged thirty-eight. Following family tradition he had become a trainee keeper at the age of fourteen at Feltwell, in his native Norfolk, and had reached the position of assistant keeper. The fields at Rothwell were, literally, heaving with rabbits, which made enormous inroads into the then meagre crops. This plague, which affected the whole area, had been dealt with in the past by professional rabbit-catchers who would pay a small rent for the exclusive right to trap, snare, and net rabbits, which they then sold. They were good at it but it was not their interest to exterminate the stock but to leave enough to breed for the following season. I decided that I would not be beaten by rabbits and advertised for a full-time warrener who would be under my control to carry out an extermination programme. Jacob applied.

He turned up for the interview with the whole of his family, his wife and two sons, Billy, aged twenty and Ben, fifteen, and I liked the look of them as sound country people. I was particularly impressed by the effort they had made to get to the interview and to arrive at the time I had requested them because the train service from Norfolk to the Rothwell area was poor and they had virtually travelled all night. Jacob had a lot of experience of trapping and clearly knew his business, so I engaged him. During the interview one of the boys spilt tea on the carpet and, on the way back to Norfolk, their mother predicted that they would not be lasting long at Rothwell! That is now forty-seven years ago!

Jacob set about reducing the rabbit plague, the rats, magpies, carrion crows and other vermin, and that was his main job. At its peak, his gibbet-line was 100 yards long but eventually I complained about the smell of it and dead vermin have never been hung up since. Billy worked as a lorry driver for me on the farm and Ben as a mechanic. Both were to be extremely important in my shooting life.

With the rabbits eliminated, we set about creating a partridge shoot, as I have described.

Father Jacob, as I call him, developed exceptional skill at driving partridges over guns and in 1952, which was an outstanding year for wild birds, he produced the record bag of over 2000 wild grey partridges out of 2342 head shot by 6 guns. He was presented with an inscribed silver salver marking the occasion – an antique of the future.

On another day, when 7 guns killed 105 brace in one drive, I was so impressed that I had a stone erected stating: 'In appreciation of the skill and devoted work of A W Jacob, head keeper to Joseph Nickerson, for 18 years, so that he and others may read and reflect that across this valley seven guns killed 105 brace of partridges in one drive on October 1 1959.'

He was equally effective when we decided to convert Rothwell to a pheasant shoot.

Father Jacob rarely carried a gun, preferring to trap his vermin and suspecting that a shot sent too many others into cover. Even when Land-Rovers became available he always believed that walking the ground was the only way to cover it efficiently and see everything that should be seen. He was particularly observant of the behaviour of blackbirds, their alarm cries warning him of the presence of stoats and other pests.

Jacob was tough with poachers and the police were rarely involved.

I learned a great deal from him and I think he learned a few things from me, such as the need not to be over-zealous, especially during nesting time. Once he had found a nest with eggs and marked it he would not disturb it unnecessarily. So long as he could see the cock-bird somewhere near the nest he could assume that all was well.

He retired on pension at sixty-five after twenty-eight years' continuous service. At least I thought he was sixty-five but he might have been a good deal older. When I interviewed him I told him I would expect him to retire at sixty-five but, incredibly, I forgot to ask his age. As many years passed and I felt that he must have totted up the required years, I asked him how long he had to go. He looked at me with a sly smile and said, 'I don't really know how old I am, Sir.'

When he did decide to go I offered him a house for life on the estate but, as his wife had died, he preferred to move a few miles away to Nettleton, where he joined his younger son, Ben, in running a shooting school. But he still returns daily to Rothwell for a hot meal with the other staff at the Nickerson Arms, which pleases me because, now he is a widower, I know that he gets at least one good meal every day and meets people.

His elder son, Billy, eventually became my keeper and continued to his retirement at sixty-five, having been associated with Rothwell for forty-five years. It must be a rare father-and-son feat, though my keeper on the grouse moor at Reeth, Mark Alderson, succeeded his father, grandfather and great-grandfather in the post.

Billy has been a wonderful friend as well as a fine keeper and acts as overseer in partial retirement. (It is important to make provision for a pension for a keeper. That is becoming a more established practice now but was not, some years back.)

Ben was, perhaps, the finest loader I have ever had and we worked as a team for many years. It was Ben who loaded for me on The Great Day.

Billy's two sons, Benjy and Will, have become splendid loaders and helpers for me and my guests so that the Jacob tradition continues at Rothwell – and on the partridge shoot in Spain.

It is customary to think of good keepers as akin to good sergeants or even sergeant-majors in the scheme of things but, for me, both Father Jacob and his son, Billy, rank as generals.

While keepers should certainly be encouraged to train dogs for themselves and their employers and should be allowed to sell off unwanted dogs from a litter, they should not, I think, train dogs for sale. This will consume a lot of time they should be spending on other work and they should be paid sufficient wages to make this unnecessary. The same applies to loading on other shoots. Some keepers spend almost as much time loading on other shoots as they do working on their own: they are being paid twice for the same day's work. This happens very rarely with my keepers. I ensure that they get fair tips from the guests and that is enough.

Nor am I in favour of paying vermin money – a bonus per head of vermin killed, because they are paid for doing that anyway and should not be encouraged to allow vermin to breed to provide extra cash.

As regards tips very few beat-keepers receive anything direct from the guests. At home I reward each beat-keeper for every day we have, and all the tips are pooled.

What should one do if and when a keeper expresses a desire to leave? In general, it is best to wish him well and let him go. To be effective a keeper needs to be happy and there is nothing worse than 'atmosphere' between a keeper and the owner. An under-keeper should be encouraged to better himself and if he comes for advice about a shoot which has offered him promotion or better prospects, I would always advise him honestly, should I know anything about that shoot or its owner. I believe that the several Rothwell keepers who have moved elsewhere have a good reputation.

It goes without saying that one should never poach a keeper from a friend. It does happen and is rarely forgiven.

There is a common belief that people come to look like their dogs. I believe that keepers come to look like birds. Father Jacob looks like a cock-partridge and Keeper Turner, a fine fellow who came in 1947 to look after pheasants for me on my late uncle's estate and now works for my brother, Sam, looks like a pheasant.

As happens on most happy pheasant shoots, a good day's shooting for the keepers, loaders and key farm staff is part of the human relations process at Rothwell. As I like to have plenty of pheasants to offer my family and friends in January, when they are strongest on the wing, more wary, and more challenging because of the weather, a lot tend to be left unshot and are available to provide a really good cock shoot on the last day of the month. About twenty guns divide themselves into two teams, one shooting one side of the property and one the other. It gives me much pleasure to hear them banging away when they have done so much for me during the season, and I join them for coffee when they have consumed their lunch at the Nickerson Arms. It is always a hearty occasion, to say the least, and true to the pattern of old-fashioned country life.

Chapter 16

Companions at the Peg

I have kept gun-dogs for as long as I can remember and life without them would be a poorer experience. Indeed, for me, it is inconceivable: there is nothing quite like the relationship between a man and his gun-dog. I reckon that about one third of my pleasure in shooting derives from working my dogs.

I probably owe my life to a gun-dog though it did not belong to me. When I was very young I was out wildfowling on marshes on the Lincolnshire coast with three rather rough diamonds, one of them an old man who had worked for my father. Fog came down and by the time we were being cut off by the tide we had lost our sense of direction in the maze of creeks, which were filling up fast. With sudden inspiration the old man shouted to his spaniel, 'Go home! Go home!' We followed him, very wet, cold and not a little frightened – to safety.

That experience should have made me loyal to spaniels for life but my preference is for labradors though I have had some excellent spaniels, both springers and cockers, and still do.

Though I love my dogs they are never allowed in my house. I know that many people derive extra enjoyment from their dogs by having them in the home – some even allow them to sleep in the bedroom. But I take my gun-dogs seriously. I want them to be professionals and I am convinced that they decline in both discipline and performance when allowed to laze in front of the fire and be petted in the house. I keep my house at 70 degrees Fahrenheit and I do not think that suits a dog's health. The house is no place for a working dog and that is what my dogs are. They see too many different people if they are indoors. They are in and out of the kitchen and tend to be overfed and generally spoiled.

I also dislike dogs in the house for hygienic reasons. What dogs will pick up and eat has to be seen to be believed and the occasion when I did see it is indelibly imprinted on my mind. I was asked by an MFH and his wife to go out with them and a pack of hounds to see if we could find and kill a fox which had a trap attached to it. We went on to some alien territory where we suspected that poison might have been laid and, as a precaution, the Master had each hound treated with soda to make it vomit. The dreadful rubbish they produced was unbelievable – all picked up during the day's hunting.

Dogs are also inclined to roll in any stinking rubbish they encounter, possibly instinctively to mask their scent, and this is a further reason why I do not permit them in the lunch hut where they can get near the food. I always require my guests to sit or peg their dogs outside the hut or put them in their vehicles during lunch. (On one occasion I recall telling a guest, quietly, 'Your dog is in the lunch hut. Would you be kind enough to remove it?' He rejoined me to say, 'Joe, that is your dog.' It was, and I was thoroughly chastened.)

Each of my dogs has a dry kennel and a run with a door that can be closed on a moonlit night to prevent howling. They are well cared for and I expect them to repay me by picking up my birds. This is not to say that I am not on affectionate terms with my dogs. I am, but only in the shooting field, when I visit them in their kennels or take them out for exercise. They need the same exercise in the closed season and, of course, on a farm this is not difficult to provide.

If you do keep your dog indoors do not assume that this will be possible when you are visiting, unless, of course, dogs have been specially welcomed. When invited to a strange shoot it is always wise, and courteous, to ask permission to take a dog at all.

How many dogs you have is a personal matter. Anyone who does as much shooting as I do needs a team. Tests have shown that a gun-dog, doing a lot of retrieving on a big day, can travel many miles, much of it at the run. I always like to start each season with a good stock – mainly labradors and perhaps a couple of spaniels. Some are at my home in the kennels, others are with keepers. My notes show, for example, that in the 1965–6 season there were twelve labradors on the estate, four with me, four with the keeper and four with the beat-keepers. Currently, I am working three labradors and a cocker. A big cocker, like my present dog, Sweep, can manage a cock pheasant or a duck with no difficulty but he is at his best on the grouse moor.

My young dogs are sent off for basic training by professionals, as neither I nor my keepers have time to do it. But they soon learn much more when working several times a week. Before buying a 'made' dog always try it out and make sure that it is not a game-eater. Occasionally, an otherwise excellent dog has this devastating vice.

My dogs are trained to walk on my left side as I carry my gun under my right arm.

Being fascinated by scientific research, and having profited so much by applying it, I have paid some attention to the results of the work done on dog behaviour. Perhaps the most important discovery is the need for puppies to be handled, regularly, between their third and tenth weeks of life. This is the time when a dog establishes a warm and affectionate relationship with man. If a pup is kept away from all human contacts until after the tenth week, it becomes increasingly difficult for it to make a bond with its eventual master, and a pup which fails to experience any contact with human beings before it is fourteen weeks old may remain permanently withdrawn. So those looking after dogs, and especially valuable gun-dogs, should take care to handle pups frequently after they are three weeks old, to establish the human bond.

I do not go in for field trials so I do not need a dog to obey long-distance signs. To react to my hand holding a handkerchief is enough.

My preference is for black labradors, which is purely personal, probably because of their glossy coats. They may be less visible than a yellow dog but any such advantage is only marginal, if it exists at all. In general, I prefer bitches but I keep both sexes, and some of my best performers have been dogs.

I like a labrador to have a broad head and jaw and a thick skin and coat so that it can go into brambles. I do not like them to be over-keen and too fast over the ground because then they will miss birds in their enthusiasm. I enjoy watching them quartering their ground and hoovering the heather, head down, with care. Some labradors these days are more like greyhounds – rat-headed, with poor shoulders.

I always insist that my dogs should look well turned out, with a good glossy coat. A little margarine in the food helps to make the coat shine and an occasional egg seems to benefit them.

The routine veterinary dosings now laid down for dogs are excellent and no gun-dog should be denied them.

I like to have two or three dogs with me on a big day, especially on the grouse moor, to clean up. I get so much extra pleasure out of watching them work. If you have more than one dog with you they must be compatible with each other. Two or three bitches can become very jealous. It is easier to manage a dog and a bitch. Occasionally two dogs take a tremendous mutual dislike and it will never be resolved. There is nothing worse than a dog fight at a shoot and I will not have pickers-up who have dogs which are temperamental in this respect.

It has been said that there are three kinds of dogs – guns' dogs, pickers-up's dogs and beaters' dogs. All have a different purpose. One of the problems with dogs among the beaters is that they turn birds back and catch a lot of unshot pheasants which go into the bag but are a complete waste. The same applies to the dogs being worked by the pickers-up. When pheasants have flown a long way in a drive they are very tired and disinclined to fly again. As a result, over-keen dogs can pick them up when they have never been touched by a shot, especially if they are holed up, recuperating in thick cover. This is why, when a sweep is held on the total number of birds, the person who has chosen a high number so often wins. On a big day, with many high birds, the pickers-up can bring in a large number which have not been shot. Some keepers encourage this unsporting pick-up to increase the bag – and the tips. If an owner X-rayed all the birds in the larder at the end of the day he might have quite a shock.

This is of some importance on let days when guns pay according to the number of birds in the bag. It means that they may be paying for scores of birds they have not shot, at anything up to £18 a bird! Perhaps the answer is to let the birds have something of a rest before the pick-up, when this is practicable.

As my dogs should be prepared to find and bring in every kind of game, I train them to retrieve starlings, which are a pest with us, because I have found that if they will do that they will bring in a woodcock, snipe, magpie or a pigeon, which some dogs simply decline. (My father's spaniel would even retrieve a hedgehog. Having found one it would roll it over in dead leaves until the prickles were completely filled and could then carry it.)

Some dogs can be cured of running in by having them well anchored on a line of about fifteen yards length. This is long enough to turn them over and they soon get sick of that treatment. A few however can never be cured of the habit and have to be pegged down or simply not used for shooting.

No dog can be expected to be absolutely steady before the age of two and a half, in my experience, and some need even longer to learn to resist temptations, particularly if used on big days.

During a drive the dog should always sit a few yards in front of you where you can see him and where he knows you can see him. That way you will eliminate the danger of tripping over him, should you chance to step backwards for some reason. Most birds will fall behind so if he is tempted to break he will have to pass you. This may be enough to make him resist the temptation, but if he does run at least you will have seen him go. You also ensure that no game falls on him.

Another reason for having the dog a few yards clear of you is to ensure that he is not showered with ejected cartridges. It will also minimize the risk of making him deaf. It is now well established that any form of shooting is damaging to the human ear, and not only do most shots wear ear plugs or defenders but so do loaders and close spectators. The structure of the inner ear of the dog is remarkably similar to that of man and, though veterinary evidence does not seem to be available, it would seem very probable that a dog can as easily be shot deaf as a man. In fairness then, some thought should be given, I think, to the possibility of devising some means of protecting a dog's hearing. It would need to be a device that would not irritate the dog while it sat waiting and could easily be removed before it was sent off to retrieve.

Deafness through shooting or natural causes may be a reason why some gun-dogs begin to squeak at the peg when they get older. A squeaking or howling dog – some of them seem to think they are opera stars – is a great nuisance to everyone on a shoot. Further, it is contagious to other dogs. There seems to be no cure, though many have been tried. One gentleman who had a very noisy dog, called Piggy, carried a soda-water siphon in his bag, mainly for its normal purpose but he also used it to squirt his dog in the face whenever it began to squeak! Sad treatment, especially if he had shot the dog deaf.

After I had aired the suggestion that dogs' ears might benefit by protection, in a letter to the *Daily Telegraph*, one reader responded by suggesting that, like humans, dogs feign deafness when they get older to avoid obeying orders. Like humans, they certainly become more stubborn as they age, which is one reason why they need replacement in the shooting field long before they become decrepit.

I always ensure that I have new dogs coming along. While some dogs age more slowly than others, they usually begin to lose their faculties after the age of ten, and few can withstand a hard day in the field after that age. I do not have my dogs destroyed when they have ended their working life, as some do. They have earned a retirement and they get it – as pensioners. But it is not a kindness to an old friend to keep him going when he is really decrepit and probably near-blind and deaf.

I have the fondest memories of my dogs because we have shared so many wonderful times. Perhaps the dog which stands out most vividly was Ben, a marvellous labrador who sired a lot of other dogs for me. He was so good that we promoted him to Mister Ben and then Sir Ben. We eventually jibbed at Lord Ben because that would have reminded me of a certain politician.

As I have already stressed, one should never pick up during a drive. A good dog knows when a drive is over. As soon as I open my gun at the end of a drive to take the cartridges out, my dogs realize their moment has come. But they have to wait to be sent, and I keep tight control over them. I therefore sometimes ask my loader to slip a lead on the dogs before I part with my gun. If I am alone I do it myself, having first unloaded my gun without letting the dogs see me do it. I can shoot 100 cartridges and my dogs will not move during a drive, so they do not need to be on leads then. They are on a lead only when a drive is completely finished and game near the peg needs picking up by hand first.

Occasionally I deliberately refrain from sending my dogs out after a drive so that they do not assume that they will necessarily be sent. It is good for their discipline just to let them sit there and await an order that does not come.

I am diffident about sending any dog to fetch a wounded member of the crow tribe, as they can peck the eyes. This is even more risky with a black-backed gull, particularly a greater black-backed, which sometimes has to be shot because it can do so much damage to game. The strength of these birds is astonishing. On the island of Skokholm, they dig rabbits out of their burrows in the shallow soil, kill them with their great beaks and then, literally, turn them inside out. When they are finished, only the skin is left, turned inside out like a glove. Never send a dog to pick one up – even if it looks dead.

A wounded heron, of course, can be even more dangerous, though nobody apart from river keepers and owners of fish-farms is likely to be shooting herons these days. (A guest of a certain prime minister watched his host put his gun up at a heron and cried, 'Protected! Protected!' 'So are my trout,' the Prime Minister replied.)

One needs to be careful when receiving what a dog retrieves while wildfowling in the dark. I witnessed an occasion when a friend accepted what he thought was a teal from his dog and found it was a live rat which bit him through the thumb. A rare experience, no doubt, but very unpleasant, especially for anyone allergic to rats, as many people are.

When I want my dogs to go into water I like them to jump in with enthusiasm, but one needs to be very careful about sending a dog into a fast current either in a river or the sea. I recall knocking down two wigeon on Read's Island which were carried away by the ebbing tide, and by the time I sent out my two bitch labradors – they were mother and daughter – one bird was about a hundred yards away and the other sixty. They were strong swimmers but I began to wonder if I had made a mistake. They swam together towards the first bird, which was on the route to the second, and it seemed to me that the mother indicated that she would go for the far bird, which she did while the young dog brought in the near one. Eventually, because of the tide the young dog finished up 200 yards down the bank while the old girl came out almost half a mile away. It was the most remarkable double retrieve I have ever seen and I still get a thrill when I think about it, but I doubt whether I would repeat the order under those conditions. It was a lot to ask.

When a river is severely iced over at the edges it can be dangerous to send in a dog because he may not be able to haul himself back over the edge of the ice, with a heavy bird in his mouth, and can exhaust himself trying to do so. A well-trained, determined dog may well do that rather than drop the bird.

I never feed my dog until we return to base, however late. Some guns take food and feed their dogs immediately after shooting is finished, but a long car journey on a full stomach can make some dogs feel sick and even vomit. Arrangements should always be made for dogs to travel in reasonable comfort, especially on long journeys. Some people carry them in the closed boot of the car which looks cruel, and probably is. A wet dog needs to be at least partly dried before the home journey or a long lunch-break, and old towels should be carried for that purpose. A dog can be put in a dry sack loosely tied round the neck. They learn to like it.

No shoot is complete without some good terriers in the keepers' hands to enter earths and other holes and bolt vermin. I ensured that my partridge shoot in Spain was supplied. Until then I never saw a terrier in Spain that would enter an earth. They have made a lot of difference to the vermin control.

Dogs remain a perennial source of wonder to me. For instance, their capacity to recognize another dog as a dog from a long distance is quite remarkable, if you think about it. Dogs vary in size and shape more than any other species of animal, yet a dog travelling at speed in a closed vehicle, and totally dependent on vision, will recognize anything from a tiny Yorkshire terrier to an Irish wolfhound as a dog and react accordingly. I suppose it is remotely possible that, even under those conditions, the dog is using its sense of smell which, according to scientists, is certainly a hundred times, and possibly a thousand times, more sensitive than a man's, and so beyond our comprehension. According to scientists, a dog can sense some substances, like lactic acid, the acid in sour milk, in a strength of only one part in a million in water and can pick out, from a pile of similar pieces of wood, the one which has been handled by its owner for only two seconds.

While nobody likes to see a blind dog, the loss of its nose would be an infinitely greater handicap. A fit dog's hearing is also more acute and can detect sounds beyond the human limit, which is made use of in the ultrasonic silent dog-whistle. It is also superior in detecting the direction from which a sound is coming. So when you tell your dog to stop barking at nothing it is almost sure to be barking at something you have failed to hear.

One of the greatest differences between dogs and humans is their respective reaction to pain. A dog can run headfirst into a table-leg or bash its tail repeatedly, in greeting, against a wall without a squeak of discomfort. This, perhaps, is one of the reasons why attempting to train a dog by ill-treating it, when it does not perform satisfactorily, almost always fails. The result is likely to be a cowed dog, which I hate to see. Rewarding a dog for good performance is a surer way of training it than punishing it for a bad one.

The greatest difference of all, of course, lies in the limited intelligence of the dog. Overestimating a dog's intelligence and expecting it to understand and respond to human standards, which is so easy to do, often leads to pointless and undeserved admonishment.

Dogs are wonderful creatures and marvellous friends but all we have done, over the centuries, is to modify their animal characteristics. The conscious acceptance of the fact that are just animals does not downgrade them but enriches our relationship with them by providing closer understanding.

Chapter 17

Shooting Abroad

Shooting in other countries is always an interesting experience and, of course, to enjoy it fully one needs one's own guns. Following the Hungerford massacre restrictions on the movement and storage of all guns have been intensified. When taking your guns through customs you must have your gun certificate and, if possible, some document such as a receipt showing that the guns are yours and with their numbers on. Your game licence may also be helpful. It is a good idea to have your guns, with their numbers, recorded on your passport, as that can save a lot of time. The guns have to travel in the hold of the aircraft so need to be carefully packed, with the case being protected against damage. The case should, of course, be locked and it is a sensible precaution to secure it further with one of those high-tensile steel bicycle security-chains and a good padlock.

No ammunition may be carried on an aircraft and must be obtained in the country where you plan to shoot.

On exit at the British airport (usually Heathrow) the guns must be shown to the customs officers who will examine the barrels to ensure that they are not rifled. After examination a customs officer will accompany the guns to the aircraft.

As so many people now travel to Spain to shoot, some details of the special procedures involved may be helpful. For shooting in Spain it is necessary to clear matters with the Spanish Consulate General well in advance of the journey. The Consulate will then issue a certificate which eases entry into Spain. On arrival at the airport there (usually Madrid) the guns, in their case, come up on the carousel with the rest of the baggage. They must then be taken, along with the certificate, to a small office, called the Intervencion de Armas. There, payment of a small fee produces a permit, which must be handed in when the guns leave the country.

A local Spanish licence is necessary and your host, or the person arranging the shoot if you are in a paying group, will usually have arranged this in advance. It is quite expensive.

On arrival back at the Spanish airport to return to Britain the guns must be checked in, along with the permit, at the office of the Intervencion de Armas and when that has been done, with the payment of another small fee, the guns can be carried to the check-in desk, with the rest of your luggage, without any escort.

After touch-down back in Britain, where the precautions are more strict, the guns will not appear on the carousel but will be intercepted and brought there on a trolley by an official who will accompany you to the customs hall. There the barrels will be examined again, the numbers checked and your shotgun certificate scrutinized.

Don't expect foreigners to behave in the shooting field as we do: their attitudes are different. It is we who must accommodate to them if we wish to be guests in their country. I have found that most Europeans, for instance, have complete disregard for protected birds and it has been pointless trying to remonstrate with them. There is, however, an increasing awareness, now, that raptors are magnificent birds worthy of respect.

Many foreigners tend to exaggerate the number of game-birds they have shot. They don't feel the necessity to look after people as we do. Sometimes my staff, accompanying me, have been accommodated in appalling conditions, though they have never complained – even to me.

My first shooting foray abroad was in 1966 after I decided to cut down on the preservation of the grey partridges at Rothwell. I found the prospect of life without partridge shooting bleak, and decided to try the wild redleg partridges of Spain. It proved to be a novel experience which I have come to enjoy very much, especially now that I have my own shoot there and can control my companions and the way it is managed and shot.

The birds are, generally, not as exciting or so difficult as the English greys but are still worthy targets. Because they are wild they are much more sporting than the redlegs in Britain, which are nearly all reared birds, and on many of my drives they are very difficult. A wild Spanish redleg from the side of a hill can offer as challenging a target as a man can want, with great acceleration, acrobatic ability and power to stand on its tail and rise or otherwise change direction. I decline to shoot reared redlegs because they are often badly shown, and if I attend a Spanish shoot and find they have begun to rear I do not go again.

On a typical Spanish shoot one has to leave the hotel early, if staying in a town, like Madrid, usually no later than 6.30, to reach the stands. There may be up to sixteen guns, though twelve is the usual number, each provided with one or more *secretarios*, who are responsible for marking and picking up their gun's birds at the end of each drive. The competition, both between the guns and the *secretarios*, is fierce and on many shoots the butts are so close together that it is rare for only one gun to fire at a bird.

There may be one or two dogs, usually a small breed of pointer, but most of the birds are retrieved by the *secretarios*.

The beating tends to be done in a peculiarly Spanish way. The beaters – as many as fifty – make a great deal of noise, blowing horns and shouting, and the birds run forwards over the dry, gritty ground. The drives may take between an hour and an hour and a half and they bring in about 200 hectares, blanking the birds into a bit of cover. Then two or three horsemen come along in line and put a few birds out at a time so that they come over the guns in waves of about eight birds. The beating line does not advance in one continuous line as in Britain. At the end of the drive the horsemen come over the hill without much warning and great care is needed from the guns. On my shoot there are no horsemen, I have many fewer guns – five or six or even less – and the beaters proceed as they do in Britain.

Spanish beaters are the only ones I know to carry umbrellas, which they raise at the slightest drop of rain and also use to protect themselves from the hot sun. On some shoots the keeper stops the drive if it rains heavily. Fortunately in the areas where I shoot there are not many wet days.

Things are done differently on Spanish shoots and this should be realized before you go. On many of them the 'poaching' of other people's birds is quite dreadful and would not be tolerated in Britain. The guns literally shoot at anything anywhere. This, inevitably, increases the danger factor. But what I most dislike is how the guns are judged, regarding their shooting ability, by the number of partridges picked up by the *secretarios* and recorded on the sheet at the end of each drive. Most foreigners are without dogs but some of the Spaniards have two dogs and up to five *secretarios* who collect everything they can from any area, often quite blatantly. Further, the spare birds from a long way behind are all deposited at the Spanish host's stand.

On one occasion I witnessed a so-called Spanish aristocrat put up his gun and threaten to fire to warn off a young boy who was picking a bird I had shot and which had fallen in front of the 'gentleman'. The frightened boy had to put up his elbow to protect his face. This 'aristocrat' is in the habit of going out with a loaded gun after a drive to protect his dead birds from the hands of anyone else's *secretarios* and to finish off anything that is wounded. Some of the Spanish grandees carry a third gun with long barrels, and fully choked, to knock down running birds, if they have been shot or not. I have even seen .22 rifles used for this purpose.

Runners in Spain really do run – much more so than redlegs in Britain. They get between rocks, down holes, anywhere out of sight, and are difficult to find. It does not take a lot of pellets to knock a redleg down but you need them in the centre of the pattern to ensure that they do not run.

There is a lot of betting between guns and *secretarios* and this exacerbates the competition. The Spanish are the worst offenders but one Spaniard, whom I like, told me that this deplorable situation is getting worse because 'so many foreigners are now shooting in Spain!' I have often shown my irritation at this cut-throat competition by handing a number of birds to someone whose intention is to have a big pile of birds, whether he has shot them or not, but the more sensible thing is to treat such people silently with contempt. Lord 'X' is remembered at one shoot where, having shot many birds, he saw his neighbour picking up everything, leaving him with only two, which he threw at the offender, who had not been shooting nearly as well. After any drive, when asked how many I have shot, I deliberately give a much lesser figure to save trouble and strife. I am there for enjoyment. And I have the satisfaction of knowing, from my counter, how many I have shot.

I fear that, in general, when in Spain one has to put up with what the Spanish do or organize one's own party or acquire one's own shoot, which is very difficult. Fortunately I am now an old hand and no longer attend such shoots as I have just described. I now have some wonderful Spanish hosts who know how to behave.

The Spanish partridges are highly variable regarding their speed of flight, much more so, I believe, than the English. Some are quite slow and one needs to shoot *at* them. Others are so fast one needs to keep swinging and see some daylight in front of them. Gauging their speed is all-important in shooting them successfully. As proper butts are not used, the birds see you and climb on their tails faster than a grouse. This must be allowed for by shooting higher than usual, especially at a crossing bird. Shoot over the top of them to kill them in the head.

Very few birds approach the line directly and the majority of the shots are angling and slightly crossing. The birds also tend to come singly or in twos and threes, which makes them easier to shoot than the English birds which come in coveys and are more difficult to pick out.

With a crossing bird at long range the gun needs to be swung and pushed through hard – almost as if you want to knock the brains out of somebody standing close to you!

The secret, with all of them, is always to keep the gun moving. It is extremely difficult to hit a moving target with a stationary gun but so many people try so often.

While wild Spanish partridges are easier to kill, on the whole, than wild English, because they tend to come over singly or in small numbers, there are exceptional days when they are as difficult as any bird that flies. One such day, recorded in detail in my shooting notes, was 23 November 1987 when, with only my wife and I shooting at Nombela, my private shoot, the birds came down from a mountainous area, very fast indeed, at all heights and rising when they saw us, as I have never seen them stand on their tails before. They gave me one of the best day's shooting I have ever had in my life. The air was dry and fresh and the birds driven over cliffs and losing height came so fast that they were like falcons. We ate lunch outside in the sun perched on top of a hill. I felt wonderful and so indescribably content that it is difficult to express in words.

The numbers of partridges killed per year on Spanish shoots are high. At a shoot in Estremadura, for instance, they expect to harvest about 13,000 partridges on about 8000 hectares and still leave a good breeding stock. The huge wild partridge populations in Spain give some indication of what the situation was like in Britain only a few generations ago.

Sixteen guns shot a record bag of 4800 partridges in a day in Spain, some years ago, but this is not really comparable with our 2159 at Rothwell with six guns because our birds were almost all greys and much more difficult.

I have been in a team as a guest with H.M. the King of Spain which killed over 1400 birds in one day and have killed 135 at one stand, my largest.

An additional joy of shooting in Spain, apart from the weather, is the number of wild birds likely to be new to the British visitor – melodious warblers, serins, rock thrushes, bee-eaters, hoopoes, rollers, eagles, eagle-owls, vultures, kites, white storks, black storks, cattle egrets, great and little bustards and birds like the great grey shrike, stone curlew and harriers now, sadly, rare with us. I would like to express my gratitude to Tom Gullick, and to his wonderful wife, Kate, for the enjoyment I have had watching birds with him in Spain, and he taught me a lot about them. I thoroughly recommend a four or five day trip with Tom.

On many pheasant shoots the cry 'Don't shoot the white pheasant!' is common but a white partridge is much rarer. I have seen them in Spain, however, in fact we have had four on our shoot at

Nombela for several seasons and now there are eight which have so far have managed to escape.

Hares and rabbits are plentiful but I do not permit them to be shot by guests because I prefer to reserve them for the locals who hunt the hares with a large type of half-bred greyhound.

There are deer and wild boar, though they are rarely seen during partridge drives. There are also some larger animals which occasionally cause excitement. During a drive on my Nombela estate in November 1988 the distant shouting from the beaters told me that something must be wrong. Suddenly I could hear the pounding of hooves and four wild cows stampeded down the hill towards the butts. Within moments there was hardly a Spaniard in sight. The loaders and the *secretarios*, as well as many of the beaters, were up the trees, one of them still carrying a gun and a cartridge bag! I have to admit that I was pretty smart myself in getting over a wire fence which happened to be handy.

When my friend who had the Nombela shoot died, and the partnership he had was dissolved, I took it over. It stretches from the mountains which border the Province of Avila, Toledo, down to the River Alberche, the nearest town being Escalona, and I have built it up to over 20,000 acres. I go there for a month's shooting in November.

As all who have travelled outside Madrid will know, the nearby countryside to the south is very flat with few trees and the partridges there have no incentive to fly high. At Nombela, however, we are in the foothills of quite high mountains and the terrain is not only undulating with little valleys but wooded, mainly with evergreen oaks. As a result, many of the partridges fly well.

The shoot is made up of many small, separate holdings so I deal with the farmers collectively through the mayor, who is very left-wing. Fortunately, my wife and others of my family speak fluent Spanish and that is a great help.

I retained the existing keepers, apart from one, and villagers do the beating and loading and *secretario* retrieving. The catering for the lunches, which are open-air barbecue picnics whenever possible, is also done locally and very satisfactorily.

The village gets a bonus for every partridge shot and this can be spent on whatever the locals decide. Sometimes, to get some concession for the shoot, we have to provide something special, such as a new village clock. The arrangement brings a lot of money into the community and, as I have been at pains to point out to various politicians and in journals, like *Country Life*, the same could be done here with pheasant shoots and especially on the heather uplands, with grouse.

I have applied English standards to the shoot and, to expedite this, Spanish keepers have been to see how we run our grouse moors, staying at Middleton, while my keepers go out to Spain.

My Spanish keepers are instructed to feed the partridges in the mountainous parts of those areas from which we drive them over the guns because food may be scarce and some corn scattered there can save a lot of driving-in over such terrain. To check that this is being done and ensure that the birds are getting enough to eat I weigh a sample of the partridges in each drive. In drought years, when nothing is green, a little extra feed is very helpful.

It has given me enormous pleasure and satisfaction to re-create Rothwell all over again in Spain, forty years later. Our bags vary with the weather and with the competence of the guns. The average bag per gun per day is about eighty wild birds. We are still building up the shoot and have had considerable success in keeping down the magpies, which invade us and do great damage.

H.M. the King of Spain has honoured us with his presence at Nombela several times and my wife and I have had the privilege of being his guests on several occasions. In November 1987 we arrived at the castle-shooting lodge of Mudela in time for dinner on the previous evening and, in a delightful custom, the King presented me with a partridge feather in the form of a hat-brooch which, at my request, he pinned on personally. I had first met him, several years before, when we were both guests at another shoot. As I had no dog, the Prince, as he then was, had helped me to pick up with his black labrador. His Majesty is a wonderful sportsman and an unselfish shot.

There is excellent duck shooting to be had in Spain and this can be fitted in with the partridge shooting. One sets off before dawn for the morning flight and the surroundings are very beautiful as the sun comes up. The duck come in very fast and they are difficult.

There are a few good places for duck in Holland but my main experience with them in Europe has been in Spain and in France, at Grand Lieu, near Nantes, where my friend, Jean-Pierre Guerlain, owns several thousand acres. He and his wife, Christiane, shoot some part of it every Saturday during the season, unless they are in Spain. When I shot there on 6 September 1980 I was told that the hide would not be big enough for a loader but, in fact, there was almost room to hold a dance in it, compared with some I have encountered. My wife was in the next hide – about two miles away. I started to fire at 7.15 a.m. and the ducks just kept coming. By the time I unloaded, at 12.50, I had clocked on the counter 239 mallard, 2 shovelers, 1 teal and 1 wood pigeon. It had become very warm and the midges were there in profusion but the repellent, Autan, was very effective.

The following year on 29 August there were not so many ducks but I had 148 and my wife, who shot really well, had 124. This earned her a gold medal which Christiane had offered for any lady who topped 100 ducks, as the donor has done herself.

I understand that M. Guerlain has left the lake to the French nation in his will, the plan being to make it a nature reserve with no shooting.

I have not done much pheasant shooting abroad but understand that some of the let days in Hungary and Czechoslovakia can provide large numbers, though they tend to be low. However, I do not like the thought of staying in the house of the previous owner who was kicked out by the Communists.

I have shot some very good pheasants on the Dutch polders, in a wind, with Prince Bernhard, and in France, where I enjoyed some good days on shoots which no longer exist. On one January day, in Austria, which was limited to cocks only, which flew well, I had the pleasure of contributing to a bag of 1200.

Twenty-five years ago, I also took part in an extraordinary pheasant shoot in Northern Italy, as a guest of the Marquis of Vistorini. I knew that H.R.H. Prince Philip had been there and, when I was invited, I asked him if I should go. 'Yes. Go once,' H.R.H. counselled. The birds turned out to be the highest I have ever seen. They were all hand-reared and were driven up to the top of a hill. There were teams of beaters doing this so that there was a succession of high-bird drives. Some of the birds had been released for several months and some for only a week or so, and they flew at different speeds. Most of them were dropping pheasants, which always fly deceptively fast – much faster than a crossing bird. There were three lines of guns – the weakest in the first row, the strongest in the third. Anyone in the back rows needed to watch out for falling birds, which could be lethal, plummeting from such a height.

In the 1960s I was a guest of the Marquis Gigetto Medici del Vascallow who had one of the summer palaces of a late King of Italy. The palace seemed to be hundreds of yards long, so long that it was difficult to find one's bedroom and one had therefore to memorise the paintings on the walls to identify it. The Marquis was a great anglophile and helped the British during the retreat of the Germans towards the end of the war. He had lots of people hiding on his estate, and he used to bicycle round to feed them. He was a wonderful host in every way who understood shooting and presented his birds beautifully.

There are syndicated pheasant shoots in Florida but I have participated in only the barbequed lunch which always accompanies these happy occasions.

My shooting in the United States, where I have a house which I occupy when the English shooting season ends, has included regular days with the bobwhite quail, a small, fast and very difficult target. It averages only about six ounces in weight.

I am fortunate to have had a friend in the late John Olin who owned Nilo (Olin spelled backwards) Plantation, a 12,000 acre estate in Georgia, about ten minutes' drive from Albany airport. It consists mainly of pine plantations planted in strips, with clover, peas and strips of maize between, grown specially for the quail. Peanuts and pecan trees provide some additional return on what is a heavy investment. They also grow some wheat on another part of the estate. I have also enjoyed days as a guest at other famous quail plantations, Pinebloom with John Harbert III, and Merrily – an area of 11,000 acres – owned by Senator Flowers.

For quail shooting one travels, most agreeably, in a wagon pulled by a pair of matching mules and with pointers in boxes underneath at the back. There are two outriders and when one of the dogs stops on point, two postillions, riding at the back of the cart, jump off, hand a gun to each of the two who are going to shoot and then grab the dog-handler's horse. The pointers are well trained and a delight to watch.

When the covey of quail gets up the guns shoot and, again, one needs to do so as soon as the gun comes to the shoulder, mounting and firing in one movement. The coveys are very big – eighteen to twenty birds being quite common. There is a noise and a sudden explosion – what they call the covey rise – as the birds jump and this can be off-putting to the inexperienced. Some go straight up in the air, some seem to fly directly at you, and they are all extremely clever at putting a tree between themselves and a gun.

Quail shooting can also be frustrating, for one can get down from the wagon, full of expectancy because a dog is pointing, and then the covey gets up way out of shot. Still, just going round on the wagon is a lovely way to spend a day, whether you get any shooting or not. Like all shooting, it can be spoiled by too many guns, for one is not down often enough if there are more than four guns to a wagon. I have had the pleasure of shooting with my son, Charles and I being the only two guns on a wagon.

John Olin, who was a brilliant shot, had a good rule that not more than four birds could be shot out of one covey. When that number had been obtained a new covey had to be found.

The weather is the major factor in shooting quail, the right wind being all-important. Bags are not large. Mr Olin averaged about 1600 for the season in the 1970s.

It is usually hot during the day, but warmer clothes may be needed for the start in the morning.

The chief enemy of the quail seems to be the opossum which eats the eggs, but rats and bobcats do a lot of damage. The guns may have problems with rattlesnakes: I have heard of fourteen being killed in one day – with a stick. The occasional horse and pointer fall victim.

Quail shooting must be the most expensive kind of formal bird-shooting in the world but it is a joy to be part of it with the horses, dogs and staff so well turned out. The standard reminded me of a meet of the Quorn Hounds in Leicestershire.

Before I went to America to shoot, in the fifties, I bought 4000 bobwhite quail eggs, incubated them and turned out the resulting 2000 young at Rothwell. They could not be driven as they do not fly far enough in one direction, but we had some fun walking them up and continued to get some over a few seasons. A few were hatched in the wild and I recall watching about twenty quail chicks with my mother who was fascinated by such tiny birds. They travelled for up to five miles around and people kept reporting that they had seen a strange bird but after four or five years there was not one to be seen. Not one of my best experiments!

I was introduced to dove shooting in Morocco in 1980. There are large numbers of birds, called tortorels, which come at all heights, mostly extremely high, in a strong wind and are very difficult – gliding, soaring, twisting and providing practice for every kind of game-bird one can imagine. A lot of them fly like snipe; others like woodcock; some like grouse or partridges or even high pheasants. On the first day I fired about 300 cartridges for 98 birds during 3 hours of shooting. We stood on a sand track near a hedge about twelve feet high on the flight-path between their feeding and roosting quarters. Apparently they can be shot at day after day from the same place during the season and will continue to come.

On the second day I got 111 down for 240 shots. The high, wide swingers were not easy to hit. We shot two more days and my wife killed over 100 in one afternoon, which was a fine performance. By deliberately trying to miss them in front I performed better, downing 151 birds with 270 shots.

I have enjoyed my shooting abroad and hope to continue to do so but have no hesitation in saying that the best all-round shooting in the world is in the lovely island of Britain.

Chapter 18

Some 'Big Shots'

The term Big Shots has come to be associated with those legendary stalwarts of the Edwardian era, like Lord Walsingham, Lord Ripon and King Edward himself. It applied to their determination and ability to shoot enormous quantities of game. In my book, the word 'Big' applies to bigness of heart as well as to skill and enthusiasm.

A high degree of skill is desirable but enthusiasm is essential and, happily, I have been endowed with that, perhaps to an unusual degree. For most of my life I have been well and truly hooked on shooting and, had I been deprived of it for any length of time, I am sure that I would have suffered from withdrawal symptoms.

From experience, some people find that they can shoot too much and become stale and perform badly. One or two days a week is ample for them. That has never happened to me. The more I shoot the better I shoot. Every bird is different and a challenge. It may sound exaggerated, after so many years, but every day that I wake up and know that I am going shooting I am still excited by the prospect. I have heard people say that if they shot for more than two days a week they would get sick of it. They could be right and the fact that I have never done so is a great blessing, for which I have been ever grateful.

My other great blessing has been my health which has enabled me to continue into old age. Sadly, some who love their shooting have to give up in late middle age for various medical reasons. They include my beloved younger brother, Sam, who was one of the finest – and quickest – shots of his generation and a delightful companion in the shooting field, as all who know him aver. We shared the experience of The Great Day, when we set the wild

grey partridge record, and many other memorable shoots. In fact
we were inseparable and planned each season together, well ahead.

Though greatly incapacitated by multiple sclerosis, he remains
cheerful and still enjoys an occasional shot or two in the line, sitting
in a chair, and was with us on the opening day of the grouse at
Reeth in 1988. When he receives my invitations he replies, 'I will
come and make a noise.' When he cannot shoot he loves to watch
and relive his old experiences, for shooting was an essential part
of his existence.

It is always heartening to see a man simply refuse to be beaten
by disability, as brother Sam has done for many years, and David
Wigan is another such admirable individual. He is a brilliant
one-handed shot who suffered severe arm damage from polio but
was not to be defeated.

The late Guy Moreton was one of the best shots of all time, being
not only accurate but very quick and rarely in need of a second
barrel at a bird. He used to tell his friends that if he dropped
dead during a shoot (which would have been his chosen way to
go) they all had to fire two wild shots each and then carry on.
Born in 1904, he found that his parents wanted him only to run
their estate, Pickenham Hall, near Swaffham in Norfolk, when it
became due to him, and meanwhile to do nothing but enjoy himself.
It was a requirement which he fulfilled brilliantly until his death
in 1987. Even during his war service in the RAF he managed to
get some excellent duck shooting in North Africa. He loved all
country pursuits, but especially shooting, at which he became a
renowned artist. While Guy was shooting grouse with Jim Joel at
Dallowgill soon after the war, an old man who had loaded for the
great Lord Ripon watched him shoot and remarked to the other
loaders, 'There goes a future Marquis of Ripon.' As has also been
said of me, 'Guy did most things he wanted to do and very few
that he did not.'

One meets a few dour people who are good shots but, happily,
they are rare. Going to happy shoots run by happy people means
meeting the same old friends every season. Pickenham was such a
shoot and we spent many days together full of laughter. As some

poet put it, 'There's little worth the wear of winning, save laughter and the love of friends.'

Guy was kindness itself and very modest about his shooting skill. He was seldom without his gun in his car in case there might be an opportunity to shoot a pigeon or two. On one occasion he came to the July open day at Rothwell to see the hundreds of acres of cereal field trials, and was asked what he thought of it all. His response was that he hadn't seen a young bird all day!

Once, when he and three friends, who were shooting cock-pheasants, came to what was believed to be a deserted church tower, he suggested that they should take the opportunity to get rid of the predatory jackdaws which inhabited it. Having stationed his friends he banged on the old oak door and shouted, 'Come out, you bastards!' The jackdaws obliged and were duly dispatched, whereupon there was a creaking sound, the door opened and a little old man put his head out to say, 'Excuse me, Sir, but we are holding a service here.'

Guy was a wonderful friend and the many hours we spent together in the shooting and hunting fields are among my warmest memories.

The late Fred Davy, DFC, AFC, was another marksman who loved his shooting. When his daughter was being born he telephoned me to say it was 'just like waiting for the geese to flight'. He was one of the six guns on our Great Day along with the Dennis brothers, Peter and Richard and Leonard Lamyman who were all fine shots. Sadly, Dick and Len are no longer with us.

Squire Hague of Grainsby Hall, who owned many thousands of acres between the Lincolnshire Wolds and the sea, was almost a caricature of the old country gentleman, and for some reason he took an interest in me, inviting me to see his remarkable collection of bird skins. They were all beautifully preserved in chests of drawers and ended up, I believe, in the British Museum. (In those days the ornithologists tended to shoot the rare-looking birds to aid in their identification – a habit which is now properly deplored and, indeed, is usually illegal.)

Sometimes he would shoot six days a week, a more formidable

programme than it is today, when the travelling between shoots is so much easier and quicker.

He used to shoot geese under the moon and he taught me a lot. He was very strong, using a double-barrelled 4 bore, with which a right and left is so satisfying, and even had a single-barrelled 2 bore which he fired from the shoulder! When he got old he had his chauffeur standing behind to prop him up when he discharged the 2 bore at a high goose.

He loved fox-hunting and he ensured that his coverts always held foxes but I never saw him on a horse. Instead he followed on foot, using a long pole for jumping hedges and ditches. His like no longer seem to exist or, if they do, I do not have the pleasure of meeting them.

Another eccentric 'marsh-man', as the farmers and landowners in that area were known, as opposed to 'wolds-man', was a rich farmer called Jack Caudwell. He was a bachelor and when he arrived home wet through after shooting would just lie in front of a blazing fire like a huge dog until he dried. He did not like women in the house and it was widely believed that this was the result of having been jilted. He treated his land with greater care than he treated himself and was an exceptionally successful farmer.

Another man who never wore an overcoat was the late Colonel Bill Stirling, who had a great reputation in the shooting world and was marvellous company – one of the best companions God ever put breath into. He and his distinguished brother, David, who founded the SAS, in which they both served most gallantly, were brought up to regard rain as an inevitable part of the Scottish scene. If you happened to be out in it you got wet but, like a sheep, you dried off eventually. When Bill, who was fairly thin, came to shoot at Wemmergill he would go out in all weathers wearing little more over his shoulders than a thin grey shirt, though, on occasion, he might don an interesting, well-worn jersey. He always wore shoes and waded through burns as though they did not exist.

He inherited a magnificent estate at Keir, in Scotland, which his family had owned for centuries and over which he drove a

Land-Rover, terrifyingly, as though it were a tank. His guests enjoyed wonderful shooting at Keir, especially on a dam between two lochs on the Ardoch beat where my brother Sam and I would shoot thirty or forty duck and then the geese – greylags and pink-feet would start to come over. On one occasion a flock of eight dark birds flew towards us and we saw that they were coots. We were shooting two guns and we managed to down the lot, taking four each and never firing at the same bird, though two of them fell to one barrel.

Bill's son, Archie, is continuing the tradition and shoots very well.

The late Felix Fenston was another kind and generous host at Druids Lodge, Helmsley and in Scotland. His widow, Greta, has learned to shoot very well.

Lord Rank, the former J. Arthur Rank, was another shooting friend with whom I shared many memorable days. I shot with him regularly in October at Sutton Scotney, where he had hand-reared grey partridges, and in January we had fine sport with the wild pheasants. For fifteen years he rented the late Lord Cawdor's 30,000-acre grouse moor at Drynachan, about twenty-two miles inland from Nairn, on the River Findhorn, and built nearly eighty miles of access roads with amusing names on it, like Trafalgar Square, Charing Cross, etc.

Lord Buxton is a keen shot and one of the few who really understand the countryside and wild life, as witness the wonderful wild life television programmes produced by Anglia Television which he controlled for many years.

One of my firmest and most delightful friends, who perpetually jokes about his shortness of stature, but is truly a big man in every other way, is Lord Forte. He took up serious shooting fairly late in life but few people are keener or secure greater enjoyment from it. A day at his shoot on his estate at Ripley or at Helmsley, which he rents for the high pheasants, is a day in the heart of a wonderful family – Charles's greatest joy. He is still shooting, though he has passed eighty, and bids fair to continue for quite a few seasons yet.

Over the years it has given me great pleasure to watch his son, Rocco, develop into a safe, clean and accurate shot. His enthusiasm, not just for shooting but for shoot management, is evident from the way he has improved the pheasant shoot at Ripley by devising means of improving the quality of the birds on what is almost entirely flat land. He is a worthy successor to his father in all respects, especially in business.

Sir Thomas Sopwith, who has recently died aged 101, was shooting into his eighties and, so long as he could see the birds, was shooting well. His wife was also a nailing shot on her day. They were determined to keep going as long as they could and that, Sir Thomas believed, was one of the reasons why they lived so long. When Lady Sopwith was over eighty she needed an electronic heart pace-maker: she insisted on having it inserted into her left side so that she could get her gun up to her right shoulder!

She was a formidable lady who wore a green shooting outfit complete with a diamond hat-brooch of whichever bird she was shooting and became known, affectionately, as the Green Dragon. She knew how to run a house so well that I begged her to pass on her expertise to others.

There have been many women who realized that if they did not learn to shoot or at least to pick up they would become shooting widows, and Lady Sopwith was one of them. She came to love the sport, as my wife does, increasing my own pleasure in the process.

The Sopwiths' last working labrador, from the Sandringham strain, was called Brandy, one of a long line of convivially named dogs which included Gin and Rum.

I greatly admired Sir Thomas's attitude when reminiscing over his days in the field: 'We spent a lot on sport but I don't regret a penny of it. I'd paid my taxes and we not only created a lot of enjoyment but a lot of employment. However long you live you are only the short-term tenant of your wealth, so why not enjoy it?'

On my list of 'big' people I must include Charles Wyvill and his wife Maggie, who are so expert at putting people up for shooting at Constable Burton, their lovely home near Bedale in Yorkshire.

Most good shots can also be described as good sports, though there are exceptions. H.R.H. Prince Philip, the Duke of Edinburgh, is high on my list as a good sport. He was shooting with me at Rothwell in October 1960 on a day when four of us shot 1680 wild partridges. He was wearing wet-weather clothing but when the rain ceased at the end of a drive he bent down to take off his over-trousers. I happened to look out of my vehicle and saw my colleague, John Denton, about to move forward in the Land-Rover which he had driven up to take the Duke to the next stand. I realized that he could not see the Duke bending down in front of the radiator and shouted to him to stop – just in time. All the Duke did was to grin and say to me, 'Thanks, that was a near one!'

On another occasion, after a very dark downpour during lunch, he exclaimed, 'It's clearing up. I can see a cloud!'

H.R.H. Prince Charles has shot partridges and pheasants with me at Rothwell, when he was undergoing pilot training at Cranwell nearby, and he has even been in July to shoot wood pigeons. He has also shot grouse as my guest at Wemmergill. He is an excellent and stylish shot with a fine sense of sportsmanship, showing great consideration to others. On 26 August 1974 he helped us to shoot $251\frac{1}{2}$ brace of grouse, taking many of them well in front, and, on 7 September 1978, 387 brace, contributing much more than his share!

H.R.H. Princess Anne, the Princess Royal, does not shoot but enjoys picking up with labradors which work well for her and accompanies her husband, Captain Mark Phillips, who has been several times to Rothwell. He really enjoys his shooting and does it well, improving every year.

King Juan Carlos of Spain, in whose company I have spent some time, is a delightful shooting companion, very friendly and popular with all the beaters, gamekeepers and staff. He shoots well and has an excellent sense of humour.

Royalty pose special problems when they are guests, not only in connection with the security which is now required. The other guests must be chosen carefully. Inveterate gossipers must be avoided when any titbit about Royals is picked up so avidly by the media. The simplest solution is to keep a visit by Royals private but if this is impossible, as it often is, it is wise to come to an agreement with the media. For example, with the Royal permission, one can agree to a photo session before the shoot begins – at the house, not on the shoot – on the understanding that there will be no more. You yourself are bound to life-long secrecy concerning anything you see or hear which could embarrass your guests, or your hosts if you are the guest.

Through my various business interests and through shooting abroad I have had the good fortune to meet some of the best foreign shots, most of whom have been to Britain to shoot with me, but have space to name but a few of them.

When eighty years of age, Jean-Pierre Guerlain, who owns the big duck lake at Grand Lieu, which I have described, drove himself and his wife down from Paris to Nantes every Friday of the whole shooting season from the end of July right through to March to shoot on the Saturday. Then he drove himself back on the return journey on Sunday via another house where they have some wild boar and shot there. You cannot stay much keener than that.

Jean, the Comte de Beaumont, now 86, is an all-round French sportsman, embracing football, steeplechasing and motor racing, as well as shooting, which he loves. He is a wonderful host.

Claude Foussier is probably the best shot in France, even though he lost one eye in a shooting accident, and is certainly one of the keenest.

Leo Biaggi de Blassi, an Italian-Swiss, who invited me to Spain and to his house at La Ronca, was immensely keen on his shooting. I went as his guest regularly, sometimes twice a year, and he came to shoot grouse with me. He lived for shooting.

Pepe Mora-Figuero, who owns the Los Quintos and Los Lonas partridge shoots in Spain, is an artist at presenting good birds and shooting them so cleanly, well into his eighties. He is a living legend. For years he has employed two people full time mounting the heads of game he has shot!

My American friend, John Olin, loved shooting and everything and everybody connected with it. He had a most inquiring mind, wanting to learn everything about the quarry, especially the quail. He is greatly missed.

Shooting with people like those I have described has given me enormous pleasure but the greatest joy and satisfaction of all has derived from shooting with my own family.

My father loved shooting and so did my mother and when my brother, Sam, and I became really keen he gave us a little shoot at Thoresway, next to Rothwell, which was one of the most wonderful things he could have done. He encouraged us in every way he could, along with my brother Ben who, though not as keen as Sam and me, is a good shot.

I have tried to do the same for my children and grandchildren. With the exception of my daughter, Diana, who plumped for riding and hunting, they all shoot and I am lucky to have a wife who loves shooting and now really excels at it. As I have said, there are occasions on the grouse moor when the whole line is made up of Nickersons and it is quite splendid, at my age, to see them all shooting so well. They all have their own dogs and derive extra pleasure from picking up what they have knocked down.

Another debt I owe to shooting.

Chapter 19

Taking Stock – Some Final Thoughts

On the first occasion when I met the late Sir Charles Clore it was on a high pheasant drive on the edge of a grouse moor in Scotland and I happened to bring down two rather spectacular-looking blackcocks with a right and left. He came to me at the end of the drive and said, 'I wish I could shoot like you,' to which I responded, 'If you could shoot like me you would not have such a big business.'

I am often asked how I have managed to shoot so much and initiate and run a successful business. Much of my work has been accomplished as a result of foreign visits which I have been able to concentrate out of the shooting season when I do most of my year's work. But the main answer is that I have good and reliable staff and have confidence in delegating work to them. One needs to pick the right people, know exactly what you want them to do, explain it to them and leave them to get on with it while checking regularly on progress. Expect efficiency but not miracles. I tell my staff that if they make ten decisions and six turn out to have been sensible they are on the right track. Then I make sure that they are, by organizing my time so that I can keep tabs on my business enterprises.

For those who might be interested, here is a typical day during the several weeks when I am at Middleton-in-Teesdale at my house where I stay for grouse shooting in the North of England:

I get up at 7 a.m., called by my man who has my clothes ready. By half past seven I am down in my study and I have the weather report, with the wind direction and speed, and talk to the keepers about the plan for the day. My secretary comes at quarter to eight and by the time I get through breakfast at 8.15 or so I have set various things in motion. Then I'm back to my study, by which time the post has arrived and I deal with that. On the way to the moor I will read the business news. On the way back from the moor, in the late afternoon, I speak on the car telephone to the Rothwell Office and deal with any immediate problems. I make regular use of my pocket tape-recorder, even in the grouse butt to put down any ideas which might surface.

I usually get about half an hour's sleep on the return journey in the Range-Rover and, on reaching home, my secretary is waiting for me with more news. I talk to various people on the telephone including, of course, my personal assistant at Rothwell. I talk to my business manager. Then I have electric massage by two men followed by a short sleep until I am awakened for a long hot bath prior to dinner.

While shooting demands concentration, it is surprising how many good ideas float into one's mind while standing waiting for the birds or moving between drives. I suppose it is because one is free from major conscious thought and the subconscious, where much is going on all the time, is able to intrude itself. This reminds me of the story that used to be told about how the Germans recruited people for government work. They divided the candidates into four categories – clever and industrious, clever and idle, stupid and industrious, stupid and idle. The top jobs were always given to the clever and idle because they were the ones most likely to produce original ideas. The important routine work was given to the clever and industrious and the rest to the stupid and idle. The stupid and industrious were never hired because they could be guaranteed to cause mayhem with whatever they touched.

Looking back, I am in no doubt that shooting has made a major contribution to the modest success I have achieved by enabling me to make many friends, far more quickly than would otherwise have been the case.

For some reason, friendships ripen on the shooting field at a rate unparalleled by any other social activity. It was my love of shooting which brought me friends at every level of society. The shooting field is also a wonderful place for learning, quickly, who you can – and cannot – trust.

I use my shoots to give pleasure to my family and friends. They have permitted me to enjoy the special pleasure of giving because so many people appreciate a good day's shooting more than anything else, especially on the grouse moor. One can see the pleasure in their faces all day long and a good day lingers in the memory like nothing else.

Running a shoot purely for pleasure gives satisfaction to oneself and joy to one's family and guests. It also enables the owner to keep a master's eye on the whole estate. My staff know that I am going to notice everything – a rickety stile, a bit of loose wire, a diseased tree that should have been removed. As a result everything tends to be in good order.

Some years ago, I took the view that, because of the impact of the Common Market and other economic factors, the agricultural value of land would go down while the leisure value would rise. It seemed that 'leisure land' would be a sensible investment for the future. I knew that moors and hill farms were not an investment on which one would get a good annual return on capital but, if properly managed and improved, they should appreciate. I therefore sold some outlying farms, keeping the shooting rights, and bought my grouse moors. I have had no reason to regret the decision to date, and the professional view is that the trend will continue in line with generally improving prosperity. Of course, it will continue to be essential to improve the capacity of the moors to hold sheep and birds by managing the heather crop.

We should never lose sight of shooting's prime purpose, which should be to provide pleasure and healthy recreation. It should be fun, not only for the guns but for keepers, beaters, loaders, drivers and everyone else involved, especially one's family.

It gives me tremendous satisfaction that twelve members of my family enjoy themselves shooting with me – two sons, two sons-in-law, three daughters, two brothers, one nephew, a grandson and my wife. As recently as the Glorious Twelfth of 1988, seven of the family accounted for over 300 brace of grouse, shooting as a team, in a high wind, in the heather of Reeth Moor, in only five drives.

Through God's goodness to me I have been extremely fortunate in enjoying robust health and believe that shooting has played a substantial role in maintaining it by taking me away from stress. I have had my full share of temporary setbacks, which were inevitable to anyone operating on the sharp edge of technology in such an area as genetics in agriculture, but have managed to weather them. Being able to forget the problems for a few hours in the shooting field, when one cannot think of anything else, has always helped.

By the time some people have reached my age, seventy-five, they find that they do not want to go on shooting, mainly because they no longer wish to make the effort or they are unable to do so for medical reasons. Poor vision is probably the commonest ageing symptom which forces people to give up the sport, though occasional dizziness is another and is a potent reason for putting away one's lethal instruments.

At the time of writing I have not yet reached that phase, thank God, either through ill health or diminishing enthusiasm, as witness the archive entry of my behaviour on 17 October 1988:

> Having returned to Lincolnshire from the grouse moor on the previous evening, my wife and I went duck shooting early in the morning. The birds flew well and we shot 106 mallard, my wife accounting for 49 of them. After lunch, at the Nickerson Arms, I received the Queen's Award on behalf of one of my companies, presented by the Lord Lieutenant. Then after making a short speech and circulating among the guests, I did some work in my study before going out to shoot duck again at the evening flight. Then at 7 p.m. we set out back to the grouse moor, arriving at Middleton-in-Teesdale soon after 9, having eaten a snack on the way. A busy day!

In any endeavour in which one has striven hard in the pursuit of competence it is not unnatural, and can be enlightening, to make comparison with some outstanding performer of the past. My obvious choice – through admiration, and perhaps a touch of envy – is Earl de Grey, who later became the Second Marquis of Ripon and has already been mentioned in my narrative. Someone suggested lightheartedly that we should look carefully at the published bags of Lord Ripon, and compare them with the archive records in my own game books. We came up with this little piece of information which I give with due modesty, at the request of the publisher. In a long life devoted mainly to shooting – he dropped dead at the age of seventy-one after killing his fifty-second grouse on 23 September 1923 – he shot a tremendous tally of game, over half a million. This total, however, included large numbers of rabbits and hares, which were abundant in those days and were regarded as an essential part of the sport at every shoot, whereas today they are much fewer and rarely engaged.

If only birds are included and a comparison is made between Lord Ripon's last twenty-four full seasons and my last twenty-four, (he died half-way through his last) and my last twenty-four from 1965 (I had given up fox-hunting earlier) until 1988 then my total turns out to be slightly greater. Documentary records show that from 1899 to 1922 Lord Ripon shot 187,763 head of birds, an annual average of 7,823. From 1966 to 1988 I accounted for 188,172, an annual average of 7,841. For the three last seasons I used nothing but 28 bores and for the fourteen seasons before those, only 20 bores (all made by Purdeys), while the Marquis always used 12 bores, so far as I know.

I draw this comparison to show what a remarkable game country Britain still is, though so much shooting land has been lost to intensive farming, development, motorways and airfields, so much heather has been allowed to waste away on the moors and so much marshland has been drained, compared with the Marquis's day. Such development is bound to continue but, with more farmland being set aside for leisure, the outlook is by no means bleak so long as the European bureaucrats and Parliamentarians, who have so little to lose in their own countries, are not allowed to call the tune as to what Britons may and may not do in their own countryside.

If my total seems excessive I can say, with certainty, that so far as pheasants, grouse, partridges and mallard are concerned I have put back far more than I have shot, through rearing and management, and with respect to the rest – pigeons, wildfowl, snipe and woodcock – I have created or improved environments for them. Scores, probably hundreds, of other people have made similar contributions.

The easiest person to delude is oneself but I hope I shall be the first to realize it if my performance begins to slip badly through age or I cease to find it satisfying or become a nuisance. That will be the time to call it a day. Pray God that sad day is still some time away. I have had so many wonderful days since I turned seventy that, being an incorrigible optimist, I go on in the belief that the best is yet to come. The past season, 1988, fulfilled that prospect for, once again, I managed to shoot more than 3000 grouse and keep my average of over 2000 wild partridges in Spain, as well as a goodly number of pheasants and duck.

Once I have given up, provided I still have my wits about me, I will have the most wonderful store of memories. In that connection I am reminded of a true story about Sir Thomas Sopwith, the aeronautics pioneer, international yachtsman, sportsman and traveller. When in his late eighties, blind and often lonely, he was asked what he tended to think about. With a uniquely varied experience to choose from he answered, 'I think about shooting and fishing. They were my golden days.'

I have never had the time to enjoy much fishing and rate myself a poor angler, but I shall have one advantage over him – the detailed archives of my shooting life which I have kept over the years and the collection of photographs of my companions in the shooting field to jog my memory.

One of the most rewarding aspects of my shoots has been, and remains, the amount of additional employment I have been able to provide, both full-time and part-time. Keepers whom I have trained are employed in many parts of Britain. Whole families have assisted me, from fathers down to grandchildren, and, if I should live long enough, great grandchildren. Shooting has played an important role in the development of Rothwell, which is a happy and friendly community.

There have been so many hundreds of days when I have been able to say to myself, in all honesty, that there was nowhere in the world where I would rather be at that time. I am what, in modern parlance, would be called a rather mature student who knows he still has much to learn and is keen to learn it.

Shooting has taught me so much, not least about human nature, including my own. It has repeatedly underlined the fact that little in life materializes without persistent effort. Along with farming, it has taught me to respect Nature. It has taught me respect for the birds we shoot and the creatures we preserve. It has taken me to so many marvellous places that the wonders of creation never cease to astonish and to awe me. If life is about fulfilment, shooting has helped to fulfil mine in rare measure.

I understand, from my editor, that some of my friends have been kind enough, without my knowledge, to pay some tributes to me. This book is my tribute to them. It is also my salute to the game-birds – the partridges from the fields, the grouse out of the heather, the pheasants from the woods and the wildfowl off the marshes.

Some Tributes to Sir Joseph Nickerson from His Friends
Selected by the Editor

On hearing that Sir Joseph Nickerson was to publish his shooting memoirs, many of his companions in the shooting field seized the opportunity to make brief tributes to him as a shot, shoot manager and shooting host. Here is a selection of some of them.

From Lord Forte:
Sir Joseph Nickerson – Joe to his friends, and he has many friends – is unique. There is no one that I have ever met or known of to rival him in the art of shooting. His is probably the best shot in Britain. His shoots are immaculate, with beautifully driven and testing birds to shoot at – a model for all of us to follow. His training of keepers is perfect.

On the commercial side, in Rothwell, a tiny village in Lincolnshire, he has created an enormous business in seeds, ducks and pigs. His farming is exemplary.

These words may sound effusive but they are factual. Joe Nickerson is a great Great Britisher.

From Sir Alex Alexander (Chairman of J. Lyons and Co. and director of many other companies):
There can be few people, if any, who can excel Joe Nickerson as a shot, as a host or as a friend. His knowledge of shooting and its environment is enormous. We became friends some thirty-five years ago and I have had the pleasure of shooting with him ever since. I must add that his wife, Eugenie, adds

to the pleasure by being such a charming – and decorative – hostess.

From the Comte Jean de Beaumont, a famous French sportsman: One of the best pheasant shoots, perhaps in all England, belongs to my friend Joe Nickerson in Lincolnshire. He produces chickens, ducks, turkeys and geese commercially and they sell in millions throughout the world. As a stockbreeder he is naturally well placed to raise his own breed of pheasant. Small in size and without a white collar, his pheasants fly extremely well. This man seems to live for game shooting. August sees him on the grouse moors and he proves to his hosts what a remarkable shot he is. In turn he invites them to shoot on his moors, one of which is highly reputed: then he leaves for Spain to shoot his red-legged partridges before returning to England to shoot his own and his friends' pheasants. But if Nickerson is a devotee of shooting he is a man no less well dedicated to all matters. He and his wife, Eugenie, make a team which spreads contentment all around them.

From Lord Prior: It was the last drive of a very warm August day. We stood in the butts waiting for the grouse and trying to keep the midges at bay. I was in the next butt to my host, Joe Nickerson. As is my experience with all great shots, the birds seemed determined to fly over his butt. I noticed a covey of eight grouse approaching him. Joe fired six shots in quick succession. No grouse flew on: he had got the lot!

He always knew and remembered where his birds had fallen and where his guests' grouse had fallen too. He is the most remarkable game shot I have ever seen.

From Viscount Whitelaw: Those who have had the privilege of being Joe Nickerson's shooting guests soon learn how much he has contributed to the sport. Not only is he one of the outstanding shots of his generation, but he is also a knowledgeable naturalist and an enthusiastic conservationist. These qualities together make shooting with him a real education. His kindness and hospitality ensure that it is an immensely enjoyable experience as well.

From Mrs Greta Fenston:
It was Joe Nickerson who taught me to shoot after I married Felix
Fenston who was a close friend of his. We were at Wemmergill
on a lovely day and he asked me to stand in his butt along
with a loader and five dogs. He insisted that I should take a
shot with one of his guns and showed me how to do it. I killed
a bird at my first attempt and was then hooked for life. It was
also with his help and encouragement that I started shooting
partridges. He has continued to invite me long after my husband's
death.

I was in a grouse butt next to Joe and I remember putting my
gun down to watch his performance. He must have been about
seventy and there he was dancing about as though he was in a
ballet with grouse falling all round him. The faster they çame the
faster he shot them. He is one of the most beautiful shots to watch,
so accurate, quick and yet calm. He is also a wonderful friend and
I am very privileged to have known him.

From Mr John Alexander, who runs the big shoot at Westwick
Hall, near Norwich:
Joe Nickerson first asked me to shoot when I was still in my late
teens. I remember the dinner party on the eve of my first day
at Wemmergill when he treated me exactly as he did the other
guests who were all so distinguished. Much of the conversation
was about business matters which I did not understand but after
dinner he took me outside to look at the sky and feel the wind
direction. He pronounced that the next day would be just right
for the grouse-ground we would be driving.

Shooting with him at Wemmergill in August 1974, the party
was rather heavily political for me, with Reggie Maudling and
Sir Con O'Neill among the guests. My relief came from Prince
'Stas' Radziwill who was prepared to bet on anything. I heard him
and his chauffeur-loader betting whether the next grouse would
be young or old, male or female. (Whether they ever settled their
debts to each other I do not know.) After listening to them wager
on every conceivable challenge, JN walked past and bet them on
the total number that the team would shoot on the next drive. He
was almost exactly correct.

That was the difference between the inveterate gambler and the master field-craftsman.

He once told me that you should set aside 100 days a year for sport and when I asked him what sport he said, 'Shooting and fishing.' When I said that I did not fish he replied, 'Well you know what you have to do then.' I have managed to do it!

Over the years that he kindly asked me to Wemmergill I tried to pick up more of his wisdom. I was always most impressed by his total knowledge of the sport. He understood what makes a bird do what it does, what encourages it to thrive and what does not. Now everyone talks of the effects of bracken infestation, conservation headlands for partridges, cover crops and natural habitat for pheasants but 'Uncle Joe' was ahead of his time by years. As a result of his example I approached the running of a shoot totally differently. If you can learn to think like a bird you can do tremendous things with the shooting on an estate.

In recent times there is one man who is famed as a shot, a host and a sage – a complete all-rounder. The name of Joe Nickerson is synonymous with the sport of shooting.

From the Rt. Hon Michael Jopling:
I do not shoot regularly and have always told Joe Nickerson that he should not be inviting me as a guest to shoot at all! However, he has always made me feel that I am the best shot in England, which is miserably far from the truth. At the same time he has always subtly encouraged me to correct my many faults and inexperience.

Among my happiest memories are those small family days at Rothwell with Joe and Eugenie and the girls. It has been said that practice makes perfect and those days have never been short of opportunity to practise!

I am delighted to call Joe Nickerson my friend.

From Michael Clark, formerly Deputy Chairman of Plessey:
My most notable impression of Joe Nickerson was of his exceptional appreciation and application of *quality*. Everything about his way of life, and particularly his shooting, was of the very highest quality. His guns exemplified this, particularly his exquisite pair of over-and-under 20 bore Woodwards, which I remember handling on

one occasion. They were the most beautiful guns I can remember in my whole life.

Equally, the sheer quality of the shooting at Wemmergill was pure perfection; there are some unbelievable stands, particularly the valley where the birds come over at an amazing height to the delight of the very few guns involved – four to six (incredibly rare on a grouse moor these days) – coupled with the quality of the presentation.

It was always a daunting experience to stand next to Joe Nickerson because he is such a brilliant shot that one always felt embarrassed by one's own second-rate performance. However he would always cry 'Good shot' if one happened to pull off a lucky one.

Staying in the house, with the finest of fare and creature comforts, was also of the highest quality and ranked with any house in the realm, not only for hospitality but for meticulous attention to detail and presentation.

From Lord Plumb, President of the European Parliament:
To spend a day on the grouse moor with Joe Nickerson is an experience no one can forget: he has the unique quality of being the perfect host, totally in control of the whole field and respected by beaters, dogs and guns alike.

But, above all, his work on moor and heather improvement, establishing an increase in bird population, sets a fine example to others and answers the critics of country pursuits.

His reputation as a shot is legendary but his pride exudes when his lovely wife and daughters show equal skill.

He is a perfectionist and a great friend.

From 'Father' Jacob, Sir Joseph's former keeper:
Nobody else has done as much for shooting as JN. Until JN set about Rothwell few people bothered with shooting in this area of Lincolnshire.

Everything he promised he carried out.

When you go out with him you feel just the same as he is – countrymen together. He always recognized that the success of the shoot was as much due to my efforts and knowledge as to his own.

It does not pay to argue with him. If he wants something done it has to be done but I've never had a wrong word from him. He looks after those who have worked for him loyally.

From Billy Jacob, Father Jacob's son and former keeper, now shoot manager:
His knowledge of wild life is something few gentlemen have. He knows as much as the keeper about game and the countryside.

You must always tell him exactly what has been happening. You can't pull wool over his eyes.

We've had a lot of fun together.

From Ian Garfoot, keeper at Westwick Hall, formerly at Rothwell 1976–85:
Anyone who has spent some time in the shooting field with JN will soon be aware of his amazing knowledge of fieldcraft, which is particularly noticeable when driving partridges or duck-flighting. One drive which comes to mind was on a partridge day at North Ormsby when, after lunch, the guns were lining out behind a good hawthorn hedge, number 8 reaching to a wood on the right.

I was loading for JN on number 1 and the beaters were bringing in four big fields, the last one in front being a wheat stubble. After a look round he said, 'We won't get a shot here: I don't think anybody will: they're not going to leave that stubble.'

I looked round for his reason but could not see it. The hedge was not too high – six or seven feet – with only a light cross-wind, though there was the possibility that they might head for the corner of the field and flick round the wood.

'We need to be on the other side of the hedge,' JN announced. After signalling to his brother, Sam, who owned the shoot, we moved in front of the hedge, kneeling down, out of sight and perfectly safe, being the first gun in the line.

As the beaters came on, one or two coveys went round the wood over number 8, as I had anticipated, but nothing flew over the hedge. When the bulk of the birds started coming, none of the coveys, either English or French, kept straight. Every time, within fifteen yards of the hedge, they tipped their wings right-handed and came over us. I cannot remember how many birds we shot but it was certainly a lot more than the main line of guns.

From Charles Hughesdon:
I first met Joe about thirty years ago and have spent many happy and instructive hours shooting with him. His accuracy and consistency as a shot at all types of game is a legend. Coupled with his skill is his remarkable ability to observe the performance of the other guns in the line. Nothing – good or bad – seems to escape him.

He is a martinet for discipline and for time-keeping. Some years ago I was his guest at Rothwell and, because of a violent storm which had blown down many trees, roads were blocked and several guests were late. At 8.55 a.m. Joe duly announced, 'The beaters are all in position: we'll have to start without them.' We did and for the first stand it was a memorable two-gun shoot.

Joe is everything a shooting man should be. As a shoot manager he is unique.

From Chapman Pincher:
Joe Nickerson is, possibly, the most widely experienced game-bird shot of all time because he is expert against every species, while the legendary 'Big Shots' of the past tended to be specialists. His style is so elegant and effective that I have long regarded him as the Jack Hobbs of shooting.

Until I met him, some twenty-five years ago, I did not really know what shooting was about – what peaks of perfection were possible, though I have never been able to attain them.

He is an original thinker with an empirical approach and has been an innovator in shooting as in farming.

From Captain Mark Phillips:
I have always very much enjoyed my times shooting with Joe Nickerson. For me it was not just the outstanding hospitality he extends or the pleasure of watching a legend in his own lifetime in action, but his outstanding knowledge of the countryside and the sport he loves. In that respect he is an example to all and I, for one, have always left his company a wiser man.

From Mr Peter Dennis, one of the original Big Six who shot the record grey partridge bag:

Having shot with JN for the past forty-two seasons I say, unreservedly, that he must be rated among the great shots of all time. Whether with an 8 bore on the foreshore or his 28 bores in a grouse butt, it is all the same to him. He takes them as they come. He seldom misses.

Of course, I shall never forget 3 October 1952 when, on a fine and breezy day at Rothwell, six of us accounted for more than 2000 wild and sporting grey partridges. But I recall all the other days spent in other places with equal pleasure. Be it moor, field or shore, Joe's enthusiasm and generosity as host knows no bounds; it is always a merry party for he is a great wit and stimulating company. His knowledge of wild life and shoot management is unique.

In spite of wide-ranging interests which take him to many countries he always finds time to listen to the problems of others. But for the kind heart of Joseph Nickerson many a lame dog would never have got over the stile.

From Charles Wyvill:
I had always hoped that Joe Nickerson would write this book as there is no one, to my knowledge, with such a vast amount of experience over so many different facets of game-shooting. His scientific interest, his keen eye for detail, his deep knowledge of the subject and, most of all, his generosity, have enabled him to make a major contribution to the study of game-birds and their habitats.

Those lucky enough to have been his guests will know of the work that he puts in to ensure the smooth running of the day and the many kindnesses shown by both Joe and Eugenie to make one's visit as pleasant as possible. A legendary shot, at over seventy he still shoots with great skill, and woe betide the bird that comes within range of those 28 bores!

I value his experience and friendship enormously and hope that he continues to shoot for years to come.

From David Donne, formerly chairman of Dalgety:
Absolute excellence in any activity is a quality that is both rare and admirable. Anybody who has had the privilege of shooting

at Rothwell will instantly recognize such excellence in everything to do with the day. Every detail – the breeding of the birds, the positioning of the guns, the presentation of the birds, the loading and the picking-up, attains a standard of absolute excellence. This is a tribute to Joe Nickerson, his dedication to and his knowledge of the sport of shooting and his generous sharing of them with others.

From Don Alfonso Fierro, a well-known Spanish businessman:
Sir Joseph Nickerson is one of the most distinguished shots I have met in my life. I compare him with the Spanish Count of Teba who, for fifty years, has been the most elegant and best gun in my country.

Both have elegance in the way they stand, handle their guns and dress, and in the cordiality offered when they receive their guests.

Joe has invited me many times to shoot grouse in Yorkshire and I am always excited by its memory. His warm character, beautiful house and the excellent food and wines are beyond any words of mine to describe.

As a man, I have always had great respect for his talent in conducting the many important enterprises which he has created and developed with tremendous success.

The following words appeared in *Shooting News* of 7 October 1988 from the pen of James Openshaw, who writes under the name of Shotgunner. They refer to the opening days of the 1988 grouse season in North Yorkshire when the wild, windy weather made the grouse fly so well that they reminded the author, who was loading for another gun, of late October birds:

A gentleman, well over seventy, was shooting with remarkable accuracy. Time after time birds came to him at all angles and the consistency of his shooting was a joy to behold. Two in front and often one or two behind were the order of the day, no matter how fast or awkwardly angled they came. I only saw him miss one bird.

Then came the crunch. At lunchtime I managed to get into conversation with his keeper/loader and learned, much to my surprise, that he was shooting with a pair of under-and-over Purdey 28 bores.

He was taking most of the birds a good thirty yards out in front of him and nearly every one was dead when picked. He was shooting in the classic style, as soon as the stock touched his shoulder the gun went off and the bird was killed.

I have seen some good shots, both with 12 and 20 bores, but never anybody who consistently used a 28 bore to such devastating effect.

Mr Openshaw has confirmed that the gun was Sir Joseph Nickerson and has added:

I have seen a lot of good grouse shots in the past, and loaded for some of them, but do not think I have ever seen anybody to compare, both for accuracy and quickness of shooting, with Sir Joseph Nickerson. As the day progressed and I observed his shooting I realized that I was watching a modern-day counterpart of the second Marquis of Ripon or the sixth Lord Walsingham.

Index

movement before shooting, 46–8
number required, 15, 33–4
obstructions, 24
position held, 46–7
safety catch, 47
stocks, 34
storing, 149
  law on, 37
taking abroad, 184–5
triggers, 33
types:
  double-barrelled 4 bore, 199
  over-and-under, 30–2
  single-barrelled 2 bore, 199
unloading, 24
weight, 49
for wildfowling, 98–9
for women, 34
gunsmiths, 36

Hague, Squire, 198–9
Harbert, John, III, 193
hares:
  chasing with lurchers, 163
  farming and, 110
  flushing pheasants, 80
  grazing on heather, 129
  hunting, 190
  infected, 92
  introducing, 123
  numbers shot, 63, 65
  records, 209
  season, 4
  shooting, 109–10
  wounded, 23
hats, 41–2
headaches, 53
heather:
  burning, 126–7
  competition for, 92
  as crop, 123
  grants for regeneration, 130
  improvement, 139–43
  lamb yield from, 130
  management, 125–30
  new varieties, 142
  Nickerson System of grazing, 134, 141
  overgrazing, 127–8
  planting by hand, 141
  rotational grazing, 133–4
  seed propagation, 140, 142
Heather Improvement Foundation, 95, 139–43
  awards, 142
hedgehogs, 158

retrieving, 179
hedges, 118
Helmsley, 200
herbicides, 128
herons: wounded, 181
hides:
  for pigeon, 103
  siting, 97
  for wildfowling, 96
Hill Farming Acts, 126
Hill Farming Research Institute, 140
Hoare, Sir Samuel, later Lord Templewood, 65
Holgate estate, 143
Holkham, 65
Holland, 192
hoods, 41–2
Hughesdon, Charles: tribute from, 219
Hungary, 192
hunting, 154

ICI, 37
infra-red beams, 164
injuries: from guns, 52–3
insurance, 36–7
invitations, 13–14
Italy: shooting in, 149–50, 193

jackdaws, 146, 158, 161, 198
jackets, 39
Jacob, Archie (Father), 64, 162, 170–2, 173
  tribute from, 217–18
Jacob, Ben, 56, 170, 171, 172
Jacob, Benjy, 57, 172
Jacob, Billy, 57, 99, 117, 170, 171, 172
  tribute from, 218
Jacob, Will, 33, 57, 82, 99, 172
jays:
  aiming at, 52
  as predators, 146, 158, 160–1
  shooting during drives, 21
Joel, Jim, 197
Johnson, Bob, 56, 64
Johnson's Wood, 159
jokes, 38
Jopling, Michael: tribute from, 216
Joseph Nickerson Heather Award, 142
Joseph Nickerson Heather Improvement Foundation, 95, 139–43
  awards, 142
Joseph Nickerson Reconciliation Project, 141, 154
Juan Carlos, King of Spain, 191, 202

kale, 119–20

keepers, 166–74, 210
  chain of command, 168
  choosing, 166–7
  control of, 168
  deterring poachers, 163–4
  holidays, 166–7
  honesty, 169–70
  judging shoot by, 16
  on other shoots, 173
  pensions, 172
  promotion, 173
  relationship with farm manager, 168–9
  shooting day for, 173–4
  tipping, 26–7, 173
  training dogs, 172
  treatment of, 112
  work, 169
Keir, 101, 199–200

Lambton, Lord, 188
Lamyman, Leonard, 63, 198
landlords: attitudes, 121–2
law:
  on game birds, 124
  on gun storage, 37
  responsibility for injury, 19
  taking guns abroad, 184–5
Leicester, Lord, 3, 65, 68
Leicester, Lord (former), 105
Llanbrynmair Moor, 144–5
loaders, 55–7
  in butts, 137
  provided by host, 27–8
  shooting day for, 173–4
  technique, 55–6
long shots, 48
Lonsdale, Lord, 135
louping ill, 92

Macauley Land Use Research Institute, 140
MacGregor, John, 131
magpies, 152
  aiming at, 52
  as predators, 146, 158, 159–60
  shooting during drives, 21
maize, 120
mallard, 98, 100, 146
  numbers shot, 65, 82, 208
marksmanship, 44–54, 58
marsh men, 199
massage, 59
mat-grass, 127–8
Maudling, Reggie, 215
merlins, 132, 145, 146
mice, 152

Middleton House, 124, 205
Milbank, Anthony, 143
mink, 149
moles, 158
moor-rush, 128
moors:
  access, 138
  drainage, 132–3
  as investment, 207
  'island', 135–6
  lamb yield from, 130
  location of butts, 136
  management, 125–43
  need for varying heights on, 135
  Nickerson System of grazing, 134, 141
  overgrazing, 127–8
  ramblers on, 123
  rates paid on, 123
  renting, 122
  resuscitating bare areas, 134
  road reconstruction, 138
Mora-Figuero, Pepe, 203
Moreton, Guy, 65, 106, 157, 197–8
Morocco, 195
muirburn, 127

National Trust, 142
Nature Conservancy, 132
Newcastle-on-Tyne University, 140
Nickerson, Charles, 194
Nickerson, Diana, 204
Nickerson, Eugenie, 213–14
Nickerson, John William, 58, 117
Nickerson, Sir Joseph:
  mentioned in *Purdey: the Gun and the Family*, 30
  records, 209
  tributes to, 213–21
  typical day, 205–6
Nickerson, Rosemarie, 58
Nickerson, Sam, 10, 63, 196–7, 200, 204
Nickerson System, 134, 141
nidderdale, 111, 133
Nilo Plantation, 193
noise: at shoot, 9–10
Nombela, 189, 190–1
North Ormesby Manor, 65, 218
nuisance: caused during shoot, 29

Olin, John, 193, 194, 203
O'Neill, Sir Con, 215
Openshaw, James: tribute from, 221–2
opossum, 194
over-trousers, 41
owls, 146, 148, 155–6
  as decoy, 160

farming and, 110
grazing on heather, 129
hunting, 190
numbers shot, 63, 108
records, 209
shooting, 4, 108–9
Radziwill, Prince 'Stas', 215
rainfall: effect on partridges, 69
ramblers, 123
Rank, Lord (J. Arthur), 143, 200
rape, 120
rats, 27, 152, 181, 194
encouraging, 120
as predators, 146, 155–6
rattlesnakes, 194
ravens, 159
Read's Island, 99–100, 107, 155
accommodation on, 124
erosion, 123
Reconciliation Project, 140–1, 154
Reeth Moor, 94, 134, 197, 208
rights of way, 123
Ripon, Lord, 3, 45, 60, 93, 196, 197, 222
rooks, 159
Rothwell, 82, 210
farming, 115–20
house, 124
improvements at, 66
introducing quail, 194–5
partridges, 74
pheasants, 76–7
pigeons, 104
pond, 96
rabbits, 108
sanctuaries, 148
shoots at, 63–5, 111, 202
Royal Society for the Protection of Birds, 145
royalty: as guests, 202–3
runners, 187

safety:
during drives, 19
in firing gun, 47
gun storage, 149
of guns in aircraft, 184
of guns in vehicles, 36
in handling guns, 19–20
for loaders, 55
of VIPs, 11–12, 202–3
when to shoot, 20–3
safety catch, 47
security, *see* safety
Sefton, Lord, 168
sewelling, 78–9
sheep:

dipping, 135
rotational grazing of heather, 133–4
threat to grouse moors, 127–31
sheep-ticks, 92, 128
sheep's fescue, 127
shoes, 40
shooting:
abroad, 184–95
accuracy, 44–54
age to stop, 59–60, 208
aiming at birds, 47–52
banning, 150
causing deafness, 42, 179–80
combining with farming, 115–20
costs in Spain, 189
fitness for, 59
friendship from, 206–7
giving up, 59–60, 208
misses, causes of, 47, 48
movement of gun, 46–8
purpose, 207
seasons, 4
selecting quarry, 20–3, 46
stance, 45
teaching, 57
Shooting News: report in, 221–2
shooting schools, 33, 52, 58
shooting sticks, 42
shoots:
accommodating extra guns, 8
behaviour at, 13–29
choosing guests, 8
competition at, 10–11, 187
costs of, 112
distances between guns, 72
effect of weather on, 9
effect of wind on, 6
equipment for, 15–16
management, 111–24
noise on, 9–10
number of guns, 7–8
organization, 6–12
planning, 5–6
poaching neighbours' birds, 22, 187
positions for drives, 18–19, 64
rented, 121–2
safety, 19
selecting quarry, 20–3, 46
sweepstake at, 11
taxes, 130–1
shot: sizes, 38
shotguns, *see* guns
Skokholm, 181
slips (slings), gun, *see* gun slips
snipe, 82, 106